Francis Close Hall Library
University of Gloucestershire
Swindon Road
Cheltenham
GL50 4AZ
Tel. 01242 714600

The BATTLE *of* VERSAILLES

The Night American Fashion

Stumbled into the Spotlight

and Made History

ROBIN GIVHAN

FLATIRON
BOOKS
NEW YORK

KT-573-561

THE BATTLE OF VERSAILLES. Copyright © 2015 by Robin Givhan. All rights reserved. Printed in the United States of America. For information, address Flatiron Books, 175 Fifth Avenue, New York, N.Y. 10010.

Prologue Interior Photo: Gala Organized by the Baroness de Rothschild for the Restoration of Versailles Castle in Versailles, France, on November 28, 1973. Photo © 1973 Daniel Simon/Getty Images.

Epilogue Interior Photo: Team Vicious performs at the Rick Owens spring 2014 show in Paris. Photo © 2013 Maria Valentino/MCV.

www.flatironbooks.com

Library of Congress Cataloging-in-Publication Data

Givhan, Robin.
    The Battle of Versailles: the night American fashion stumbled into the spotlight and made history / Robin Givhan.
        pages   cm
    ISBN 978-1-250-05290-2 (hardcover)
    ISBN 978-1-250-05385-5 (e-book)
    1. Fashion shows—France—Versailles—History.   2. Fashion merchandising—United States—History.   3. Fashion merchandising—Social aspects.   4. Social change.   5. Château de Versailles (Versailles, France)   I. Title.
    TT502.G585 2015
    746.9'209443663—dc23   2014040369

Flatiron books may be purchased for educational, business, or promotional use. For information on bulk purchases, please contact the Macmillan Corporate and Premium Sales Department at 1-800-221-7945, extension 5442, or write to specialmarkets@macmillan.com.

First Edition: March 2015

10 9 8 7 6 5 4 3 2 1

This book is dedicated to

my parents,

Robert and Stella,

whose love makes all things possible.

Contents

The
BATTLE
of
VERSAILLES

Liza Minnelli and models performing "Bonjour, Paris" at the gala organized by
Baroness De Rothschild for the restoration of Versailles Castle, November 28, 1973.

Prologue

On November 28, 1973, the world's social elite—men in dashing tuxedos and women dripping with diamonds—gathered in the majestic Théâtre Gabriel at the Palace of Versailles. Originally conceived as a publicity stunt and fund-raiser for the dilapidated French landmark, the Grand Divertissement à Versailles had become an international fashion extravaganza, bloated with pomp and passion. Style writers and society columnists; royalty, tycoons, diplomats, and politicians; the crème de la crème of the jet set; stagehands, set designers, burlesque dancers, ballet stars, drag queens, glamorous models, famous choreographers, and one Academy Award–winning triple threat all watched in eager anticipation as five kings of French fashion faced off against five unsung American designers. By the time the spotlight dimmed and the curtain came down on the evening's spectacle, fashion history had been made and an industry had been forever transformed.

In the Wings

A t the close of the twentieth century, there was perhaps no brand that better represented the swaggering confidence of American fashion than that of Bill Blass. In his golden decade of the 1980s and into the early '90s, Blass was a household name synonymous with American style as personified by society dames and tomboyish beauties. He was a smooth gentleman walker, chum to First Lady Nancy Reagan. And he had grown his company to a $500-million-a-year business fueled by licenses for everything from luggage to the Lincoln Continental Mark series of fancy sedans. But it wasn't always that way. Like most designers of his generation, for much of his career, Blass was nothing more than a workaday guy trying to get a little respect in an industry dominated by the French. He stood in the wings of the industry, waiting for his chance at center stage. When it came, in the late autumn of 1973, he and four of his fellow American designers grabbed it and forever altered the course of fashion history.

Blass was a handsome midwestern fellow who came of age at a time when Indiana wasn't just flyover country; it was nowhere. Fresh from the army, he arrived in New York in the late 1940s wanting to work in fashion and live a glamorous life. With a hint of a fake British accent picked up from the Hollywood films of the day, he found his first job as a sketch artist—a kind of entry-level position once occupied by some of the now-great names in the business. But he quickly discovered that fashion, as it was practiced in New York's Garment District back then, was nothing more than a daily grind of kowtowing to the demands of grim factory bosses, rather than the boldly creative career he had envisioned. When he won his first big promotion, he went from sketching to designing, but designing meant merely producing cheap copies of Balenciaga and Christian Dior dresses for American manufacturers like Anna Miller and Co. and later Maurice Rentner.

Invention didn't happen in America; it happened in France.

From the days of the French monarchy through World War II, French designers dictated fashion with a confident strut born of fiercely protected tradition, national character, and mythology. A shift in hemlines in the Paris ateliers reverberated throughout the retail world like an encyclical from the Vatican. Whatever Paris said, the wealthiest and most beautiful—and thereby the most influential—women all over the world took heed. Other ladies across social and economic classes then fell in line.

But by the 1960s, society had evolved and world politics had disrupted the fashion system. A handful of prescient retailers in New York and Chicago recognized an opportunity and opened their doors to a new kind of fashion: American. Homegrown designers began slowly crawling from the backrooms of manufacturers and into the light. For the first time, American designers were beginning to find their voices. And what they had to say was being published by the newly prominent trade tabloid *Women's Wear Daily*. The American fashion industry had sprung to life.

In 1960, Blass's name was added to the label at Maurice Rentner; he was now being publicly credited for his work. He continued to claw his way forward. He excelled at the art of socializing. Sexually ambiguous, he made himself indispensable to a group of wealthy women in constant need of going-out companions who posed no threat to their distracted husbands. By 1970, Blass had established himself as a man-about-town with important connections and an eye for jaunty style. He bought out his employer, and Maurice Rentner was renamed Bill Blass Ltd. He was crawling toward the light.

But being seen as a competent businessman and being respected as a titan of imagination, sophistication, and influence are two separate things. It wasn't until a snowy evening in 1973 that public perception of Blass shifted. On November 28, about an hour outside Paris at the historic Palace of Versailles, Blass, fifty-one, made a play for dignity. By the end of the evening, Blass and four other American designers went from being considered merely savvy industrialists to being thought of as innovative, creative, and significant. And their influence reverberates today.

Working alongside Blass that night was his old friend Oscar de la Renta, forty-one, who had built his career the same way Blass had— catering to America's social elite, all the while nibbling at the edges of French dominance. With them stood Halston, forty-one, a tall, slender, handsome gay man who had created a famous public persona for himself and catered to celebrity clients. His eyes shielded by sunglasses, his grooming impeccable, his ego outlandishly plus-size, Halston's identity boiled down to a single moniker. Before his Versailles debut, the French had known of his fame, but he had not yet won their respect. The woman among these gentlemen designers, Anne Klein, had made a name for herself by catering to the burgeoning population of professional women; her designs had an artistic edge and a dollop of plain old fun, and the strategy had paid off handsomely. By the time her work was shown on the Versailles stage, the fifty-year-old Klein was a financially successful businesswoman who had kick-started the industry habit of vanity sizing—that naughty practice of cutting a dress with the generous girth of a size 14, but labeling it a 10. Like all the Americans, Klein made sportswear, which the French considered practical, commercial, and banal. Her mix-and-match, industrially produced separates were the lowest of the low in fashion's hierarchy, which was topped by French haute couture. But her sportswear was also disrespected by her own colleagues as it was wholly utilitarian, in service to women, rather than in celebration of the designer. Fifth in this group of aspiring American designers was Stephen Burrows. At thirty, Burrows was a young African American whiz kid at home in the seventies party atmosphere. News of his daring use of color and rhapsodic baring of the body had made its way to Paris, and the French were curious. Burrows was both naive and self-absorbed; he was on the hunt for an adventure.

Each of these designers came to Versailles with a story to tell. Blass and de la Renta had specters of insecurity to silence. Halston was looking to prove that his star power was not parochial but international. Klein wanted to add critical success to her commercial triumphs. And Burrows wanted to dress the world.

They were a group of friends, rivals, and total strangers who had been brought together to represent the American fashion industry. They were competing egos. They were disorganized. For four months leading up to this Wednesday night, there had been tears, screaming matches, backbiting, and demands to just "shut up." They'd come with three dozen professional runway models to present their ready-to-wear to an international audience. Ten of those models were black—an unusually high proportion that reflected 1970s politics, fashion economics, and social tensions.

The American designers were ostensibly guests of five of their French counterparts, the kings and princes of the industry: Hubert de Givenchy, Yves Saint Laurent, Emanuel Ungaro, Pierre Cardin, and Marc Bohan of Christian Dior. Unlike the Americans, these Frenchmen were rooted in the painstaking craftsmanship of haute couture, a tradition that had dominated French fashion since the nineteenth century. Where the Americans came to Versailles trying to prove something, to show the world their scrappy, boundary-breaking creativity, the French arrived confidently prepared to impress by stature and extravagance.

The French were the star attractions; the Americans were the chorus girls. But in this case, it was the chorus girls, their stomachs knotted with fear as they prepared to take the stage, who stole the show.

One

French Rules

If a tourist arrives in Paris during the period of ready-to-wear runway shows in March or September, a taxi driver stuck in the inevitable traffic jam on the trip into the city from Charles de Gaulle Airport is likely to offer commentary on the world-famous fashion labels Christian Dior or Chanel in the same manner that a New York cabbie might kibitz about the Yankees. Fashion, after all, is one of France's national treasures. Even those who do not consume it at its highest levels are interested in its well-being.

France's reputation in the world of fashion is bound up with the industry's early links to the monarchy, its importance to the developing republic, and the enduring tension between the two. From the days of Marie Antoinette, in the eighteenth century, French fashion, like fashion throughout Europe, was dictated by nobility. "The rules were established by the court in every country. Spanish fashion had nothing to do with French fashion. When French fashion was pale blue for men and women, Spain was black," explains Didier Grumbach, the author of *Histoires de la Mode*, his book about the history of French fashion. "In every country in Europe, the king or queen was making fashion. Marie Antoinette had a couturier but only to give her advice. It was the queen deciding."[1]

Any well-bred French woman, even those who were not part of the royal court, employed a dressmaker. As a result, there were some 350,000 couturiers working in France up until the end of the 1920s. In addition, all commoners who could not afford a dressmaker sewed, so that the production of basic clothing occurred at home. But there was no ready-to-wear, no off-the-rack, in the manner we think of today.

The monarchy ruled over clothing aesthetics—everyone simply copied or paid homage to what the nobles wore. There was no creativity in fashion—only in textiles. The fabric merchants were the artists in what could only barely be called a fashion industry. They dealt in jacquards, brocades, and silk taffetas, as well as notions: button making, lace weaving, and embroidery. They perfected crafts that continue on at such lauded firms as Maison Lesage embroidery and Maison Lemarié, where artisans work magic with feathers.

Breaking from this tradition of the royal court determining the styles and women collaborating with their own dressmakers was Charles Frederick Worth, who arrived in Paris in 1845. An Englishman with significant chutzpah, Worth established what we now consider couture: something that is born in the imagination of the designer and offered to the client.

As a young man, Worth worked as a salesman at Gagelin, a textile firm. While there, he began to make dresses for his wife, who was a saleswoman in the shop. He built a small business designing dresses, which won prizes at various fabric exhibitions and contributed to Gagelin's success. With the rise of the French Second Republic in 1848, Worth encouraged his employer to expand even further into dressmaking. But Gagelin refused. Dressmaking was still perceived as lowly, inelegant, and beneath the status of a textile artist. So Worth found a partner and started his own business, calling it the House of Worth. He set about the process of developing new shapes and conjuring fresh ideas. He even had the audacity to present his creations on live models. His brazenness didn't go unnoticed—or unrewarded. It created a scandal.

"It was unaccepted that someone was inventing new shapes," Grumbach explains. "The rules were very clear about what women wear—before forty years old and after forty; when she is married, when she is widowed. Everything was imposed. There was no freedom in fashion."[2]

For a time, Worth's daring paid off. All was fine and lucrative, and destined to get even better. But then Louis-Napoleon Bonaparte, who had been elected the president of the Second Republic, led a coup d'état and, in 1852, began to rule as Napoleon III. With a new emperor and a new royal court, Worth had to rethink his business plan. Wily and savvy, he dispatched his wife, Marie Vernet, to visit the wife of the Austrian ambassador. Vernet arrived with a book of sketches. At first she was met with skepticism about this Englishman's skills, but Worth's creativity prevailed. The ambassador's wife placed an order for two dresses, one for day and another for evening, for the grand sum of three hundred francs.[3]

Soon after the dresses were completed, the diplomatic corps was invited to a ball at the Louvre. When Napoleon's wife, Empress Eugénie, got a look at the Worth gown—white tulle, embroidered with silver threads—she was smitten. The next day she summoned Worth to the Louvre, the emperor's city home, to shop his wares. But instead of arriving prepared to acquiesce to the empress's desires, with a sketchpad and sample fabrics, Worth arrived with a fully made brocade dress.

"The empress sees the dress and hates it because she thinks it looks like curtains. And she's absolutely insulted because the dress hasn't been negotiated. It's all made. He's proposing a creation where she didn't interfere," Grumbach explains. "She sends him back; she sends [the dress] back. But by chance, the emperor arrives. And Worth, who is not shy, quickly explains: 'The brocade is from Lyon—a republican city—so I think it's good politics if the empress wears it a few times.'"

Politics won the day, as it still so often does, and Empress Eugénie gave in. And Worth, a consummate rainmaker, made sure that anyone with money knew that he was the couturier for the empress. During the reign of Napoleon III, from 1852 to 1870, France saw robust growth both industrially and economically. Its influence and power spread around the world. Worth's position as the exclusive dressmaker for the court was incomparable publicity. He was deemed the ne plus ultra creator of evening gowns and began to dress Russian and English nobility, as well as the wives of American millionaires.

Worth's business model and his determined self-promotion set the foundation for what became haute couture at the dawn of the twentieth century. Worth would create a collection of designs, which he presented to potential clients. They would make their choices with Worth's counsel. And he would tailor-make the garments to each client's specifications through a series of fittings.

This would be the process by which generations of well-to-do women would dress. And while those women would still collaborate with the great couturiers, because of Worth, the balance of creative power increasingly tilted toward the designers.

Today the term *couture* is used loosely in reference to clothes that are expensive or especially luxurious, but from Worth's day well into the 1970s, it had a particular meaning—and in France it still does. Formally, haute couture refers to a manner of construction, one dedicated to handmade quality and personalized fit. The rules of haute couture are strictly dictated and overseen by the Chambre Syndicale de la Haute Couture, which was established in 1868 and essentially codified Worth's design process. In France, haute couture is a legally protected designation and the Ministry of Industry regularly reviews which design houses are allowed to use the nomenclature.

A couture show was and remains a singular event—intimate, dignified, and glamorous. The attire of the guests can be breathtaking, not for its opulence or its ostentation but for the sheer perfection of its construction: the purity of fit, the unspeakable chic. The audience is filled with clients as well as retailers, editors, and, today, stylists.

The guests arrive quietly and in due time. There are no hordes of people clogging doorways. No pushing. No snarling guards. There is no conjuring of faux frenzy. The anticipation is palpable but silent.

If haute couture shows today are calm and respectful, up until the late 1960s they were like religion, a cross between Easter Sunday and Holy Communion. The models were not especially beautiful, but they were elongated, birdlike creatures who floated gracefully through a room filled with clients perched on little gilded chairs. Each model held a number in her hand to identify her look. There was a hush over the room. At Balenciaga, there was utter silence.

Haute couture greedily consumes a woman's time, as a garment requires multiple fittings—in practice and by legislation. It demands patience and a willingness to bother with details. A woman has to appreciate the perfect little hand stitches on the interior of a garment, the handmade lace and embroidery—or at least relish the admiring glances that an exquisitely constructed garment can attract.

Following each couture show, clients make an appointment with their *vendeuse*, or saleswoman, for the next day. The process has not significantly changed since the time of Worth. Clients select their style, request tweaks, and then proceed through a series of fittings. From a rudimentary muslin to the final product, the garment is handmade, embroidered, beaded, and feathered by a group of artisans who have learned their trade over the generations. This is not disposable fashion. Clients keep garments for years, often altering them slightly to freshen them up.

Historically, clients maintained close relationships with their *vendeuses*, who were not just salespeople, but also social arbiters, gatekeepers, and meticulous businesswomen who kept track of who bought which garments and how those orders were progressing through the atelier. The *vendeuse* was a diplomat who knew which social circles overlapped and was abreast of the current hierarchies. She could discreetly dissuade a client from an ill-advised purchase. If so moved, she could offer a client the discounted sample garments worn by the model in the show. And if the *vendeuse* was the sort of woman who herself came from relatively rarefied circumstances, she could bring in influential, big-spending, important women who could raise a design house's notoriety by association. The *vendeuse* was a celebrity wrangler long before the first Hollywood red carpet was unfurled and the swag suite was opened.

In its most serious form, couture is a way of life. And in its heyday, the 1930s to the 1960s, when there were some twenty thousand couture clients, wealthy women made multiple costume changes a day, going from a dressing gown to a luncheon suit to a dinner dress. The couturier often developed a personal relationship with his clients. For example, designer Hubert de Givenchy sometimes traveled with his American clients Rachel "Bunny" Lambert Mellon (whose grandfather invented Listerine) and Betsey Cushing Roosevelt Whitney (daughter-in-law of Franklin D. Roosevelt and later wife of John Hay Whitney, the U.S. ambassador to the Court of St. James).[4] Indeed, Mellon once sent her private plane to fetch Givenchy from Paris so that he could create uniforms for her entire household staff—including the gardeners.[5]

You had to be *someone,* not just someone with very deep pockets, to wear couture. Couture was a world defined by relationships and lineage, in addition to money. A woman was introduced into this world by her mother, a socially prominent friend, or a representative of the house who'd taken note of the woman's stature in the community and her healthy bank account. One did not simply turn up at an atelier, ring the bell, and expect to be welcomed. *A fool's errand!* Haute couture was an exclusive club. And once admitted, a woman tended to remain loyal to one or two couturiers for a lifetime.

Paris's fashion industry provided the wardrobe for the Western world's great, striving, and influential beauties. And in the decades straddling

World War II, beauty was as all-consuming and revered as any career. Beauty was a profit center for those who were genetically endowed or determinedly self-creating. It helped women attract the most suitable sort of husband. And thus, it could improve a woman's social standing, fatten her bank account, and enhance her cultural clout. And of course, her beauty reflected well upon her spouse, lending him both virility and admiration.

In today's judgment, relying on one's appearance for advancement may be disdained, but throughout the 1940s and '50s, a woman would be declared foolhardy and unambitious if she failed to exploit her valuable gift of beauty, just as a musical prodigy would be deemed a disappointment if he shunned the concert stage.

The French fashion capitol had a symbiotic relationship with these aspiring women. The Parisian designers used their great skill to help them dazzle men of means and impress (or intimidate) their fellow sojourners. In return, as their appearance won compliments and their prominence rose, these women reflected the spotlight back on their French *créateurs* whenever their portraits appeared in the pages of *Vogue*, which debuted in America in 1892, and when their names were included on the International Best-Dressed List, which began as a poll orchestrated by Paris couturiers.

Haute couture set the standard of beauty in all of fashion, and the women who wore it set the standard of style for the masses. The American women who patronized the couture ateliers of Paris came from all parts of the country, from the East Coast to the plains west of the Mississippi to the oil fields of Texas to the California coast. They availed themselves of couture because it was the most personal expression of creative design. They admired the couturiers' techniques, understood couture's history, respected its perfectionism, and relished its enduring iconography. But they were also drawn to couture because of social expediency, family tradition, and simply because it was expected of them.

Among the most memorable of these women were Mona (née Strader) Schlesinger Bush Williams von Bismarck, who was enshrined in the Hall of Fame of the Best-Dressed List. She was born in 1897 with little fanfare in Louisville, Kentucky, but she died a countess in Paris after she'd made an impressive and lucrative habit of marrying up. The designer Hubert de Givenchy, who says she was both "beautiful and elegant," often dressed her.[6]

Barbara "Babe" Cushing Mortimer Paley, the wife of a Standard Oil heir and later of the founder of CBS, was another darling of the haute couture world. Born in 1915 in Brookline, Massachusetts, she made her first appearance in *Vogue* in 1934, where she was described as having a "special talent for wearing clothes."[7] By 1958, Babe was also welcomed into the Best-Dressed List Hall of Fame.

"There's a story about her walking out of a famous New York restaurant and she had a scarf and didn't know what to do with it so she tied it on her handbag. And scarves on handbags became a thing," recalls fashion editor Marylou Luther.[8]

Hailing from Texas, the blond socialite and philanthropist Lynn Wyatt was the granddaughter of the founder of the Sakowitz department stores. She was divorced with two children when she married Oscar Wyatt, the smooth-talking wildcatter, in 1963. A friendly and exuberant woman with a birdlike physique, large, round eyes, and a rollicking Texas twang, Wyatt was introduced to couture—specifically, Hubert de Givenchy and Emanuel Ungaro—and the glamour of Paris by well-meaning friends who took her social well-being in hand. They invited her to all the right parties, and she would pack ten evening gowns in her suitcase for a ten-day trip to Paris. "It was never exhausting to me, ever. I don't care how many times I see something. I am never blasé. I am never blasé about anything. Beauty is beauty is beauty," Wyatt says of herself. "I get energized by things like that.[9]

A pure and unabashed clotheshorse, Nan Kempner, wife of New York investment banker Thomas Kempner, was a wry and self-deprecating character who maintained a "social X-ray" physique, which was akin to that of a very hungry-looking twelve-year-old boy. She grew up in San

Francisco in the 1930s and '40s with a mother who shopped couture. The daughter quickly picked up the habit.

And there was Muriel Newman, the legendary Chicago art collector, who used to say that she always chose the top pieces from a couture collection so that her dress would speak eloquently for her and help secure her rightful place in society regardless of her having come from the former cow town of Chicago.[10]

But the grandest presence among this genus of American women is the regal Catherine "Deeda" Blair. A great thoroughbred, she was born Catherine Gerlach and grew up in Chicago, with her social coming out occurring in 1949. She was a devotee of Cristobal Balenciaga, and it was his work she'd saved up for when she arrived in Paris in 1959 for her first couture show.

Deeda was recovering from a failed marriage when family friends Eunice and Sargent Shriver introduced her to a lawyer named William McCormick Blair Jr. Mr. Blair was the son of an investment banker and a member of the family who once owned the *Chicago Tribune* and gave Chicago's McCormick Place its name. He was also an associate of Adlai Stevenson and part of the Kennedy circle.

In 1961, not long after Kennedy appointed Blair ambassador to Denmark, Blair and Deeda were married at Frederiksborg Castle, which dates back to the seventeenth century.[11] Balenciaga designed Deeda Blair's wedding dress. In keeping with an aesthetic considered the epitome of austerity and elegance, the gown was a restrained eggshell color with a subtle satin sheen, a modest off-the-shoulder neckline, and a gentle waistline. During one fitting, Balenciaga sent the bride-to-be around to a young designer he was mentoring to have him construct her veil. That designer was Hubert de Givenchy.

"I did not know it was Mr. Balenciaga who sent me Mrs. Blair, but I do remember that there [were] a lot of fittings," Givenchy says. "I was delighted to dress [her]—a beautiful woman."[12]

After living abroad for many years, the Blairs eventually moved to

Washington, where Deeda began a career in pharmaceutical consulting and medical philanthropy. Decades later, they settled in New York. In her twilight years, Blair remains a tall, slender woman with the upright, calm bearing of a ballerina. She does not walk so much as glide. She is a regular swimmer, which no doubt serves as a preventative to the appearance of frailty despite her reedlike figure. Blair's voice is a perfectly modulated and subdued alto that lacks any hint of her Saratoga cigarette habit. Her hair remains as it always has been, an immovable raven halo streaked with silver.

As a young woman in the 1960s, she bought from Christian Dior, Givenchy, and Balenciaga. Later, she grew to embrace Saint Laurent and Chanel. Today, her style of dress is classic, reserved, and expensive, from the drape of her silk trousers to the featherlight texture of a cashmere sweater. Even as the numbers of women around the world with the money and wherewithal to indulge in couture has shrunk to a few hundred, Blair has remained a couture client, although her attendance at the annual January and July shows has waned.

But of all the beautiful women who supported and were supported by the business of haute couture, the Baroness Marie-Hélène de Rothschild was the socialite nonpareil. Born in 1931 in New York to a Dutch diplomat father and an Egyptian mother, she headed to Paris after graduating from Marymount College. She married twice, first to a French count and then to Baron Guy de Rothschild of the French banking family, who was a distant cousin. The couple had a thick web of connections to political power brokers, social heavyweights, artists, and various members of the gilded jet set.

With a tidal wave of strawberry blond hair, a sturdy nose, and strong jolie laide features, Rothschild had the most highly valued social cachet in France. She was a woman to whom few could say no. She was imperious, exhausting, imaginative, and vengeful. The stories about her would make Miss Manners alternately smile and recoil in horror. She was both mean girl and Good Samaritan. She could be so far beyond politically incorrect that she risked being a caricature. She gave her *vendeuses* at Christian Dior compacts from Van Cleef & Arpels as Christmas presents. In a fit of pique, she slapped a man in the middle of the Paris restaurant Fouquet. She suffered for years from a form of degenerative arthritis and sometimes received guests in her bathroom while soaking in her tub.[13]

As the baroness came into her own as a socialite, she received a good deal of attention for her party-throwing acumen—a skill she put on full display in 1971 when she hosted a costume ball to mark the one hundredth birthday of Proust. When she died at sixty-five, her various obituaries included commentary on her reputation as "one of Europe's most imaginative hostesses."[14]

These women and their peers considered their *vendeuses* and their preferred designers to be indispensable. The gowns worn by these admired ladies helped to solidify their social standing. At the same time, their social standing served to burnish the reputation of their chosen designers.

"I got on well with my *vendeuse* and was sold samples the models wore," Blair recalls of her early days in the ateliers. "I went to Dior and they had this room upstairs where they kept all the old samples. This was the year of the famous Dior gowns with twenty or thirty layers of net with the four top layers all embroidered.

"There was a dress up there, strapless. It weighed about twenty-five pounds. It was boned. White. It fit perfectly. I got it for nothing," Blair remembers. "During Marc Bohan's time at Dior, I bought a white organza wedding dress. He added a pale green belt. They'd let you buy the dress for $700. They wanted you to wear them."[15]

Specifically, designers wanted Mrs. William McCormick Blair Jr. to wear their clothes. And $700 would be the equivalent of about $5,300 today. The cost of haute couture has risen far faster than the rate of inflation, as the designs have become more lavish and ostentatious, and the skills required to produce them increasingly endangered. The prices of contemporary haute couture gowns—those Cinderella red carpet fantasies—can spiral up to $75,000 and beyond.

Wealthy clients weren't the only ones bolstering the reputations of the haute couture designers; occasionally it was the *vendeuses* themselves who lent panache to the houses with which they worked. "I started with Givenchy at the beginning, when he was at [Elsa] Schiaparelli," recalls Dreda Mele, a former *vendeuse* renowned for her taste and connections. Beginning in 1943, Mele developed a relationship with Givenchy that lasted ten years, until she moved on to the atelier of designer André Courrèges. Mele was a true rainmaker.[16]

Born in Bordeaux and educated at the Marymount School in New York City, she was quite beautiful in her youth and remains a striking woman in her eighties, a brunette with deep-set eyes. She was married twice and, as she merrily shares, could have acquired husbands on countless other occasions. She met her first husband in Capri. Her second husband adored yachts. She has most recently been in a decades-long relationship with Philippe Stern, a Frenchman who has a home in Switzerland, which is where she lives when she is not in her stately Paris apartment on Cours Albert Premier.

Mele was lucky enough to have been born into a family of means, and she could have enjoyed a lifetime of leisure. But circumstances demanded otherwise. Her father wanted her to occupy her time with something other than parties. So at age fourteen, she promised her father, on his deathbed, that she would work.

Her mother added another impetus for employment. Not particularly generous with the family funds, her mother had been a beautiful but cold apparition in her daughter's life. "My mother was dressing at Balenciaga. She was very chic. I had the eye of my mother *and* my father. He was very, *very* good looking. I started to realize I could bring Hubert [de Givenchy] a lot of friends," Mele says. "I brought him Jackie Kennedy."

The influence of wealthy clients; the taste, social standing, and business savvy of the *vendeuses* who serviced them; and the skilled craftsman-ship and creativity of the designers all came together to make haute couture a dominant and influential cultural presence from the 1950s to the beginning of the 1970s. But today, even as Mele recalls those years, she admits that the moss-colored tailored suede jacket she wears is from Ralph Lauren. An *American!* How times have changed.

To fully understand how a woman like Dreda Mele could come to wear Ralph Lauren, one must look at a single event in November of 1973 at the Palace of Versailles.

Two

Copycats and Salami

In the early twentieth century, America's wealthiest women were crossing the Atlantic to assemble their wardrobes because there was little to be found in the way of high fashion closer to home. The United States fashion business was comprised almost entirely of the garment trade—factory work. The New York fashion industry, one of the biggest employers in the city, consisted of musty workrooms filled with striving immigrants from countries like Poland, Austria, and Italy who were trudging toward the middle class one laborious stitch at a time.

Clothing production had always been dangerous work. In 1911, the devastating Triangle Shirtwaist Factory fire killed more than one hundred young women and men. Trapped behind locked doors, they perished—many of them leaping to their deaths from the building's highest floors to escape the lunging flames. Witnesses watched in horror as girls plummeted toward the cobblestone streets, their bodies hitting the pavement with gut-wrenching thuds, because the firefighters' ladders proved too short to reach them.[1]

In the shadow of that tragedy, unions grew in size, vitriol, and moral authority, among them the International Ladies' Garment Workers'

Union. Union bosses fought to rid the city of its soul-sapping, deadly sweatshops, but they also used their mighty membership, which at its peak reached into the hundreds of thousands, to influence the politics of the day. By the mid-1920s virtually every aspiring politician felt compelled to parade through the Garment District in hopes of securing the support of the unionized dressmakers, patternmakers, fabric producers, and the like.[2] In the years after the Triangle Shirtwaist Factory fire, the American fashion industry had influence and scale, but not much in the way of original style. It was safer work, but it was a world of cigar-smoking ruffians and callused seamstresses, whirring sewing machines and clacking mills. With few exceptions, there was little enviable or glamorous produced in the Garment District, which was centered around New York's Seventh Avenue.

Those exceptions, however, hinted at what was possible. A handful of women and men were striding down a more refined path and making names for themselves. Hattie Carnegie, who began her fashion career as a milliner, opened her own dress salon in 1928, selling original designs.[3] She established an enviable reputation with high-end, ready-to-wear, and a deep backroom that served as the training ground for designers Norman Norell, Claire McCardell, James Galanos, and others who would go on to fame and influence.

Elizabeth Hawes, a contemporary of Carnegie's, was an early fashion populist, believing that well-designed, functional clothes should be readily available. She was convinced that creativity could flourish outside the French ateliers. Hawes ran her company from 1928 to 1940, first with her partner Rosemary Harden and then on her own.

And Nettie Rosenstein was, for a time, the American queen of fancy ready-to-wear. She opened a dress house that bore her name in 1916 and kept it in business until 1961. Along the way, it grew into a million-dollar company trading in dresses that retailed from $98.50 to $500—quite expensive for the time. Paris prices, actually. But Rosenstein built her business, in part, by embracing a quintessentially French idea: the little black dress, which had originally been declared fashionable by French designers. Rosenstein made it accessible to middle-class American women.[4]

In the mid-twentieth century department stores had more brand recognition and cultural influence than any individual designers. Stores like Lord & Taylor, Ohrbach's, and Bergdorf Goodman dictated the fashions of the day, not the designers themselves. Rosenstein was one of the first exceptions to that rule. Department stores competed to carry her dresses, which could be supremely chic with narrow waists and buoyant skirts. Stores were eager to advertise the Rosenstein brand. Such was Rosenstein's prominence that she created Mamie Eisenhower's 1953 inaugural ball gown, a pale pink, sleeveless peau de soie confection embroidered with two thousand rhinestones. More debutante sweet than sophisticated, the dress now resides in the Smithsonian National Museum of American History.

Into this small but burgeoning world of American fashion waltzed a young woman who would later transform the industry. Eleanor Lambert grew up in Crawfordsville, Indiana, a tiny city about 150 miles southeast of Chicago and home to Wabash College, a private liberal arts school for men. With $100 tucked in her little handbag to fund her new life, Lambert arrived in New York just before the start of the Great Depression. She was only twenty-two years old, but she was endowed with bulldozer determination, a love for the arts, and the soul of P. T. Barnum. (Her father had been an advance man for the Ringling Brothers Circus.) She came east, as so many did, looking for glamour, prospects . . . herself.

She had studied at the Chicago Art Institute and aspired to be a sculptor. She adored antique furniture and porcelains. She was captivated by contemporary painting. But she was obsessed with fashion. While in school, she'd dabbled in fashion writing and served as a freelance fashion illustrator for local department stores.

Lambert was neither exceedingly wealthy nor was she a classic beauty of *Vogue* standing. She was a brown-eyed midwestern girl of modest means who needed to work for a living and who hid her fine, lank, sandy brown hair under a turban.

When Lambert went looking for her first New York job, she did not land at any of the young, quixotic fashion firms. Instead, the art school graduate patched together the beginnings of a career with two part-time engagements. In the morning she helped design book jackets for Franklin Spear, a small public relations and advertising firm, and in the afternoon she worked in consumer research for a retail consultant.

She crossed the threshold into public relations when she began to bring her own clients into Franklin Spear. From the moment she arrived in New York, Lambert had been drawn to the city's artists and art galleries. She headed to Fifty-seventh Street, where there were rows of galleries, and pitched herself to the art world. With a combination of charm and determination, she formed relationships with photographer Cecil Beaton, sculptor Isamu Noguchi, and painters Jackson Pollock and Salvador Dalí.[5] Her new art clients each paid her $10 a week.

For years, Lambert concentrated her energy on artists. She threw herself into helping to create the Museum of Modern Art and the Whitney Museum of American Art, where she became the press agent. She became the public relations representative for the American Art Dealers Association, which she'd help found. In 1934, on a trip to Europe to help promote the American Pavilion of Contemporary Art at the tenth Venice Biennale, she met journalist Seymour Berkson. They married two years later.

As the years passed, the American fashion industry began to change, in part due to World War II. The upheaval during the war, along with rationing of materials and the closure of France's great fashion houses, served as an opening for American designers. Women needed clothes and stores needed to fill their racks.

The American fashion industry had another growth spurt. Hattie Carnegie's former employees Claire McCardell and Norman Norell, as well as Chicago-born Main Rousseau Bocher, all launched their own businesses during this period.

Norell made a name for himself as the dean of bourgeois American taste. His showroom at 550 Seventh Avenue was entirely black and white, with a reception area that smelled of his signature fragrance and a desk adorned with orchids. For the pleasure of visitors, there was a little satin bench, a mirrored table, and an enormous arrangement of calla lilies. His workers wore white coats and would carefully drape garments across their outstretched arms to present them to clients. It was every bit as overwrought as it sounds.

Norell was the rare American designer who had his own *cabine* of models, just as the French did. He worked consistently and exclusively with the same group of women, *his* women. Norell was enthralled with the work of French painter Kees van Dongen and inspired by the artist's stylized depiction of women. All the models in Norell's showroom resembled van Dongen's 1920s flappers, with dark eye makeup, three sets of false eyelashes, and slicked-back dark hair. Norell was not a fan of blondes.[6]

"He was my first idol," admits designer Louis Dell'Olio. "What a naive kid I was—a kid from Long island with a summer job at Norman Norell!

"I thought everything on Seventh Avenue was like this," says Dell'Olio, recalling his 1966 internship. "What a rude awakening. This was not the norm. This was the exception."[7]

Decades later, First Lady Michelle Obama wore a vintage Norell cinched-waist black party dress to a Washington Christmas celebration in 2010. It was a fine reminder of the kind of 1950s decorum that guided the era's well-dressed ladies. But it was also a look that was derivative of French taste.

Although he was unquestionably American, Main Bocher set up shop in Paris, calling himself Mainbocher and pronouncing the name with a

French twist. He became an international sensation thanks to his fine fabrics, simple silhouettes, and the snob appeal of being based in Paris. He created the pale blue gown American socialite Wallis Simpson wore to marry the Duke of Windsor.

Claire McCardell became one of the most influential founders of American ready-to-wear by emphasizing function, practicality, and ease. She made signature use of brass hardware, patch pockets, the Empire waist, and madras plaids.

These designers all had gumption and a marketing strategy. But in large measure, it was Dorothy Shaver who elevated their stature. Born in the small Arkansas town of Center Point in 1893, Shaver eventually became president of Lord & Taylor—a major feat for a woman—and was dubbed "Fifth Avenue's First Lady" by *Time* magazine in 1945. She championed American designers with a public relations blitz called "The American Look."

"She made them happen," recalls fashion editor Marylou Luther. "In those years, you really needed a store to send you off. Stores were gods."[8]

It was a designer who wanted to make a name for herself, rather than rely on the power and largesse of department stores, who was responsible for nudging Eleanor Lambert into the fashion world. Annette Simpson, an American designer who had participated in a fashion show at Lord & Taylor in 1932, had gotten a taste of applause and adulation. She wanted more. She'd seen the newspaper stories that Eleanor Lambert had engineered on behalf of artists and she wanted Lambert to represent her.[9] Lambert agreed, but the difficulty in doing so was a lesson. Lambert learned that Lord & Taylor had opened women's eyes to American products, but with the exception of a few standouts—designers like Norrell, Mainbocher, and McCardell—consumers and the media remained uninterested in the individuals and personalities behind them.

"Shopping in the forty-odd stores we had in New York, it wasn't about designers, but about classifications of merchandise. If you wanted a dress, you went to the dress department. If you wanted a sweater, you went to

28

the sweater department," explains Joan Kaner, who retired from the retail industry in 2005 as fashion director for Neiman Marcus.[10]

In the 1950s and '60s, companies such as Bonwit Teller, Ohrbach's, Lord & Taylor, Bergdorf Goodman, and Saks Fifth Avenue were the names that carried prestige. Yet most of the clothes they were selling weren't original designs; they were copies of Paris's creative output. Copying was not just standard practice for American stores and designers, it was formalized and conducted in the light of day.

Regularly one could open the pages of *Vogue* magazine to find a photo story offering "Paris Copies—for U.S.A. Wearing." In it, image after image would depict original garments from haute couture designers such as Christian Dior, Nina Ricci, Pierre Cardin, and Guy Laroche, along with helpful captions detailing where a reader might find the American imitations.

Dior red wool coat, with incisive seams making the point of a very controlled flare. This, imported and copied by Saks Fifth Avenue.

In wool fleece, a pair of Dior coat-points—well-shaped flare, the colour taupe. Copied by Frank Gallant for Saks Fifth Avenue.

Wide-flaring yellow-orange wool double-breasted coat, copied by Frechtel for Lord & Taylor.

Coat of red chinchilla wool with a long fling of scarf, no collar, rounded skirt. Imported by, and copied for, Macy's.

The idea that the industry so openly copied Paris designs may seem shocking today. The American fashion industry has spent years lobbying Washington for copyright protections on its most original designs, and the protection of intellectual property is a principle concern of trade negotiations with countries such as China. And in Paris, design houses like Chanel once experienced such paroxysms of paranoia about photographs of their collections becoming instantly available by computer that they have gone so far as to ban online media outlets from shows and bring legal action against photographers who post unauthorized images online.

But two generations ago, the American department stores pioneered the system of approved copies. The French fashion unions signed off on the scheme because it meant more money for its members and it magnified France's influence in the marketplace. By the 1960s, these commercial entities—retailers, not individuals—accounted for the bulk of couture purchases.[11]

To enter the system, a store was vetted for cachet, aesthetics, and financial solvency. Then it paid a *caution*—French for a kind of security deposit against future purchases—for access to the haute couture ateliers. That fee might have been a promise to purchase a minimum number of ensembles, or it could have been a flat dollar amount. In her detailed analysis of the business, *Couture & Commerce*, scholar Alexandra Palmer notes that the *caution* at Balenciaga was a minimum of two ensembles, while at Dior it was $300 for store buyers and $1,000 for manufacturers.[12]

Bergdorf Goodman, for example, paid its *caution* and sent its representatives to Paris twice a year. They bought original couture designs from Yves Saint Laurent, along with the patterns and high-quality fabrics used by the couturier. Once back home, the new season's offerings were presented to the local well-to-do clientele in a "mini haute couture show."[13] Customers made their selections and then had fittings as required by the agreement with the design house, with the construction carried out by the store's own in-house dressmakers. Clients could ask for changes and tweaks, but the finished garment would bear the label YVES SAINT LAURENT FOR BERGDORF GOODMAN.

The store could also buy the Saint Laurent dress in a simple muslin and commission Seventh Avenue manufacturers to reproduce it in a variety of reasonably priced fabrics. The label in these dresses would simply read BERGDORF GOODMAN. It would be modeled after Saint Laurent, but it would not bear his imprimatur. And its cost would reflect its more distanced connection to the original Paris atelier.[14]

Marshall Field had a particularly close relationship with Christian Dior.[15] Its lead buyer attended the Dior couture shows and purchased entire collections for the store. In the 1950s, Marshall Field was one of the largest couture customers. In Chicago, the store organized three fashion shows. One was to educate the staff about the season's trends; the second was for American designers and manufacturers who could not attend the Paris couture shows; and the third was for special clients.

The designers and manufacturers attending this second show would receive a detailed packet with line drawings of the garments, technical measurements, and in some instances, the matching fabric itself. This booklet gave manufacturers a clear directive for the new season so they could produce copies of couture designs that Marshall Field and other stores peddled to the masses. For the fall 1952 season, for example, the look book titled "Couture Collections: Marshall Field & Company" read "There's a new fashion feeling abroad! In essence, it's effortless elegance. Each important designer interprets it in his own way." What followed in the eleven-page booklet were detailed descriptions of the collections of Christian Dior, Cristobal Balenciaga, and Madame Grès. A Dior coat "looks deceptively simple but actually achieves the streamlined curves of an ideal feminine figure." It has a molded bodice, rounded sides, and a belt that is curved but "never tight." A Balenciaga suit has "lower pockets," "longer skirt," "absence of detail," "lowered, square neckline," and a "touch-me-not waistline." For each garment, the booklet included instructional sketches highlighting the shape of the sleeves, the type of fabric, the cut of the skirt, or the volume of the coat. Every part of a woman's wardrobe was discussed, from coats and jackets to suits and dresses, along with a full-page "Paris Headlines" section dedicated to hats.

The special clients attending the third show were allowed to order individual and personalized looks that were produced in-house, usually with a shared label, like CHRISTIAN DIOR FOR MARSHALL FIELD.[16]

For the American customer, there was no shame in buying copies. Everyone did it. Even at the height of haute couture's popularity, only a small group of exceptionally wealthy and influential American women traveled to Paris to purchase wardrobe selections for the season. Most well-off women simply waited for the copies to arrive at their local department store—that moment preceded by gushing advertising campaigns and breathless reports in the pages of *Women's Wear Daily*, which would pinpoint the exact day and hour the new styles would reach these shores. Women of modest means and more frugal types were even further down the delivery chain, but they still took their marching orders from Paris.

As late as 1972, two fashion presentations at Ohrbach's department store in New York drew more than four thousand women "from all over the country, many of whom supplement their original couture designs with Ohrbach's 'translations,'" *Washington Post* fashion editor Nina Hyde wrote.[17]

The shows drew not only middle-class and upper-middle-class strivers, but also public women of note, such as Eunice Kennedy Shriver and her sister-in-law Jean Kennedy Smith. Both women made hefty purchases, such as Dior suits, Saint Laurent dresses, and Ungaro coats.

Ohrbach's buying team had paid $3,000 for a Christian Dior suit in gray flannel, lined in electric blue. The fee was twice what a private client paid, Hyde explained, and it gave the store the right to copy the design—but not use the Dior name. Ohrbach's publicity office simply referred to Dior as "Monsieur X." Customers paid $395 for the reproduction.

A Valentino two-piece black chiffon short dress with a beaded top cost a couture customer $3,500. The Ohrbach's client paid $199.95 in the original fabric and only $155 in an alternative one.[18]

The purchases of prominent women were reported upon in a manner that underscored fashion's importance in matters of decorum, status, and acceptability. Fashion was a respected measure of cultural change, a reflection of social order, and a point of pride. Well-chosen fashion, even made-in-America copies of Paris originals, could provide an entry point into society for a woman who was not well-born. One American woman's dress might be couture and another's might be a Seventh Avenue reproduction, but both ladies were engaged in the same conversation. Fashion had not yet diverged into countless stylistic tribes, each with its own codes and hierarchies. There was a kind of democracy embedded in the fashion industry's tyranny.

Fashion's rules could be cruel and unrelenting for everyone. The language of fashion focused on the new shapes, the right hemline, *the* seasonal color. To be appropriate meant wearing the appropriate silhouettes, whether that was the wasp waist of Dior's "New Look" or the shapeless sack dress and pillbox hat as defined by Balenciaga. Fashion was not a choice. It was a requirement, handed down not by a royal court but by ateliers located all the way across the Atlantic.

Occasionally, American women fought back. Fashion historian Timothy Long recalls news clips from the 1940s and '50s that chronicled a trip Christian Dior made to Chicago. Women rose up in protest, declaring, "We abhor Dior! We abhor skirts to the floor!"[19] One can imagine them, with their hands clenched into tight fists that pumped the air.

But as much as those fashion rebels might have abhorred Dior, opting out was not much of a possibility. American closets featured styles conceived in Paris; the backrooms of Seventh Avenue manufacturing houses and the grand department stores were filled with talented men and women charged with copying Paris originals. Even American designers who had made names for themselves owed a debt to Paris.

"They always talk about Norman Norell as a great American designer. I remember Norman Norell paying his *caution* to go look at the [Paris] collections and getting his toile from Balenciaga," recalls Oscar de la Renta. "American fashion was copying French haute couture clothes. That was the basis of American fashion."[20]

For all the fillips of respectability and laudatory shows in the United States, American designers were cogs in a mom-and-pop industry of knock-offs and industrial production. Even in the late sixties, one could walk out on Seventh Avenue and find clusters of tailors sitting on the street curbs munching on a lunchtime meal of salami sandwiches.[21] There weren't restaurants to speak of in the Garment District. Fashion was overwhelmingly blue-collar work. Everyone brought his own lunch. And then went back to copying.

Three

Four Gentlemen
and a Powerhouse

Although she failed to get the public and the press to recognize Annette Simpson's talents, Eleanor Lambert believed that Simpson and her peers on Seventh Avenue had stories to tell. She continued to work with artists, but by the early 1940s she began focusing on fashion. As a publicist, she essentially had the field to herself.

Lambert began constructing a foundation that would eventually elevate American designers in the public eye. She involved herself with the unions that represented the dressmakers and the blouse producers, pitching stories to the press that would encourage women to keep shopping despite the fabric rationing during World War II. She courted political power brokers such as New York senator Jacob Javits, a liberal Republican who pushed to position fashion alongside visual arts and music in the public imagination and in federal legislation.

In the fall of 1963, Congress held four days of hearings to debate the importance of the arts in American society. Lambert testified on October 31, encouraging legislators to include fashion in their thinking: "Americans today are artists, honored and respected in many fields. Yet American fashion is still far from assuming its rightful place as a vital cultural force in our life, as a part of our world image."[1]

The result of the hearings, the National Foundation on the Arts and the Humanities Act of 1965, provided for education, protection, and advancement of the arts. But it did not set out budgets, nor did it specifically define the arts. There was no mention of fashion. Still, in the years surrounding its passage, there was an active effort on the part of Washington to promote American fashion. Under the auspices of the U.S. government in 1959 and again in 1967, Lambert organized shows of American fashion throughout the world, including one in Moscow.[2] She expanded her Rolodex of social contacts by producing charitable shows in support of the March of Dimes and for the 1964 World's Fair in New York.

"It was 1967, 1969 when it all started to happen," remembers designer Stan Herman. At that time, John Fairchild, whose grandfather founded *Women's Wear Daily* in 1910, began touting unheralded American designers in the publication's pages. He felt it was far more interesting to write about the charismatic creators of fashion than the grubby manufacturers and unimaginative bean counters. And with a ready outlet for stories about designers, Lambert's obsession only grew. "*WWD* made designers and designers made *WWD*," Herman says.[3]

Lambert was working feverishly to establish American fashion as an admirable institution. Yet with all her political machinations in Albany and Washington, D.C., in the late 1950s and '60s, she may have sowed her most important seed even earlier. In 1943, Lambert organized Fashion Press Week at the Plaza Hotel, the precursor to today's massive biannual fashion circus. Lambert set a single period in New York when fashion editors from around the country were invited to view the new collections in an orderly manner—and in a time frame that Lambert herself determined. Before she stepped in, designers presented their collections on their own schedule, with all the expected chaos. Without a critical mass of news, few papers bothered to cover the endless trickle of debuts.

Fashion Press Week consisted of tightly orchestrated presentations of clothes scheduled after the Paris shows and after the stores had made their selections for the coming season. Lambert provided photographs to the regional press—a little something different to each outlet so that it could claim exclusivity. She hosted luncheons during which she wooed editors. She doled out access to the designers, most of whom she eventually signed up as clients. She whispered conspiratorially to editors. She distributed her own regular column in which she announced the seasonal trends. She exerted a controlling authority over the media, aspects of which endure today.

Modern fashion publicists and the media are forever engaged in a power struggle that is fraught with false intimacy and ambiguous intentions. Lambert didn't aspire to a mutually beneficial relationship with the press; she wanted writers to be committed to celebrating American fashion, American designers, and, in particular, her clients. As Fashion Press Week became a habit within the media, Lambert's power expanded.

"So here we are sitting at the Plaza watching the clothes go by. They were all [Lambert's] clients. It would happen over several days, for hours. Lunch was served. We would be sitting on a little gilded chair," recalls Marylou Luther, who was a sweet-faced cub reporter at the *Des Moines Register* when she first began attending Fashion Week. Lambert rounded up sponsorship for the week and financed trips to New York for members of the regional press—at least those who would accept her largesse. Luther did not.

"I was sublimely happy. As my husband would say, 'fat, dumb and happy.' Then I went to work for the *Chicago Tribune* [about 1954] and I had this amazing boss: Eleanor Nangle. And Miss Nangle said, 'This doesn't make any sense. If you told a sports reporter that you can't cover the World Series until three months after it happened, he'd say you were crazy.' But that's what we were doing. We were seeing the clothes three months after the buyers had seen them.

"So we—Miss Nangle, me, the illustrator for the *Chicago Tribune*—we'd go to the showrooms. I got to Ben Zuckerman or Ben Reig. They were two of [Lambert's] clients. They asked you to sign in. I got to M-a-r-y-l and they said, 'Are you Marylou Luther from the *Chicago Tribune*? We're clients of Eleanor Lambert and she's asked us not to admit you.'"

"I said, 'Fine.'"[4]

Lambert was in complete control of the American fashion industry. The press saw the collections when and how she dictated they would. And Lambert doted on her clients, determined to make them the biggest stars of all.

The same year Lambert established Fashion Week, she dreamed up the Coty Awards—sponsored by the cosmetics company—to honor the work of designers. The winners were voted on by editors who attended Fashion Week. Eventually, the Coty Awards became so overtly commercial that designers protested. Tension also grew between emerging designers and the manufacturers who employed them. So in 1962, Lambert helped to found the Council of Fashion Designers of America, which became her operating base. The CFDA went on to become the lead trade organization for American designers. It now oversees its own version of Fashion Week and hands out awards each year in a celebrity-drenched gala at Lincoln Center. But for almost forty years, the Cotys were the premiere American fashion award. Frankly, they were the only award. And Lambert's clients were duly honored.

Lambert had no competition. If a designer wanted publicity, if he wanted to become a fashion personality, if he'd crafted an especially dynamic collection, he turned to Lambert because she knew all the editors. And she was relentless. She represented the groundbreaking generation of designers that included Hattie Carnegie, Lilly Daché, Norman Norell, and Mainbocher. Her roster included manufacturers such as Maurice Rentner, as well as designers like the French-born but New York–based Pauline Trigère, Herbert Kasper, Adrian, Ben Zuckerman, and Donald Brooks. If French designers such as Christian Dior needed someone to guide their publicity in the United States, they also turned to Lambert.

* * *

Almost forty years after first arriving in New York, Lambert had grown into a strong-willed matron who favored red dresses and blackamoor jewelry from Venice. Not exactly imperious, but relentlessly, gently manipulative, Lambert was a master cajoler and diplomat—and, sometimes, a yeller. She had one foot in the socially constrained past and another in the blustery whirlwind of change.

In the late 1960s, Lambert began putting the full force of her marketing skills and political savvy into a self-created bully pulpit to bring fame to Seventh Avenue and raise the stature of fashion in the public consciousness. Once again, she turned to the nation's capital.

In 1968, under the patronage of Lady Bird Johnson, Lambert produced a fashion show at the White House. The historic show took place Thursday, February 29, in the State Dining Room. It served as an addendum to Mrs. Johnson's beautification project and the administration's "Discover America First" campaign, which encouraged folks to spend their vacation dollars at home rather than overseas.[5]

The fashion show highlighted summer looks from twenty-five American designers, including Norman Norell, James Galanos, Adele Simpson, Geoffrey Beene, and a young Oscar de la Renta, whom Lambert had just added to her client roster. The show was timed to coincide with the midwinter meeting of the National Governors' Conference. Of course, the audience for the show and accompanying luncheon included just the wives, not the governors, who were all men.[6]

Mrs. Johnson's opening remarks focused more on road trips and postcard sites than hemlines: "Gathered in this room are some of the most accomplished tour guides in the country. I know because many of them have helped me discover their own state: from the white church steeples and covered bridges of New England to the wide open space of the American west."[7]

Against a backdrop of American landscape photography, models moved demurely in red and white day dresses with matching coats, white chiffon evening gowns, and prim picture hats. Their clothes were lit by the glow of chandeliers and wall sconces.

"I remember Mrs. Johnson wore white, and Pauline Trigère dared to wear red," reminisced writer Barbara Cloud, who was there. "Try as I might, I don't remember what I wore, but I know I carried white gloves. Didn't everybody?[8]

The nature of American fashion was evolving. People began to see it not merely as a trade but as a point of national pride, a source of empowerment, perhaps even a salve for some of what was ailing the country—the world—as the 1960s staggered into the '70s.

By the late 1960s, Eleanor Lambert had almost single-handedly established a fashion industry in America. She had a client roster full of aspiring designers and manufacturers; she held tight control over the reporters and illustrators who covered fashion in the press; and she wielded considerable influence with union bosses, politicians, and cultural heavyweights. Lambert was in the unique position of being able to bring an entire American industry to the world's stage—and no one would benefit more from her clout than five of her favorite clients: Oscar de la Renta, Bill Blass, Halston, Anne Klein, and Stephen Burrows.

Of all her American clients, the one with the most experience was de la Renta. Born in the Dominican Republic, de la Renta was the only boy of seven children. His father owned an insurance company. De la Renta could be shy and he sometimes stuttered, but he was also charming and tirelessly competitive. At twenty, he left the Dominican Republic and moved to Madrid, intending to become an artist. But he soon turned to fashion sketching, and ultimately to design. Working in the Spanish studios of Cristobal Balenciaga, de la Renta longed to be in Paris, the home of haute couture and a city he idolized. When he finally made the move, he realized he wanted financial success even more than the romance of history.

"I was working for Lanvin in Paris. I was making $400 or $500 a month in Paris. There were already some assistant designers who had gone to New York and Los Angeles and they were making in a week what I was making in a month," de la Renta remembers. "I came to New York because I felt the future and the big money in fashion was not in couture but ready-to-wear."[9]

Over the years, de la Renta built an empire, one that now brings in hundreds of millions of dollars a year in revenue. He is known for his ladylike clothes and his ability to make any woman, whether an awkward young starlet or a dignified dowager, look and feel pretty. His aesthetic is predicated on the simple thesis that a woman—no matter her age—wants to be wooed. And for those women lucky enough to engage directly with him, they are on the receiving end of Old World manners, easy flirtation, and unabashedly dishy humor.

Tall, tan, with a Roman nose and dark eyes, de la Renta came to New York in 1963. He had several prospects for employment: the American office of Christian Dior was looking for a designer to help with its nascent ready-to-wear line, and he had an opportunity at Elizabeth Arden to design a couture collection. De la Renta was also armed with a letter of introduction, an old-fashioned version of polite networking, to Diana Vreeland, who had just become editor in chief of *Vogue*. On his fifth day in New York, Vreeland invited him to Sunday tea at her Park Avenue apartment.

The aspiring designer was intimidated meeting Vreeland, who was well on her way to becoming a fashion legend thanks to her discerning taste and influence. She styled herself as a kind of fashion sphinx, with raven hair, scarlet-slashed cheeks, and a vocabulary laden with inscrutable aphorisms. De la Renta was even more unnerved when her booming voice squawked: *"YOUNG MAN, TELL ME WHAT YOU WANT TO DOOOO? WHAT DOOOO YOU THINK IS IMPORTANT?"*

He shared his belief that the future of fashion lay in ready-to-wear. De la Renta recalls that Vreeland had a particularly astute assessment of his two job offers: "Dior is ready-to-wear; Arden is couture. If you're interested in ready-to-wear, go to Arden. At Dior you'll be behind a big name and never able to emerge from behind it. Arden is not a big name. You will be able to make a name for yourself much quicker working there."[10]

De la Renta spent a little more than two years working for Arden, where he demanded a starting salary of $700 a week and then tried to convince her that she should begin a ready-to-wear line. She was intrigued by the idea. The ambitious young designer went to the Seventh Avenue office of Ben Shaw, a manufacturing dynamo and financier who had backed the collections of countless American designers. Shaw was interested. "Then Arden changes her mind," de la Renta recalls.

"So I came to tell Ben Shaw: Arden changed her mind. He says he's not interested in Arden; 'I'm interested in you.' So I left Arden and cut my salary in half."[11]

In 1965, de la Renta took a job at Jane Derby, an upscale ready-to-wear label that had been around since the 1930s and was located at 550 Seventh Avenue—Shaw's building, the building that through much of the 1970s and '80s housed the crème de la crème of American designers. The deal was that the label would read OSCAR DE LA RENTA FOR JANE DERBY.

His work bore the mod simplicity of the 1960s, but incorporated lustrous fabrics and glittering rhinestones. A typical dress, for example, was a chemise with an A-line silhouette in aqua silk. The bodice was trimmed in crisscrossing lines of pastel-colored paillettes. Another dress from that period was a sleeveless metallic sheath with undulating bright orange stripes. It was accompanied by a matching coat with bracelet sleeves and a Nehru collar.

De la Renta was still a salaried employee, but his name was on the label and he had an option to buy in. When Derby died less than a year after de la Renta's arrival, he did just that, with Shaw's help. By 1973, the business was renamed Oscar de la Renta.

On his own, de la Renta's work gradually became more luxurious and exuberantly romantic. Today, his dresses and suits are devoted to lady-like formality. They do not hug the body but are politely acquainted with it. His eveningwear makes lavish use of ruffles, organza, and taffeta. The skirts can be voluminous, the shoulders bare, but the décolletage always respectful.

"The handsome, dark-haired designer's efforts have been hailed as almost couture, particularly his recently shown fall and winter collection," declared a 1967 story in the *New York Times*. "In it, Mr. de la Renta ranged from the splendor of imperial Russia (a calf-length coat bordered in fur) to Buck Rogers tunics worn over little pants."[12]

De la Renta made his mark among wealthy social swells with the help of his first wife, Françoise de Langlade, who was the former editor of French *Vogue* and ten years his senior. Born in Paris, she had dual French/American citizenship, thanks to her first husband, who had been a U.S. diplomat.

She recalled first meeting de la Renta at a dinner at Maxim's in Paris in honor of the Duke and Duchess of Windsor. He remembers meeting her under far more prosaic circumstances: when she was an editor at *Vogue* and he was a sketcher.[13] The two married on Halloween in 1967. He was thirty-five and she was forty-five; she was an influential editor and he was just setting out on his own as a designer. She was comfortable on the society circuit and in the upper echelons of French fashion. She had a penchant for entertaining, a skilled eye for more-is-more interior design, and an elegant sense of personal style. If de la Renta was her charismatic Romeo, she was his rock of Gibraltar and his passport to rarefied worlds and the ladies who would ultimately wear his clothes.

As de la Renta's star rose, Eleanor Lambert made sure to sign him as a client. Lambert was de la Renta's stalwart champion. She'd worked with Jane Derby and she supported him when he took over Derby's business. Whenever there was a charity fashion show, an opportunity to spotlight American designers, Lambert made sure de la Renta had a chance to shine.

William Ralph Blass was another one of Lambert's earliest clients—and one of the most loyal. Just as she had done with Derby and de la Renta, Lambert had represented Blass's boss, Maurice Rentner. She was waiting to support Blass when he stepped out on his own.

Blass, a jaunty young man who led a self-described "colorless" childhood in Fort Wayne, Indiana, did a stint in the army and entered the New York fashion world as a sketch artist making $35 a week—the most common entry point into design studios. Fashion illustration was the industry's preferred form of communication before it was shunted aside for photography. In a design studio, the sketch was the intermediary between idea and functional pattern. It was the fantasy of the frock put down on paper and doled out to the press.

In the 1960s, Blass moved up to cranking out daywear, first at Anna Miller and Co. and then for Maurice Rentner. "At that time, designers were kept very much in the backroom, almost something to be ashamed of. The minute a collection was over, we were encouraged to take long holidays, which gave the manufacturer a chance to totally change the collection," Blass said.[14]

From the moment he arrived in New York, Blass proved himself an expert negotiator of the beau monde. In short order, his life took on the rhythms of a Cole Porter soundtrack. Starting in the 1950s, he moved through café society as if he'd invented it, making connections all along the way. According to Blass: "Society then was built on being out and being seen."[15] He became a regular at the Stork Club, El Morocco, and the Bombay Room—the watering holes of the day. He engaged in what he called "verbal roughhousing," a kind of rigorous repartee during

44

which he played the teasing but adoring big brother to a class of women often treated like glass figurines. He went to their parties, and when their husbands begged off, he escorted them to dinners and kept them entertained during luncheons. If Ernest Hemingway, with his macho swagger and charisma, had been a designer, he would have been Bill Blass.

Blass walked a fine line between the public world he'd crafted for himself and a true sense of pride and comfort in those accomplishments. It would be years before he would admit to his profession, often telling people that he was in advertising instead of fashion. "You see, in those days, there was a stigma about being on Seventh Avenue, which I've always felt had a lot to do with anti-Semitism. There was also a stigma, of course, about being a designer, because there was a stereotype of a designer—an effeminate man who wasn't any good at business. The combination of the two would have been socially deadly. Never mind that one, I'm not Jewish, and two, I certainly don't think I fit that stereotype."[16]

If that was his deepest personal insecurity, his greatest professional one was that he never worked for a Paris couture house—not like his constant rival and friend de la Renta. Blass was never tutored in couture's painstaking technique.[17] But like every other American designer, or copyist, he had plenty of experience with French fashion.

"We absolutely became dependent on Dior's New Look, because that's what everybody wanted. You might get an idea or two from Balenciaga's tailoring or from Madame Grès, but no question about it, everything we did was derivative of Paris. In those days, that was considered the norm."[18]

Blass emerged from the backroom in 1970, when he bought out the Rentner name. His clothes developed a quiet confidence that was proudly American in its temperament and beloved by the locked-jaw, horsey set. The clothes had ease and panache and were considered by critics to be the most chic and wearable creations of the rising Seventh Avenue talents. "Women should always look terribly clean and healthy and fresh," Blass said.[19]

A quintessential Blass look included a jaunty pair of gray flannel trousers and a tailored tweed or velvet jacket with a hint of menswear bravado or a sweater set transformed into an easy-to-wear skirted suit. He loved herringbone and pinstripes for day, and his eveningwear was full of glamour. He was not shy around sequins, but his clothes were never fussy or precious. His style was American—not New York. He was firm about that.

Certainly no one was more adept at selling his clothes than Blass himself. He made himself available to his ladies, and they loved him for it. He traveled the country to sit with them at their teas and charity luncheons and helped them make selections for their seasonal wardrobes. His dazzling road shows helped him to eventually build his business into a $500 million behemoth.

Like Blass and Lambert, Roy Halston Frowick was a midwesterner. He was born in Des Moines, Iowa, and educated at Indiana University, but his trajectory as a fashion designer began in Chicago, where he was a hatmaker and window dresser for Carson Pirie Scott. He came to New York in 1957 and worked for milliner Lilly Daché, who was one of Lambert's clients. Lambert took notice of Halston's skill in interpreting Daché's outré sensibility.

In a Liberace-esque showroom, with walls lined with mirrors and upholstered in pink, tufted satin, celebrities such as Loretta Young could try on Daché's hats: some adorned with fruit and fowl, one with an attached "complexion veil," dyed green where it skimmed the eyes and pink at the cheeks.

In 1959, Halston moved on from Daché to the custom hat salon at Bergdorf Goodman, a second-floor space of mirrored tables where well-heeled ladies sat and tried on hats at a time when hats were de rigueur.

Halston, as he called himself, became Lambert's next-generation designer. He was tall and dashing, with a made-for-fame ego. He was also blessed with good taste, fancy friends, and luck. While at Bergdorf, Lambert began to broadcast his talent to editors and writers. She wove stories about his rise from Indiana kid to Bergdorf star. By 1962 he'd won his first Coty Award.

At Bergdorf, Halston met some of the city's wealthiest and most socially prominent women, one of whom provided him with $125,000 in seed money so that he could leave Bergdorf and set up his own business in 1968. The first customer in his new East Sixty-eighth Street showroom was Babe Paley. There was arguably no bigger fashion fish to hook than this perennial member of the best-dressed set.[20]

Nine months after launching his own ready-to-wear line in 1972, Halston passed the $3 million mark in orders.[21] His name was synonymous with ankle-grazing cashmere sweater dresses, shirtdresses cut from a newfangled microfiber called Ultrasuede, and tunics. In August of 1972, Halston's favorite model, Karen Bjornson, appeared on the cover of *Newsweek* wearing a purple Ultrasuede hat with a wide brim along with the headline EASE AND ELEGANCE DESIGNED BY HALSTON. That same year, when he received his fourth Coty Award at New York's Alice Tully Hall, the Andy Warhol character actress Pat Ast—two hundred pounds of artful, frizzy-haired kitsch—sang "Happy Birthday" to him from a giant fake cake rolled onstage.

Halston had become a celebrity, one surrounded by a coterie of models (the Halstonettes) and stars such as Liza Minnelli. While Blass conquered café society, Halston set out to dominate the burgeoning 1970s nightclub scene. He became impossible to ignore.

In early 1973, Halston sold his company to the Norton Simon conglomerate, which was in an acquisition frenzy, for $16 million.[22] The sale was huge and became the talk of the fashion industry. Lambert did not broker the Norton Simon deal, which pushed Halston into the stratosphere, but she ballyhooed it to the press.

* * *

Sportswear designer Anne Klein was Lambert's gal. Simple female kinship explains much of Lambert's mama-bear ferocity when it came to Klein. But Lambert also recognized that Klein was creating clothes for a newly independent, professional, glass-ceiling-shattering woman—the kind of woman that Lambert had become by default.

Klein was born Hannah Golofski in Brooklyn, New York, in 1923. She was a fine-boned, trim woman with gray-green eyes and wavy hair. She worked behind the scenes as a freelance sketcher (everyone, it seemed, had been a sketcher at some point) and did a stint at Varden Petites. Bill Blass worked briefly as her assistant there, a job from which he was fired after less than a year. He recalled Klein telling a colleague, "He has good manners but no talent," to which he retorted, "Isn't that funny? She has no manners *and* no talent."[23] The two eventually became friends, but Blass retained a habit of condescendingly noting that she designed *sportswear.*

Using herself as a model, Klein transformed the silhouette of petites from short and matronly to lean and well proportioned. Indeed, she pushed petites toward their modern-day cut, which assumes a woman is not only short, but also a gamine.

In 1948, she and her first husband, Ben Klein, a clothing manufacturer, created Junior Sophisticates, which became a rousing success. Klein transformed junior fashion into something grown-up and stylish, shifting it from a look defined by ruffles and bows to one that was youthful, leggy, and chic. For more than a decade Klein worked behind the scenes at Junior Sophisticates, even after she and Ben divorced in 1958.

For a long time, she and Ben worked outside the insular fashion circle ruled by Lambert. While Lambert held sway over how and when fashion editors gained access to new styles, the Kleins went rogue. Lambert wanted the buyers to see the collections first, but the Kleins allowed them and the press to see their work simultaneously.

"I'll always remember the designers who would show to us," says fashion editor Marylou Luther. "Ben Klein . . . he was totally amazing and really smart. He'd say, 'Yeah, why wouldn't I show to you?' "[24]

Anne Klein was hardworking and focused. She was not a social gadabout. Instead, she was a realist interested in the needs of working women, who were not just taking on jobs, but embarking on careers. If she thought a silhouette was compelling, Klein didn't hesitate to borrow it wherever she found it. Luther once visited Klein's showroom wearing an orange canvas raincoat. It was vaguely Scandinavian in feeling, in keeping with the look of the moment. Klein loved it. She asked if she could borrow it for a few minutes. Klein immediately took it into the sample room so pattern-makers could copy it.

"She was a garmento," Luther recalls. "She was very aggressive and very outspoken. But she was always smiling; she wasn't mean. She was just really sure of herself."[25]

In 1965, Klein and her new husband, Matthew "Chip" Rubenstein, co-founded Anne Klein and Company. They hired Lambert to promote it. The new label was a full flowering of Klein's ideas about the contemporary woman and her relationship to clothes—the desire for ease, accessibility, and sophistication. Contemporary young women, who now rely on brands such as Ann Taylor for their work wardrobe, owe a debt of gratitude to Klein. She didn't create clothes to boost a woman's social standing or help her land a husband. Instead, she produced one of the earliest versions of chic career dressing, a luxurious mix-and-match sensibility that preceded the 1976 launch of the more down-market Liz Claiborne.

In that way Klein's work was controversial. It wasn't in the tradition of Paris. And it wasn't coolly glamorous. One of her looks from 1969 included a pair of russet and white wool knickers paired with a rust-colored wool safari jacket and a white turtleneck. It was vaguely horsey with a smidge of urbanity. Some saw it as brilliantly prescient. "The workforce for women was growing and growing, and these women needed clothes. They could go buy a suit, but that's not what they needed," explains

49

designer Louis Dell'Olio, who worked at Klein's company from 1974 to 1993. "She introduced a new type of dressing. It wasn't just a nice-fitting jacket and skirt. A maxi, suede skirt, a poor boy sweater, a hip-hugger belt—you'd go to Anne for that."

"What she was doing was so relevant," Dell'Olio continues. "She dressed the new workforce of women."[26]

Others saw it as a bore. The stuff of a dull nine-to-five life.

"I had to cover her when I was at *Glamour*," says former fashion editor Frances Patiky Stein. "We didn't get along at all. We eventually got to be very good friends. And she made nice sportswear. But it wasn't anything historical."[27]

Klein borrowed from menswear; Chanel inspired her; and she was firmly rooted in the commercial ethos of Seventh Avenue. She wasn't a fragile artist struggling to turn out one collection after another. She wasn't a charismatic member of the social set. And she wasn't a hip party girl. She was a bit of a workaholic. But she was building a company that was intended to be larger than a single personality. And she was fighting an industry that remained enamored with the male gaze and a French hierarchy that was dismissive of practicality.

Klein's focus and drive were part of her nature. But she'd also had a health scare—the kind of event that brings mortality into clear focus. In the late 1960s, Klein fought a battle with breast cancer and came out the other side. She was lucky; by the mid-seventies, the standard of treatment for breast cancer was mastectomy, and the five-year survival rate was only 75 percent. More than thirty years later, the survival rate is 90 percent, and treatment options now include lumpectomy and hormone therapy.[28]

In early 1973, Klein signed up with new investors: Tomio Taki, a Japanese textile and apparel mogul, and his business partner, Frank Mori, who would help the company expand. Klein, Taki says, was constantly thinking about design—not just form, but also function.

"There's an ultimate kind of designer who thinks you can improve anything. Anne went through a mastectomy and she was ready to redesign the hospital to make it more efficient and more comfortable," Taki recalls.[29]

Klein's focus was on the longevity of her company, and she took great pains to make sure the press knew its creative bench was deep. The brand was not wholly reliant on its namesake. As proof, she often pointed to her talented young assistant: a Long Island girl from a garment industry family named Donna Karan.

The fifth designer Lambert would eventually invite to Versailles was such a rapidly rising star that he wasn't even her client when she extended her invitation—though she made sure he had been added to her roster by the time they crossed the Atlantic. Blass and de la Renta had gotten to know Lambert when she represented the manufacturing bosses for whom they once worked. She'd seen Halston and Klein's work early, when they were still young assistants, and had declared them talents worth watching. But Stephen Burrows sort of snuck up on her. He did so because his arrival in the spotlight was not by the typical route. Lambert didn't introduce him to editors; they pointed him out to her. He showed his first collection during her Fashion Press Week because pretty much everyone did, but he was not yet her client.

Burrows was an exciting young designer with an aesthetic no one had ever seen before. His fresh sensibility had nothing to do with Paris; it had nothing to do with what the magazines were showing. It was straight from the street, the dance clubs, the neighborhoods. And it was deliciously hip. Burrows was also a black man at a time when "blackness" was a riddle that the white social establishment was trying to decipher, a problem the government was working to solve, and a form of exoticism attracting adventurous cultural tourists. At the time of Burrows's rise to prominence in the fashion world, black was beautiful.

Even today Burrows moves with the elongated posture and lightness of a dancer. He has a boyish face, with eyes hidden by schoolboy glasses with dark-tinted lenses. He has a disco body, lean and narrow. He is, perhaps, the least introspective, navel-gazing, self-analytical person in our era of reality television narcissism and public confessionals. Friends who have known him for forty years attest to his unnerving tendency to live a wholly unexamined life.

He is not so much private as he is unwilling—or unable—to assess his own existence. What went right and what went wrong over the course of his career remain unsolved and uninteresting mysteries to him.

Born in 1943, Burrows began life as a bridge-and-tunnel kid, growing up in Newark with his mother and grandmother. His father, whose roots reach back to Trinidad, lived in Harlem at 147th Street. His mother spent her weekdays in Washington, D.C., where she worked as a government typist. She commuted back to Burrows and his four siblings on the weekends. His paternal and maternal grandmothers had been sample hands in the garment industry, which was how his parents first met. As he puts it, "My parents were together for a minute—long enough to conceive me."[30]

In the late 1940s and '50s, Newark's West Side, where Burrows lived, was an enclave in a midsize city that felt almost surburban. It was decades before the riots, violence, and drugs of the 1970s and '80s turned Newark desolate and dangerous. In Burrows's youth, Newark was vibrant and lively, and his neighborhood was a diverse mix of Italian, Spanish, and black residents.

Burrows's creativity must have been born of both nature and nurturing. "My father used to paint," he remembers. "My father used to take me to the bars in Harlem and I'd sit on his lap and he'd caricature everyone in the bar." His mother, whose family came from Greensboro, North Carolina, loved to draw. His maternal grandmother was crazy about dancing, and so was Burrows. He even studied dance for a short while at the Fred Astaire Dance Academy, thanks to the generosity of his grandmother. "My mother had a fit when she found out I was in dance class." She worried it would make him effeminate, but he kept dancing.

"On Sundays, we got mambo fever, my friends and I. We'd go to the

Palladium on Broadway and [Fifty-third] Street. It was a Latin club," he recalls. "I don't know how we got in! We didn't have fake IDs. We couldn't drink. But we weren't there for the alcohol."

Burrows, his creativity evident as an adolescent, attended Newark Arts High School, a magnet institution specializing in the visual and performing arts. He planned to become an art teacher, and after graduation, he headed to the Philadelphia Museum College of Art with funding from his grandmother and student loans.

He switched from art to fashion after catching a glimpse of a design class in a neighboring studio. He left Philadelphia and in 1964 enrolled at the Fashion Institute of Technology (FIT) in New York City. It was there that he connected the dots between the three key elements that would inspire, shape, and popularize his fashion: disco, drugs, and sexual freedom.

They were intertwined, one ineffectual without the others. Music stirred his emotions and encouraged him to express his creativity. Drugs diminished his inhibitions. And the era's breakdown of sexual taboos and labels gave him an eager audience for his gender-bending work, as well as a level of comfort in living his life as he chose without having to define himself as gay, straight, or bisexual. He could just be. No one asked questions.

From the beginning, Burrows was the quiet one in his group of FIT friends. He was a natural introvert and lackadaisical in demeanor. He was an unlikely ringleader. And yet, he was. He was creative and stylish in a way that his friends were not—more eccentric, sexually provocative in a naive way. He had a knack for stitching up interesting frocks with a look that no one had seen before. Before a night of dancing, friends and flatmates would come to his room searching for something to wear. He gravitated to bold colors, festive adornments like feathers and fringe, and the idea of genderless dressing.

In the late 1960s, when he was still a student at FIT, he began spending time in the Pines community of Fire Island. Roz Rubenstein, a buddy from FIT, introduced him to the idyllic setting. She shared a group house there and invited Burrows to come to the island one weekend in 1965. "It was a magical place," Burrows recalls. "It was like the Garden of Eden. No cars were there. I'd never been to a place like that before."[31]

Burrows soon became a regular on the island. And when he wasn't lounging with his pals, they were heading out to a party. "We would go out dancing in wild colors and walking down the boardwalk in Fire Island in these fabulous clothes," remembered Burrows's friend Vy Higginsen. "We became like a family, a sort of fashion family."[32]

The aspiring young designer was enthralled with the Age of Aquarius and Janis Joplin. But it wasn't just Joplin's voice that made an impression on him, it was listening to her through an acid haze. Burrows first indulged in drugs during his early days on Fire Island.

"It was great!" he remembers.[33]

Burrows's experimentation was typical of the era. This was the calm interlude before crack cocaine caused entire communities to implode. Drugs represented fun and enlightenment. Some even argued they were therapeutic. Hippies smoked pot and reveled in their meditative, self-absorbed self-discovery. And while Vietnam veterans were returning home addicted to heroin, the pathology of drug addiction had not yet been fully recognized.

"I think everything that happens to you contributes to what you expel when you're designing. You can't get away from it. It's part of you," Burrows says of his drug use. "I can't say it was bad or it was good. It just was. I was a product of the generation. I did everything."[34]

Burrows's career was also built on the cultural shifts that created disco and fueled its popularity. Disco was a soundtrack for showing off, a prelude to a one-night stand. In some cases, the seductive lyrics, the moaning voices, the drugs, and the body-against-body crush of a dance floor could turn a disco party into a full-on sexual encounter. Disco could not have existed without the invigorating, newfound sexual freedom of gay men, the primal heat of soul and rhythm and blues, and the power vocals of female singers flexing their sexual authority.

Burrows loved disco's underpinnings of soul and R&B. He could lose himself in this hypnotic music. He even had his own idiosyncratic way of dancing, with one hand raised in a kind of rapturous salute.

One looks at some of Burrows's clashing color combinations, liquid silhouettes, and childlike sexual innuendo and imagines the kaleidoscope of images that might swirl through a mind in the midst of an LSD trip. His bold, unsubtle colors looked good under a spotlight, set in high relief against the dark shadows of a club's corners and against dark skin. Cartoon characters and sexual humor captivated him. His colorful patchworks often made reference to phallic symbols. He'd use geometric dots to draw attention to breasts. At times, his work read like the immature jokes of a twelve-year-old boy. "He loved tits and ass," laughs designer Diane von Furstenberg.[35]

Burrows's clothes were best worn by someone with a dancer's body, or at least a dancer's willingness to reveal it. They were sexy, but Burrows used a different vocabulary to talk about sex. He didn't deal in curves or cleavage. His interest was not in the voluptuousness of the body but rather in the way in which a body could move when it was unfettered by social mores, gender definitions, girdles, brassieres—fat. He loved the idea that men and women could reach into the same pile of clothes and pull out something to wear.

Burrows worked on his own terms, creating wild dance club dresses, body-conscious tunics, and androgynous fringed leather pants, and remained happily ignorant of anything that was going on elsewhere. His creativity was fueled entirely by his surroundings. He wasn't influenced by history or tradition. He was utterly disengaged from what was happening in Paris.

Burrows's rise to prominence was breathtaking in its velocity. He graduated from the Fashion Institute of Technology in 1966. By 1973, he had won a coveted Coty Award and was settled into his own atelier in New York's most adventurous store, Henri Bendel. It was an invaluable connection.

Even in the early 1970s, merchants remained the dominant force, the stars of fashion. Some stores even removed the designer's label and replaced it with their own. The designers' relationship with American stores needed to change before the designers could claim their place on the world stage. The stores were not keen on ceding that control, but due to Lambert's increasing clout, they were being forced into it.

Through Lambert's savvy public relations, American designers were beginning to establish themselves in the public consciousness. Klein's focus on working women fueled her success and gave her the financial leverage to negotiate in-store boutiques bearing her name. Halston's friendships with celebrities had made him a celebrity in his own right. And Blass and de la Renta's popularity among socialites eventually thrust them into the spotlight, lending value to their brands.

"I don't remember the exact date. I get a call on the telephone—Mr. Adam Gimbel [of Saks Fifth Avenue] would like to see me at five o'clock in the afternoon. I was terrified," says de la Renta of a call that came sometime in the late 1960s. "I was just starting to sell a few clothes and I think he's going to tell me my clothes are not good enough and he's not going to buy them.

"I walk into a reception room and I meet Geoffrey Beene. Why are we here? Mr. Adam Gimbel was going to announce . . . that from then on the store was no longer going to remove our label from the designs."[36]

At the same time, Halston was blazing a new trail as a boldface name, with social footholds on Fire Island and among the new demimonde of Broadway stars, artists, and media titans such as Barbara Walters and Katharine Graham.

"I remember having a big fight with management because we were carrying Halston and not telling anyone. The name that mattered was Saks," says Ellin Saltzman, a former executive at the specialty store.[37]

And while Burrows was a coddled, salaried employee at Henri Bendel, it is impossible to ignore his contribution to the store's mystique. His arrival was celebrated with a two-page spread heralding his "happy palette of the rainbow" in the August 1, 1970, edition of *Vogue*. To churn up excitement, he'd put on fashion shows using mostly black models and they'd dance down the catwalk to contemporary music. He once mounted a fashion show on the sidewalk, during which he turned the street into a public disco. That was Burrows's style. And it dazzled Lambert.

Four

Cities in Flames

Burrows's joyful approach to life, his multiethnic "family," and his let's-all-get-along politics formed the perfectly timed antidote for a tumultuous time. A series of devastating riots exploded across America during the summer of 1967. It seemed that virtually every major American city was going up in flames fueled by racial inequity, disenfranchisement, and poverty. On June 11: Tampa. June 12: Cincinnati. June 17: Atlanta. June 20: Newark. July 22: Detroit.

The Detroit conflagration, which lasted five days, began when members of the predominantly white police force raided an after-hours bar at the intersection of Twelfth Street and Clairmount. Onlookers on that July summer night protested the police action and the department's aggressive tactics. As the crowd taunted the cops, windows were broken, a mob soon formed, and businesses were looted and set aflame. Dozens of black citizens were shot and killed by police officers and National Guardsmen. Residents hunkered down, afraid to be caught on the streets, let alone run afoul of the cops.

In search of causes and solutions, on July 28, 1967, President Lyndon B. Johnson called for the creation of the National Advisory Commission on Civil Disorders. It was an eleven-member, bipartisan commission co-chaired by Illinois's Democratic governor Otto Kerner and New York's Republican mayor John Lindsay. It also included representatives from business, labor, law enforcement, and the NAACP. The commission members hailed from the "moderate and 'responsible' Establishment," and critics complained that it lacked representatives of the black radical movement, academic leftists, and militant youth.

In March 1968, the commission issued the Kerner Report, which, despite its moderate lineage, opened in famously unsparing terms: "Our nation is moving toward two societies, one black, one white—separate and unequal. Reaction to last summer's disorders has quickened the movement and deepened the division. Discrimination and segregation have long permeated much of American life; they now threaten the future of every American. This deepening racial division is not inevitable. The movement apart can be reversed. Choice is still possible."[1]

The report went on to characterize the rioters as desiring "fuller participation in the social order and the material benefits enjoyed by the majority of American citizens." Rather than rejecting the American system, they were anxious to find their place in it.[2] It also described a new mood that had arisen in young "Negroes," noting that elevated "self-esteem and enhanced racial pride" had replaced "apathy and submission to 'the system.'"[3]

Perhaps most important, when the Kerner Report offered its healing and preventative tonic, it looked at the media, among other forces. It encouraged newspapers, magazines, and television to broaden their content and become more inclusive. The report urged the media to "recognize the existence and activities of Negroes as a group within the community and as a part of the larger community. It would be a contribution of inestimable importance to race relations in the United States simply to treat ordinary news about Negroes as news of other groups is now treated. Specifically, newspapers should integrate Negroes and Negro activities into all parts of the paper, from the news, society, and club pages to the comic strips. Television should develop programming which integrates Negroes into all aspects of televised presentations. . . . Negro reporters and performers should appear more frequently—and at prime time—in news broadcasts, on weather shows, in documentaries, and in advertisements. Some effort already has been made to use Negroes in television commercials. Any initial surprise at seeing a Negro selling a sponsor's product will eventually fade into routine acceptance, an attitude that white society must ultimately develop toward all Negroes."[4]

Whether or not one agreed with the findings of the Kerner Report, it had the effect of heightening cultural sensitivities to race. The government itself had found that there was an urgent need to open the doors of social access and visibility to black Americans. There was even an undercurrent of fear: What would happen if the disenfranchisement continued? What powder keg would explode next?

The anger and resentment that had poured into urban neighborhoods and fueled the ongoing Black Power movement enthralled a generation of radical young people, experimental artists, and the fashion industry, which was increasingly influenced by the street and by popular culture. Fashion didn't like getting political, but it loved being subversive.

Black politics was spawning a black aesthetic that was confronting and changing mainstream culture. In 1971, Melvin Van Peebles helped give rise to a new black cinema movement when he directed *Sweet Sweetback's Baadasssss Song*. The title character, played by Van Peebles, is a black man who brutally attacks a racist policeman and flees for his life. The guerilla film is full of bell-bottoms, velour jackets, afros, sex, and black male heroics. In the final scenes, Sweet Sweetback escapes the police and crosses the border into Mexico. The film was dedicated to "brothers and sisters who have had enough of the Man." The hero's survival was seen as a revolutionary conceit.

When the original film was released, only two theaters would even screen it. One was in Atlanta; the other was the Grand Circus Theatre in Detroit. It was so enthusiastically received by black audiences that there were reports of moviegoers sitting through it two or three times in a row.

The film, with its Black Power themes, was an enormous success considering its meager budget of $500,000 (including a $50,000 loan from comedian Bill Cosby) and went on to gross more than $15 million.

The action was everywhere. *Julia*, starring African American actress Diahann Carroll as a widow and single mother working as a nurse, made its groundbreaking appearance on television in 1968. In literature, writer Amiri Baraka instigated the Black Arts Movement in Harlem. Maya Angelou published *I Know Why the Caged Bird Sings*. In 1972, Alma Thomas, at eighty, became the first African American woman to have a solo show at the Whitney Museum of American Art. And on the dance stage, Judith Jamison was mesmerizing audiences with her emotional and regal performances with the Alvin Ailey Dance Company of New York.

The world of fashion was similarly looked to as a place where the culture could find signs of racial progress. Expressions of beauty and glamour mattered. Good race relations required taking note of who was selling women lipstick and miniskirts, which meant that advertisers and designers began looking for black models.

A current of earnest, idealistic do-goodism had been stirred. People believed—*hoped*—that with a positive attitude, with the right words and the right government programs, the anger could be quelled and injustice eradicated.

So while Lambert equated fashion with patriotism in order to bolster the economy, New York's Bergdorf Goodman used it to make a pitch for racial harmony. In the spring of 1969, the specialty store, with its rarefied air, deep stock of French haute couture, and high-society clientele, hosted a fund-raising fashion show saluting black designers.

Bergdorf is housed in an imposing beaux arts building on Fifth Avenue and Fifty-eighth Street. From its founding in 1901, it was never a store known for edgy, experimental fashion. Rather, it trafficked in chic, patrician, *expensive* sophistication. We have never been a culture comfortable admitting to having an aristocracy, but we do. And Bergdorf ministered to the members of that aristocracy's inner court. Indeed, in 1961, its fashion director collaborated with Jacqueline Kennedy on the creation of her inaugural ball gown.

Yet in 1969, Bergdorf Goodman, the favored haunt of the elite, turned its spotlight on half a dozen black designers.[5] More than five hundred broad-minded New Yorkers paid at least $15 each to attend the show, which was dubbed "Basic Black at Bergdorf's." It paid tribute to Arthur McGee, Jon Haggins, Maybelle Lewis, Jon Weston, Luretha Williams, and a young, rising designer named Stephen Burrows, who had just started his professional career.

The Bergdorf party was rip-roaringly popular. Both the black community and white society clamored to go. Governor Nelson Rockefeller, a moderate Republican and arts supporter, purchased a block of tickets. Guests included singer Dinah Shore and actor Raymond St. Jacques. And the clothes were youthful and charming: white crochet minidresses with geometric details at the waist, plaid pajama pants worn with a midriff-baring top.

The show benefitted Harlem's Northside Center for Child Development, which was founded by psychologists Dr. Mamie Clark and her husband, Dr. Kenneth Clark. In the 1940s, the Clarks became famous for their "doll test," which revealed children's alarmingly biased attitudes about race. The couple's testimony on the damaging psychological impact of segregation on children had weighed heavily in the 1954 Brown v. Board of Education Supreme Court decision that desegregated schools.

The Jothan Callins quintet, a jazz ensemble whose members were costumed in dashikis, entertained the audience. Guests nibbled on corn bread, fried chicken, collard greens, and chitlins. In 1969, soul food was pure radical chic, and serving it up at a celebration of black designers did not seem to strike any of the organizers as painfully condescending—or vaguely horrifying. But even then, passing chitlins around the fifth floor of Bergdorf went several steps beyond authentic and well down the slippery slope to minstrelsy.

Guests arrived convinced that it would be an electric evening, before anything had even happened; the store hadn't seen such excitement since it hosted the Duke and Duchess of Windsor two years earlier. "I guess people were interested because they want to endorse something constructive in black-white relations, which everyone is very concerned about right now," mused Lorna Bade Goodman, daughter-in-law of store president Andrew Goodman.[6]

Her husband, Eddie Goodman, third generation of the New York retail dynasty, had recently left the family fold to focus on business development in the predominantly black neighborhood of Bedford-Stuyvesant in Brooklyn. Eddie assured the press that his new role had not been the impetus for the uptown show. Rather, thanks to the nightly news, the deafening social chatter, and the mood of the country, his father's "consciousness of what's going on in the world, just sort of expanded."[7]

Eddie Goodman was not exaggerating. Race, as part of the cultural dialogue, had become inescapable. It was practically all anyone could talk about. Raised voices, wringing hands, and caustic words were signs of passion, honesty, and commitment. Back then, people believed verbal sparring could be meaningful and productive.

The sixties had ushered in crunchy-granola liberalism and navel-gazing self-criticism, bold political activism and racial diplomacy. This was the era that spawned Tom Wolfe's *Radical Chic & Mau-Mauing the Flak Catchers*, which assessed liberal guilt and black anger. It would not have been surprising had the white guests arrived at Bergdorf wearing Black Panther berets and Aunt Jemima head wraps, proclaiming them all the rage.

By the time soul food was being served on the fifth floor of Bergdorf, the race problem was part of dinner table chatter, church pew politicking, college campus protests—and the popular culture.

There were no easy or obvious answers to solving it, but what made the Basic Black show even possible was the fact that people were actively looking for them. And as unlikely as it seems today, they were looking everywhere, from legislatures to television, literature, and even fashion.

Race matters were woven into the culture. In October 1969, *Life* magazine ran an advertisement for Sylvania color televisions that equated picture quality with kumbaya racial diversity. In the ad, the central image is a lineup of four women—white, African American, Asian, and Hispanic—each staring proudly from a television screen. The copy reads, in part:

> *Presenting life the way it really is. White people aren't white, black people aren't black, yellow people aren't yellow, brown people aren't brown. Not in real life. Not on Sylvania color TV.*
>
> *Everyone's color is different. That's a fact, which has caused some problems. In the color TV business, the problem is to accurately reproduce all these different colors (things, too, not just people) and keep them accurate from scene to scene and channel to channel. . . . Together, the Sylvania chassis and picture tube give you reds that stay red, blues that stay blue, yellows that stay yellow, and flesh tones that are true and natural. That's the way life really is.*
>
> *Regardless of race, color or place of national origin.*

The cover of that issue of *Life* featured model Naomi Sims with the headline BLACK MODELS TAKE CENTER STAGE. Inside, there was a group shot of thirty-nine black models—men and women—represented by a new agency called Black Beauty, which was run by a white former model named Betty Foray. The story also touted the success of Charlene Dash, a twenty-year-old black model represented by the Ford Model Agency who'd done commercials for, among others, Clairol. Racial progress was measured in a multitude of ways, even by the color of the elegant faces that smiled from the pages of fashion magazines and by the race of the men and women who dressed them.

Basic Black at Bergdorf's was exemplary, not simply because it celebrated black designers, but because people believed that fashion could change this country for the better. People believed American fashion, in its choices and depictions of beauty, could help everyone get along. Basic Black was not merely raising money for a cause; it was a way of standing on the right side of history—albeit with a cocktail in one's hand and the smell of collard greens in the air.

F rance, too, was grappling with tumult, both social and economic. In the spring of 1968, a massive student uprising that broadened into a worker revolt and labor strike brought the country to its knees. Under the government of Charles de Gaulle, France in the 1960s had settled into a period of stability and affluence. The population was more urban, less religious, and better educated than it ever had been. Paris West University Nanterre La Défense was founded in 1964, just as France's rural population was declining and vast numbers of citizens were moving into the cities and suburbs. With that shift came a growing number of university-age students ready to be educated in the ways of a cosmopolitan society. In 1938, France had 60,000 university students; by 1961 there were approximately 240,000. And by 1968 there were 605,000.[8]

Nanterre developed a reputation for a left-leaning atmosphere and would count among its alumni French president Nicolas Sarkozy; head of the International Monetary Fund Dominique Strauss-Kahn; the woman who replaced him, Christine Lagarde; and French prime minister Dominique de Villepin.

Despite the country's growing wealth and shifting demographics, France remained a paternalistic culture, one that created a sense of oppression and malaise for anyone who was not male, middle-aged, and bourgeois. From women to blue-collar workers, the country was roiling with discontent. The issues were minor to significant, aesthetic to substantive, both political and cultural.

In March of 1968, students at Nanterre began protesting against university rules that prohibited men and women on campus from after-class fraternizing. Fresh to adulthood and the freedoms that implied, students wanted to have sex in the privacy of their dorm rooms. They wanted to be unbound from the strictures of a conservative, structured, Father-knows-best culture. They were railing against Frenchness, as it was then perceived.

Thanks to the development of the birth control pill, modern medicine had given students a warrant for sexual liberation. In 1960, the U.S. Food and Drug Administration approved the Pill for use. Its popularity was instantaneous, sending millions of women to their doctors demanding it, so much so that in July 1968 Pope Paul VI declared the church's opposition to the Pill in the *Humanae Vitae* encyclical. The sexual revolution was at full tilt. The Nanterre students' sense of sexual oppression lit the fuse for the spring aggression, but a host of other issues led to the explosion.

The Vietnam War had unleashed, in France, a complicated mix of colonialism, communism, and nationalism. And while capitalism had stoked the French economy, the benefits were not trickling down to the workers. A cultural revolution was under way, and the protests of 1968 reflected the diffuse anger, frustration, and longing that grew from every little indignity. Even fashion could be exasperating. A law originally passed in 1800 that prohibited women from wearing pants was still honored in France. "In the sixties, women . . . couldn't wear trousers," fashion historian Pamela Golbin explains. "It's difficult for us today to grasp that."[9]

Indeed, when trousers first began to appear on the runways of André Courrèges and Yves Saint Laurent, the stir among the fashion press and consumers was not so much because of the silhouette but because of the subversive idea that a woman would defy the law by appearing publicly in a forbidden garment. "You couldn't wear [pants] in a lot of places. You couldn't wear them at the [restaurant] Côte Basque [in New York]. I had to drop my pants and go in in a tunic, and this was the early sixties," socialite Nan Kempner said before her death in 2005.[10]

It wouldn't be until January 31, 2013, that France would finally remove the 213-year-old anti-trouser law from its books.[11]

The student protests at Nanterre soon spread to the Latin Quarter and the neighborhood surrounding the Sorbonne, as frustrations exploded into the light. The students were joined by faculty members, who were joined by union workers, who were joined by sympathetic bystanders. The angry throngs began prying up the cobblestone streets and hurling the rocks at police in riot gear. The police responded with tear gas and billy clubs.

Protesters—"Trotskyites, anarchists and revolutionary students"[12]— attempted to burn the Bourse, the Paris stock exchange. They shattered windows along the Boulevard Saint-Germain, where history had seen Jean-Paul Sartre, Pablo Picasso, and Albert Camus take coffee and libations. Cars and buses were overturned, tires slashed, and gas tanks torched. Streets were barricaded by both police and the insurgents. General mayhem ruled the city for weeks as angry crowds ran from neighborhood to neighborhood seething with fury and discontent.

According to one contemporary account, "Red Cross workers with helmets ran through exploding tear gas grenades to give first aid treatment to the hundreds of casualties. As the police slowly drove the demonstrators up the Rue de Rennes, Red Cross workers carried youths and girls, with heads streaming with blood. Policemen and journalists with long years of experience of Paris riots almost disbelieved the evidence of their eyes as they viewed the scene of destruction."[13]

Soon there was a total work stoppage as clock-punchers occupied their factories and fell in line with the students. France was grinding to a halt. "Everyone was concerned," recalls Givenchy. "Americans, at that time, would not buy in France."[14]

De Gaulle had to end the gridlock and the rioting. By early June, the trade unions had negotiated a 10 percent increase in all wages, as well as a 35 percent increase in the minimum wage. They won a shorter workweek and "mandatory employer consultations with workers."[15] And of course, the sexual revolution rolled through Paris unhindered. The streets were alive with emotion. The young men and women who had begun their protests properly attired in jackets and neat dresses ended them in jeans and with a decidedly scruffier look. If fashion is the costume of social tribes, society was at war. And it was clear who was winning.

Five

Apostasy

While haute couture had captured the attention of the world's wealthiest and most style-savvy women in the twenties and thirties, during World War II, French industrialists looked across the Atlantic Ocean to the United States. The challenges of war ushered in a new mind-set and the French began embracing the idea of mass-manufactured clothes—albeit on a very small scale befitting their market. As France became increasingly industrialized and the possibility of reaching a global audience became more enticing, French businessmen started to hire young "stylists" to work in a new category the French called "confection," aimed at dressing a wide range of women. A "stylist" however was not a designer and "confection" was several rungs beneath couture and suggested something more commercial than the inventive work of a true master.

Postwar couture clients were a different ilk than their hothouse mothers. Their lives moved faster; they were more independent. They didn't want to emulate the old guard. Industrialization offered them more possibilities. The fashion industries of London and Milan were beginning to stir with, respectively, youthful rebellion and matter-of-fact beauty—a *bella figura* ease.

All the significant French designers began making their way from haute couture toward ready-to-wear. They had little choice. But there was still tremendous tension between the two crafts, with ready-to-wear perceived as industrial, less creative, and, occasionally, embarrassing.[1]

Like so many things in bureaucratic France, where every idea seems to require a thick dossier of paperwork inked over with official stamps from one union or another, the two approaches to fashion were governed by separate entities, each dictating the rules of engagement. Indeed, the unions sorted French fashion into an endless variety of categories, with varying degrees of quality and originality, that included haute couture, demi-couture, confection, and ready-to-wear. Ready-to-wear was poised to be the ultimate moneymaker, but it was wholly disdained as little more than derivative widgets, produced for the masses.

"Ready-to-wear started in 1950, not as everyone thinks with Pierre Cardin in 1961," explains fashion historian Didier Grumbach. "It started with five houses: [Gérard] Pipart, [Robert] Piguet, Cardin, [Jean] Dessès, and [Pierre] Balmain. Those five went into ready-to-wear under a licensing system. And their colleagues were ashamed and curious. It was a French war. Typical! The most furious was Balenciaga, who considered it the worst of the worst."[2] But it was too late. The door had cracked open.

Soon all the designers were walking through it, from protégés of the master himself, Balenciaga, to fashion's most promising talent, Yves Saint Laurent. Even at Christian Dior, once the most successful haute couture house of them all, the ground was shifting. The house's place in history was secured in 1947 when Dior created a wasp-waisted, rounded-hip silhouette called "le Carolle," or popularly, "The New Look." The luxurious style was credited with reviving haute couture after World War II had forced so many houses to temporarily close. By 1948, Dior had lent its prestigious name to ties and hosiery through licensing agreements. It had offices in London and New York that oversaw the diluted, mass-market versions of its couture designs.

Then, in 1956, Christian Dior died unexpectedly and his assistant, Yves

Saint Laurent, took over. In January 1957, Laurent showed his first haute couture collection for the label and the public went wild. The twenty-one-year-old, slightly built designer "came out on the balcony of the house of Dior and traffic stopped. People were yelling and screaming in the streets. It was like a national event," marvels fashion editor Marylou Luther, who witnessed the cacophony.[3]

However, Saint Laurent's success was cut short. After multiple deferrals, in 1960 he was finally drafted into the army. A few days following his conscription, Saint Laurent suffered a nervous breakdown and had to be hospitalized. When he recovered, he was determined to build on his success at Dior. He opened his own design house in 1962 with his partner in business and life, Pierre Bergé. They had defined public roles: Saint Laurent, who died in 2008, was the creative half of the duo, the delicate, tortured artist; Bergé was the strong-willed businessman who provided him with a solid foundation.

Saint Laurent became fashion's rock star thanks to his unorthodox influences and flamboyant personal life. He'd bowled over the old guard with his work at Dior. But in his own atelier, he quickly allied himself with modernity and youth. He embraced art as a point of reference in his work, popularized trousers, and participated in a glittering nightlife surrounded by an indomitable entourage of friends.

"Haute couture was too expensive," Bergé recalls. "[Yves] had girlfriends who were young; he was young. He decided to create a ready-to-wear line because haute couture was only for rich women."[4]

In 1966, Saint Laurent opened his Rive Gauche boutique, which was solely devoted to ready-to-wear. The culture demanded it and so did his bottom line.

When Saint Laurent left Dior to break out on his own, he was succeeded by a more reserved talent. In 1961, Marc Bohan, who had been leading the house since Saint Laurent's conscription, took charge officially. He was thirty-four years old.

Bohan, who was born in the town of Versailles to a milliner mother and businessman father, had been called to the majors from London, where he had been in charge of Dior ready-to-wear. Bohan led the house until 1989, presiding over it through the sexual revolution, the feminist wave, and the rise of eighties narcissism. It was Bohan who oversaw the opening of the first Miss Dior ready-to-wear boutique in 1967.

"I was very proud and happy to be working for Dior. . . . I felt free to evolve in my career," Bohan says.[5] He also made full use of the Dior name to expand the business in inventive new ways.

Dior may have been the first of the major French fashion houses to benefit from licensing deals, but it was Pierre Cardin who took licensing to its unholy extreme. By the 1980s, Cardin would have some eight hundred agreements to his name.[6]

Born near Venice into a large and poor family, Cardin came to southeastern France as a toddler when his father was looking for work. By age fourteen, Cardin himself was working for a tailor during school vacations. He was not a brilliant student, but he managed to graduate and began performing in local theaters. He headed to Paris, hoping to become an actor.

World War II stopped him in Vichy, where he began sewing at a local clothing store. When he finally arrived in Paris at twenty-three, he found work as a costumer. A fortune teller urged him to look for a position in the haute couture salons, and so he did. He eventually landed at Christian Dior during the season of the New Look, which he helped to create.

In 1950, Cardin opened his own atelier on rue Richepene, where he would rack up daily sales of $60,000. Three years later, he moved to the exclusive Faubourg Saint-Honoré.[7] Cardin was always keen on making money and made no bones about that. "Why shouldn't my clothes be sold in normal shops and worn by ordinary women? Don't women who aren't wealthy have a right to dress elegantly?" he once said.[8]

He leapt at the opportunity to create a ready-to-wear line and eventually bore criticism of it with a shrug, recalls Renée Taponier, who has worked with Cardin for more than fifty years, first as a seamstress's apprentice, then as a *vendeuse* in Cardin's haute couture atelier, and now as curator of his archives. Cardin was "not always understood," Taponier says. "When he started his [ready-to-wear] collection, he was very criticized. I think it hurt him. But he continued."[9]

Cardin was a resolutely modern designer who brought a sleek, mod look to menswear and a pop sensibility to women's clothes. The costumes from *Star Trek* could have been plucked from one of his collections. The quintessential Cardin "look" was a brightly colored, sleeveless, A-line shift, structured and geometric, its high-on-the-thigh hemline rendered nearly asexual thanks to opaque contrasting tights.

Cardin was also a marketer extraordinaire, brimming with confidence and bravado, and, of course, he was not the least bit diplomatic. Well on his way to becoming one of the richest men in Paris, he was impossible to ignore. He would eventually be thought of as one of fashion's great megalomaniacs, which, of course, may very well be redundant.[10]

Cardin attracted an impressive clientele of actresses and political luminaries: Jeanne Moreau, Charlotte Rampling, and Claude Pompidou, the wife of French president Georges Pompidou. "We dressed the wife of the president for free, which was normal," Taponier says. "Once she wore an outfit, she would give it back to us [without being asked]. She had a lot of class and was very thoughtful."[11]

These couturiers, who had been cautiously moving into ready-to-wear, understood the freedom and ease that the 1968 protesters were demanding. They were concerned by the upheaval, but also inspired by the way in which the ground was shifting and forcing them to question their aesthetic certainty.[12] Average workers had joined the surging demonstrations in search of greater dignity in their day-to-day life. Ready-to-wear would dress them.

These were the designers the ladies of couture had always trusted; gradually, the more daring couture customers began to follow their lead and dabble in ready-to-wear.

As the 1960s came to a close, haute couture was in upheaval, and it was only getting worse. During this period of heresy, if the religion of French couture had an Opus Dei of the faithful, Balenciaga would have been the most devout, cilice-wearing member. "He was my master, the greatest couturier," enthuses Givenchy. "The perfection! The most complete couturier, [he] could make a coat, lace dress, or suit with great sobriety and simplicity. Never bad taste."[13]

When Balenciaga retired in 1968, he was prescient in understanding what was coming and he could not bear to watch.

Today, design houses do not shut down; they simply fall into disrepair until they are resurrected by an ambitious—or delusional—businessman and a pop-culture-savvy designer. In contrast, Balenciaga shuttered the doors of his company. He anointed no one to follow in his footsteps. He couldn't countenance it. He had no desire to go where it seemed fashion was headed: into ready-to-wear.

Balenciaga closed his doors. *Closed his doors.* Balenciaga was religion. He was continuity. He was control. But no more. "It was the end of an era," says Pamela Golbin, chief curator at Paris's Musée des Arts Décoratifs.[14]

Balenciaga sent letters to his staff alerting them that he was retiring. "The *vendeuses* literally had nervous breakdowns. Most had spent all of their life working for Balenciaga and couldn't believe the house had actually closed," Golbin says. Golbin remembers interviewing one of the women who had been working there at the time. "Florette was ninety-six years old when I talked to her. She was crying. Even the death of her husband wasn't as traumatic as the closing of Balenciaga. It was really, really hard."[15]

The news was made even more trying because the staff didn't receive Balenciaga's letters until months after he'd mailed them. With the strikes and rioting, the nation had ground to a halt. Mostly employees learned about the fate of the company from Belgian radio and from American customers who'd read the news in *Women's Wear Daily,* which had treated

Balenciaga's retirement like the death of the pope. Those inside the world of couture weren't quite gnashing their teeth, but they were in deep distress. Their religion had ceased to exist.

In another blow to couture, on June 10, 1971, Gabrielle "Coco" Chanel died. That same year, Saint Laurent created a couture collection inspired by the war years: *"Hommage aux Années 40."* The collection created a scandal of the sort that could only occur in the world of fashion—particularly in France. It was criticized and reviled by editors and couture customers who had no desire to relive the war through aesthetics. Critics did not like the brightly colored, streetwalker furs, the turbans worn to hide untended hair, the men's tailoring and curtainlike skirts that had been a stopgap during the lean years of rationing. They did not want to be reminded of the Nazi occupation, the collaborators, the desperation, and all the rest.

But the failure of that collection also signified a generational shift. Saint Laurent had stopped speaking to the couture customers. He was engaged with his twenty-something friends, who had no memory of the war and who scoured the flea markets on weekends and saw the war frocks as fun retro fashion ready to be revived.

"I was the fashion editor of *Glamour,* and we had to find things to photograph in couture that would appeal to [young] *Glamour* readers. We often had to sort of fake it," remembers Frances Patiky Stein. "Ready-to-wear happened and it was like manna from heaven. We went crazy. I remember when Yves opened his ready-to-wear shop. I couldn't afford couture. I walked out of that shop with half the collection. It was suddenly another world. You could buy absolutely wonderful clothes at a price you could afford."[16]

Also in 1971, Didier Grumbach founded Créateurs & Industriels, an organization aimed at connecting young designers with manufacturers. That decision allowed men and women such as Dorothée Bis, Chantal Thomass, Jean-Charles de Castelbajac, and Sonia Rykiel to emerge as influential designers. Their sheen has dimmed over the years, but at the time, they were the hot young commodities. They produced accessible clothes that were fun, sexy, and filled with the kind of feminist independence that had been part of the 1968 uprising.

Grumbach's family was firmly rooted in the French fashion and social establishment. A slender, elegant man of modest height and discreet bearing, with gray hair and basset hound eyes, Grumbach's resting expression speaks of bemusement. His family tree includes Pierre Mendès France, a former prime minister. But his family also owned the great manufacturing firm C. Mendes, which produced Saint Laurent's Rive Gauche line. With the founding of Créateurs & Industriels, Grumbach had begun chipping away at the future of couture even as the ground was shifting under it. He led the way in making French fashion more industrial and more international.

Meanwhile, across the Atlantic, American designers who'd felt the sting of a judgmental and snobbish French fashion establishment were reveling at what they saw as the decline of couture.

In the early 1970s, the tension in the French fashion world had nothing to do with the Americans. While the Americans were always looking to Paris, the French wouldn't deign to glance toward New York. The United States didn't warrant consideration other than as a lucrative market filled with wealthy women. The tug-of-war in Paris was between haute couture and ready-to-wear. Which would prevail as the exemplar of French aesthetics? Would artistry fall to commercialism? Wealthy American clients were reading stories in their local press asking, "Is Paris couture losing its image of primal power?"[17]

The devaluation of the dollar was also making French haute couture impossibly expensive. In the 1950s, Deeda Blair bought a couture ball gown—a sample—for $700. But as the value of the dollar began to tumble, that same ball gown, in 1973, would have cost about $1,000. Throw in inflation, and suddenly the cost is $1,500.[18] The declining value of the

dollar against the French franc would stymie the fashion industry throughout the 1970s. The exchange rate would dip to four francs to the dollar
and would not begin to improve until the 1980s; by 1985 a traveler could get
ten francs to the dollar, making even middle-class American tourists feel
flush.

Haute couture had other problems aside from inflation and exchange rates. The Chambre Syndicale de la Haute Couture, the organization overseeing couture, had been around for a century and was
as protective as ever. But in 1973, a new, renegade group formed. The
Chambre Syndicale du Prêt-à-Porter des Couturiers et des Créateurs
de Mode supported ready-to-wear designers, and Saint Laurent's influential partner Pierre Bergé became its president.[19] The couturiers had
history on their side, but the ready-to-wear designers were an ever-
growing lot.

Such was the rise of ready-to-wear in France that even American
wholesale manufacturers, the ones busily producing copies of couture for
a mass audience, were beginning to worry. What would be the value of
their copies if even the greatest French couturiers were diluting and selling their own work as ready-to-wear? In 1971, a ready-to-wear exhibition at the Porte de Versailles had American retailers "swarming around
the shows like ants on a cube of sugar."[20] The garment manufacturers'
unions in the United States accused European design houses of paying poor
wages, thus luring American stores with low prices. The unions also complained that American retailers were snubbing domestic goods even when
their prices were competitive. They thought the French merchandise was
new, different, and exciting. Paris was where it was at: style, savoir faire,
inventiveness, pure but oh-so-effortful chic.

After decades in the shadow of the French fashion industry, Eleanor
Lambert and her clients thought they had carved out a modest niche. Now
upheaval in the French fashion world was threatening even that. It was
time for the Americans to fight back.

* * *

Years of experience had given Lambert an understanding of the fashion industry's fragile egos, insecurities, and competing players. She was comfortable with the workings of the elite social sphere with its unspoken hierarchies and petulant rivalries. And she had the stomach for creative chaos. She could be both firm and politic. She knew how to get her way without leaving a fingerprint. For decades Lambert had been working to make American designers world famous; with tensions brewing in France, the time had come for Lambert's vision to become a reality.

Because of her background in both art and fashion, and with her influential circle of friends, Lambert was prepared with the perfect idea when opportunity presented itself. That moment came in late July of 1973. Visiting the home of Lady Kenmare, one of the many forgettable aristocrats on the social circuit at the time, Lambert sat poolside, chatting with Gérald and Florence van der Kemp. Gérald, born in the Val-de-Marne region southeast of Paris, was the chief curator at Versailles.

Tall and dark-haired, with a gently curved nose, perfectly groomed hair, and an athletic build, Gérald was Dutch by lineage but French in upbringing. He wore a boutonniere daily. He was the quintessential curator—both charming and erudite, with a sure manner capable of persuading moneyed acquaintances, especially Americans, to open their wallets and make substantial contributions to Versailles.

He also had an alluring mystique thanks to his swashbuckling actions during World War II. At the battle of Dunkirk in 1940, he was taken prisoner, but managed to escape. According to legend, Gérald walked 125 miles over two days. During the journey he tore several tendons in one leg, which left him with a permanent limp.

As the war continued, he was assigned to protect a collection of artwork—including Leonardo da Vinci's *Mona Lisa*—that the French had stashed at the Château de Valençay in central France.[21] This assignment wasn't as random as it might sound. As a young man, van der Kemp studied at the École du Louvre. In 1936, fresh out of school and before being called into the war, he'd been an assistant at the famous museum.[22]

While at Valençay, van der Kemp was a dedicated bodyguard, often keeping the *Mona Lisa* in his own bedroom.[23] When the German forces marched through, they set fire to the château and threatened to kill van der Kemp and the staff. In a scene straight out of an Indiana Jones film, he appealed to the Nazis' revulsion at being perceived as cultural barbarians and begged them not to destroy the priceless artworks. He convinced them to let him extinguish the flames. He also managed to not be executed.[24]

After the Liberation of Paris, van der Kemp rode into the city in a convoy carrying the crown jewels of civilization. It was reported that he personally carried the *Mona Lisa* back into the Louvre.[25] A year later, in 1945, he was appointed assistant curator of Versailles. In 1953 he became the chief curator.

By the time he was lounging by the pool with Lambert, he had overseen the enormous restoration of the Grand Trianon, one of the smaller châteaus at Versailles, which served as a country getaway for the French president (then Charles de Gaulle) and as a guest house for foreign heads of state. The repairs were estimated to have cost $10 million, raised primarily from private donors, both French and American.[26]

Gérald had an aggressive and unabashed fund-raising partner in his wife, the former Mrs. Florence Harris Downs. It was a second marriage for both of them, their previous ones having ended in divorce. Florence van der Kemp was American—*very* American, as Deeda Blair, an acquaintance of hers, notes.[27] She was tall and solidly built, always well dressed, and free of the distinctly French tendency toward circumspection. She was filled with energy and enthusiasm, not for staid antiquities, but for people, conversation, and fun. Florence was larger than life. And when she spoke, she did so in great lapping torrents. With her flat vowels, apparent even when she spoke French, she gestured broadly with her hands and had a tendency to ruffle her short-clipped hair as if its very presence was getting in the way of her thoughts.

When de Gaulle once invited the van der Kemps to a private reception, Florence was wildly excited, even though she regularly brushed up against the famous and powerful. Uniformed aides flanked the president as Florence was formally introduced. She was so overwhelmed that she curtsied—as if she was meeting a king—rather than just shaking his hand. The verbal floodgates soon opened and she began to blather about everything from Versailles to the weather. She had to be politely shushed into silence and gently moved along.[28]

Florence was born at the Brooklyn Navy Yard. Her father had been an admiral in the U.S. Navy and her mother was a well-practiced hostess. When she was an adolescent, the family moved to Washington, D.C., where they lived in a house on Embassy Row. She was groomed to be a proper and decorous young woman and a savvy hostess. She attended the private girls' school Holton-Arms, as well as various schools in Europe. In the 1930s, she briefly worked as a society writer for the now defunct *Washington Star* newspaper, penning a column called "By the Way."[29]

One of the tools used by the van der Kemps for successful fund-raising was their apartment at Versailles (once used by Colbert, Louis XIV's minister of finance), which sits in the Pavillon Dufour at the southeast corner of the Cour Royale.[30] The van der Kemps furnished the apartment in a conversation-starting blend of the lofty and the mundane. While they were able to borrow certain works of art from the collection of the palace, most of the furnishings in the six-bedroom, two-and-one-half bathroom apartment were their own, accumulated during their time in Washington. The housewares, including the bedding and kitchen cookware, were from Bloomingdale's. At dinner parties, Florence would occasionally use one of the château's antique chamber pots as a gravy boat—an unorthodox accompaniment to her Bloomie's bargains.

The couple hosted countless dinner parties for personal friends as well as friends of Versailles. Florence had strict rules about entertaining, including adhering to one of about twenty-five set menus, several of them taken from her mother's notes. In 1967, *Vogue* published a feature about her husband that included several of Florence's recipes, along with helpful hints for organizing an elegant dinner party. She believed in plenty of champagne, and flowers from her husband's private garden. Enormous cabbage roses, peonies, and delphiniums regularly filled the rooms.

"I consider that the best quality food, simply served and well prepared and served on a gold plate is what makes a party," Florence said in a *Washington Post* story.[31] Who could argue with macaroni and cheese on a gold plate?

While Gérald was a deft fund-raiser, Florence was much more blunt. She went for the money with a warm heart but a heavy hand. Florence understood that wealthy American families had a history of giving to Versailles. Inscriptions of donors' names on the wall in the Hall of Statues date back to 1837 and include recognizable Americans like John D. Rockefeller, Barbara Hutton, Marjorie Merriweather Post, Brooke Astor, and Mr. and Mrs. Alfred Bloomingdale. She had the idea of creating a French-American foundation to benefit Versailles to make it easier for Americans to claim a tax deduction. "I'd be around when she'd be pursuing these targets of opportunity among both the French and Americans," Deeda Blair says, an amused smile drifting across her face at the memory. "She never pretended to be knowledgeable about Versailles itself, or eighteenth-century furniture or sculpture. She loved people. And she adored Gérald."[32]

Together, Gérald and Florence van der Kemp used their connections and natural social charm to raise money for the restoration and upkeep of the Palace of Versailles. The dowager landmark had begun life as a hunting lodge constructed by Louis XIII. His son, Louis XIV, expanded it and transformed it into a mythical, golden, ornate fantasyland in celebration of the French state. Beginning in 1682, it served as the home of the French monarchy and government. The French Revolution, however, put an end to such aristocratic opulence.

Today, the Palace of Versailles is a museum dedicated to the history of France, a major tourist attraction, and, since 1979, a UNESCO World Heritage Site. Its Hall of Mirrors, a 960-square-yard gilded gallery lined with 357 mirrors, hosted the signing of the Treaty of Versailles on June 28, 1919, which ended World War I. But in the early 1970s, the landmark needed help.

The yearly government stipend set aside for its upkeep was the equivalent of a few thousand dollars—not nearly enough to return it to its regal glory. The palace needed close to $60 million of restoration work.[33] Gérald was devoted to Versailles. And Florence was a steadfast fund-raiser devoted to her husband.

Chatting poolside that July day, Florence suggested that Lambert might help with the Versailles restoration. And Lambert saw an opening. Her thoughts went immediately to her American designers. Well, Lambert replied, the only thing she could really think to do would be to put on a show.

Lambert's daring idea was to have American designers display their talents on fashion's most hallowed ground, the land of haute couture. In France, Lambert's designers could have a formal, international coming out on one of the most glamorous stages in the world: the Palace of Versailles. The Americans would share that stage as equals with French designers, and the crème de la crème of high society would gather in the audience. Lambert would spin, weave, embroider, and package the story with a perfectly tied bow . . . and present it to the media.

The idea had been brewing in Lambert's imagination for decades. This would be the perfect denouement to all the fashion shows she'd organized, at the White House and for charity. She would ask five American designers to participate; she already had a list of names in mind. And to create a sense of international partnership, the American designers would be billed as "guests" of their French counterparts.

The designer personalities would have to be managed, of course. Fashion, by its nature, attracts creative individualists, unruly rebels, and exasperating narcissists. Organizing them would be akin to herding cats. Patience and a stern hand would be required. No one was better suited to the task than Lambert.

She knew that to make it an event that would draw international press coverage, she would have to pull in the most glittering society names and the great beauties of the era. Despite their affection for Versailles, their peripatetic lifestyles, and their access to all that was new and shiny, wrangling them and impressing them would require some heavy lifting. Lambert understood these women. She was familiar with how and where they socialized. She recognized their power and understood the role fashion played in their lives. If the standing of American designers on the world stage were to change, it first had to change in their eyes.

Theirs was a social world of lucky royals, middling nobility, talented celebrities, wealthy businessmen, high-minded philanthropists, and, of course, the clubby inhabitants of the International Best-Dressed List—which Lambert herself codified in 1940 and later willed to *Vanity Fair* magazine. The list was like a Venn diagram of overlapping, golden circles. Everyone knew everyone and summered or wintered in the same cozy châteaus, villas, and palazzi in Europe.

Lambert had made herself indispensable to the fancy crowd. She was an ambitious worker bee among queens. She helped build institutions, fostered relationships, conjured up publicity, and maintained an unflagging enthusiasm for the creative class. All of those talents could help raise the money the van der Kemps needed for the restoration of Versailles. Together, she and the van der Kemps decided to organize the glitzy, star-studded event Lambert had in mind.

First Lambert set about building the American host committee, filling it with the same names that regularly graced the society pages. C. Z. Guest, a noted horsewoman, hostess, and beauty, chaired the American committee. "With her pale skin, blue eyes, ash-blond hair and trim figure, she is cut from the same cool, silky cloth as Grace Kelly," a *New York Times* story noted upon her death in 2003. "It is a patrician beauty that is indigenous to socially registered enclaves like Palm Beach and Southampton, a sporty, outdoorsy look that eschews makeup, hairspray and anything trendy. She has an outspoken, coolly self-assured manner and a throaty, well-modulated voice with a trace of a British accent."[34] Other American committee members included now former *Vogue* editor Diana Vreeland, Babe Paley, Princess Lee Radziwill, Lynn Wyatt, Nan Kempner, Deeda Blair, and Betsy Bloomingdale.

The French committee was helmed by the Duchess of Brissac and included at least three other women of comparable nobility, including the Duchess of Windsor. The French sprinkled their committee with other notable names like L'Oréal heiress Liliane Bettencourt; São Schlumberger, the Portuguese-born wife of oil industry tycoon Pierre Schlumberger; author and former minister of culture André Malraux; and, a social butterfly if there ever was one, Baron de Redé.

The most notable distinction between the two lists, aside from the plethora of nobles on the French side, was that the entire thirty-seven-member American committee was female. The thirty-member French committee was almost evenly split by gender, a reflection of the universal importance of and respect for the role of fashion in that nation's culture.

Also on the list of distinguished French participants was the grande dame of the international social set: Marie-Hélène de Rothschild. Politically connected, extravagant, and controlling, Rothschild made things happen.

Almost as soon as they had hatched the idea for the show, Lambert and the van der Kemps called Marie-Hélène de Rothschild and asked her to serve as the events chairwoman. Rothschild's participation would open every door, attract every big spender, and make even the most petulant snobs beg for an invitation. She was also a couture client par excellence who knew every noteworthy French designer. She was emblematic of French fashion's history and its present. And the choices the French would make about who would represent their industry and how their work would be presented were a direct result of Rothschild's imposing authority.

84

"Marie-Hélène was the queen bee of Paris," recalls Deeda Blair. "She had the last word on everything. She did things in a very grand way."

Rothschild's houses were filled with treasures that sound ludicrously luxurious, shockingly ostentatious, but absolutely stunning. Rembrandts hung in the bedroom. "You can't imagine the imagination and creativity of some of the rooms and the way she lived in them," Blair says. "You know rare Limoges enamel? She had Limoges enamel plates and platters mounted right into the boiseries."[35]

Rothschild was known for her lavish parties, most famously her Proust Ball, in December 1971, which she presided over with her husband at their country estate, Château de Ferrières. The guests, including the Duchess of Windsor, Audrey Hepburn, and Princess Grace of Monaco, arrived—as requested—in costume and were photographed by social chronicler Cecil Beaton. Some 350 people came for a dinner that included quenelles of lobster and duck stuffed with foie gras. Another 350 came for a late-night supper.[36]

The party made such an impression on the popular culture, at least the part that cared about high society, that tales of it figured prominently in obituaries following Rothschild's death in 1996. Hostessing was not merely her avocation; it was her profession.

Dreda Mele, the former Givenchy *vendeuse,* was a close friend of Rothschild's who attended the Proust Ball and was among the guests photographed by Beaton. More than forty years later, as other events have slipped from her memory, the Proust party and Rothschild's handling of it remain vivid.

"Marie-Hélène used to sit people so well at her dinners. And it's very important to know how to place people," Mele says with a knowing nod.[37] "She was so unbelievable. She loved artists; so suddenly during the dinner, somebody would be singing. The music was extraordinary. We'd dance all night. There was always an orchestra. It was unbelievable. She was the best. People were begging to be invited to her parties."

Mele dotingly described Rothschild as a "giver," someone who recognized the responsibility of great wealth and who was wholly engaged in using it and her connections to support cultural institutions and the French republic. Those who are less admiring—or perhaps just more frank—note that Rothschild was the ringleader of a pack of people who often served as little more than decorative objects. Rothschild was authoritative and particular; she was a snob. In other words, the "giver" could also be quick to take.

But she recognized the power and responsibility of the Rothschild family, the fading beauty of Versailles, social opportunity, and the possibility of a good time. When she agreed to be the show's chairwoman, the event instantly took on another dimension.

The tension between French fashion's storied past, full of rules, hierarchies, and elitism, and its globalized future, rooted in democracy, street style, and mass production, was expressed by dueling trade unions. The Chambre Syndicale du Prêt-à-Porter des Couturiers et des Créateurs de Mode, headed by Pierre Bergé, and formally founded November 15, 1973, supported ready-to-wear. The Chambre Syndicale de la Haute Couture, presided over by Madame Grès, continued to protect haute couture. But the opposing factions were not walled off from one another; designers such as Yves Saint Laurent were invested in both worlds.

On November 21, 1973, these unions were joined under a larger, umbrella organization called the Fédération Française de la Couture, du Prêt-à-Porter des Coutouriers et des Créateurs de Mode. Two decades later, businessman and historian Didier Grumbach would lead it into the twenty-first century. Like most of the French in attendance, Grumbach did not expect the Versailles gala to be particularly noteworthy, other than for its social aspects. American design was presumed to be a bore. But unlike most of the other guests, Grumbach, who was a young fashion businessman at the time, understood that Versailles might well be one

Fall, 1952

Couture Collections

Marshall Field & Company

the moulded "Profile" line of Dior

cut and construction create a new "formed narrowness". It looks deceptively simple, but actually achieves the streamlined curves of an ideal feminine figure

- moulded bodice
- manipulated seams
- belt curved and threaded through but never tight (often waistlines are higher or back, belts vanish into sides)
- subtly rounded sides and back
- longer, slimmer skirts

the easy, elongated cut of Balenciaga

gives you freedom of body- great flare

- lowered square neckline
- non-clinging bodice
- touch-me-not waistline
- lower pockets
- longer skirt
- casual fabric (tweed)
- absence of detail

the bloused look of Grès

essentially casual in feeling- expertly clever in cut

- deep, easy sleeves
- soft falling skirt
- deflated balloon back
- soft light fabric

A 1951 look book from Marshall Field & Company provides details of Paris fashions to be copied.
The Chicago History Museum

Stephen Burrows (seated, in fringed shirt), hangs out with his pals on Fire Island. CHARLES TRACY

For his portion of the Versailles show, Stephen Burrows encouraged his models to dance and let their personality shine. CHARLES TRACY

Josephine Baker performed "J'ai Deux Amours" during the French portion of the Versailles show.
CHARLES TRACY

Left: The invitation for the Grand Divertissement à Versailles, with its gold script, reflected the lavishness of the gala. Fashion Institute of Technology|SUNY, FIT Library Special Collections and FIT Archives, New York, NY, USA

Bottom: The centerpiece of Oscar de la Renta's presentation at Versailles was a magician, played by model Billie Blair (foreground). © Alain Dejean/ Sygma/Corbis

Grand
Divertissement
à
Versailles

of the last hurrahs for the dominance of haute couture. He knew that French fashion was changing; he was helping it along.

When the unions and committee members set about selecting the designers who would represent French fashion on the stage at Versailles, the lines between the country's stylistic old and new guards were thrust into the spotlight. Although an abundance of cultural signs pointed to the rise of ready-to-wear, the Versailles gala would showcase only haute couture.

Sensitive to Rothschild's considerable influence, the French organizers determined that the young, commercial upstarts who had begun their solo careers in ready-to-wear would not be included. Rothschild was in her late forties. While she was not a dowager, she was not part of the rising generation of avid ready-to-wear customers. And as chairwoman of the Versailles show, she was to be wooed, not crossed. There would be no Paco Rabanne, with his jazzy Judy Jetson sensibility. No Sonia Rykiel, who had emerged as a Left Bank character-about-town and champion of a young, liberated, and independent French woman. And no Jean-Charles de Castelbajac, whose clothes luxuriated in deep, rich color. The French designers who were most simpatico with the Americans would not be invited to participate. The ones who were striking fear in the union halls of New York's Garment District would not show. They were not grand enough.

The French committee decided France's great couturiers would go to Versailles—the men who had apprenticed with Balenciaga, Schiaparelli, and Dior himself. But the French wanted to have it both ways. These couture designers had all also launched ready-to-wear collections and were part of Bergé's forward-thinking trade group. But since ready-to-wear still had the whiff of crass commercialism in France, the French would show only couture.

It was Bergé who signed off on the participants. The list of French designers was not surprising. Hubert de Givenchy, Christian Dior's Marc Bohan, Pierre Cardin, Emanuel Ungaro, and Yves Saint Laurent. These five men were part of the old order, and they counted among their clients the most prominent and wealthiest women in the world.

These designers didn't merely respect the past; each man was intimately connected to it. For them, the past was omnipresent. Every decision they made about their future within the fashion industry was in tension with French history, national pride, and basic economics. Each aesthetic choice was momentous, and it reverberated not only across the Atlantic but through the consciousness of France.

Givenchy is a tall, imposing, distinguished, and elegant man with a fine sense of humor whose interests beyond fashion run to French antique furnishings and gardens. Born a count, he studied under designers Lucien Lelong and Elsa Schiaparelli, but his greatest influence was Cristobal Balenciaga. Although he never worked for Balenciaga, the two developed a friendship and professional kinship. So deep was their relationship that when Balenciaga closed his atelier in 1968, he referred all of his most loyal clients to Givenchy.

Givenchy was forty-six at the time of the Versailles show. He was well known for his work with actress Audrey Hepburn, who epitomized the youthful chic of his aesthetic. As a designer, Givenchy focused on line rather than embellishment. A Givenchy gown was infused with the restraint and control of Balenciaga. His couture work boasted a sumptuousness that somehow did not inhibit its wearability. Popular culture will always remember Givenchy's sophisticated, minimalist little black satin dress from the 1961 film *Breakfast at Tiffany's,* with a neckline that sweeps around the shoulders to gracefully reveal the curves of a woman's back.

Givenchy's relationship with his clients was discreet and rather old-fashioned, but it was the essence of his work. In fact, much of his legacy is dominated not by a certain line or silhouette he created, but by the clients he dressed—women such as Marie-Hélène de Rothschild, Lee Radziwill, and, of course, Audrey Hepburn.

"Hubert was full of talent," says Dreda Mele, his former *vendeuse.* "Right away I was amazed; it was beautiful what he did. I was enamored by the beautiful evening clothes he did. He did the most extraordinary evening clothes for balls."[38]

The antithesis of Givenchy's cinematic glamour, Marc Bohan was a shy, wonkish fellow. If any of the Frenchmen would have had empathy for the Americans, who had spent so many years working in the shadows, it was Bohan. His name never appeared on the Dior label or the collection programs handed out in his own atelier.[39] His name didn't even appear on the invitation for the Versailles show; he was invited as the man behind Dior—the brand name mattered above all else, including the designer.

In 1963, Bohan was quoted in *Vogue* as saying, *"N'oubliez pas la femme."* Don't forget the woman. Alas, fashion has almost forgotten Bohan. "He was so self-effacing and quiet," remembers Deeda Blair, a client. "He was underappreciated."[40]

Bohan was the most sober of the French designers at Versailles. He tended to dress like a banker in gray flannel suits of his own making, and he was not quick with a smile.[41] He was a reserved man who was both nurtured and tormented by his work.

During his time at Dior, Bohan lived in a beige, art-filled apartment in a building adjacent to his atelier, which allowed him near constant access to his studio. He was often tense, irritable, and prone to headaches in the days leading up to one of his couture shows. He could look at three hundred models just to select one. Like Balenciaga, he preferred to work in silence. And he detested it when models spoke to him during fittings. If there was any hint of a fun-loving side, it was his propensity to zip around Paris in a white Porsche.[42]

"I may have been a little shy, but it did not interfere with my working and social life, nor did it get in the way of my contacts with my clients, with whom I always enjoyed a close and trustful relationship," says Bohan, who now lives in the Burgundy countryside.[43]

His point of view was profoundly woman-friendly while adhering to the decorum of couture. When he arrived at Dior in 1961, he quickly became famous for what editors dubbed the "Slim Line." It was a welcome counterpoint to the volume and froth that dominated so much of fashion at the time. The skirts of his little suits had a subtle flare at the hem, and his dresses were quietly pleated. These styles were more comfortable and pragmatic for the women who wore them. The suits worn by Jackie Kennedy during her White House years, with their simple collars that highlighted a swan neck, speak to the Bohan aesthetic.

"My clients were mostly social and international women who enjoyed a very busy social life and appreciated high-quality couture clothes in which they felt confident and comfortable," Bohan explains. "My goals were to offer my clients total satisfaction."[44]

Bohan established a loyal group of customers: Blair; Lynn Wyatt; Evangeline Bruce, wife of globe-circling diplomat David Bruce; and Betsy Bloomingdale, wife of the department store magnate. He was less inclined to flashy displays of imagination and more controlled. He described his winter 1971 collection, which was inspired by his daughter, as "a reaction against the over-creativeness of designers who have allowed their imagination to run wild."[45]

One of the first French couturiers to embrace ready-to-wear, Pierre Cardin put no limits on his imagination, his ambition, or his ego.

Cardin's flagship boutique remains where it has always been: a stone's throw from the Élysée Palace (the French equivalent of the White House) at number 59 rue du Faubourg Saint-Honoré. It is a pine green structure with doors that curve outward as if welcoming you into a rocket ship. The spacious boutique holds only a tiny percentage of the Cardin oeuvre: menswear, women's ready-to-wear, children's clothes, perfume, accessories, and luggage. There are myriad examples of color blocking, such as simple jumpers in black with red polka dots marching single file down the front. A straightforward dress will cost you about $2,500. The men's coats have high collars that call to mind Jimi Hendrix. Fey tweed blazers are paired with coordinating belts. Wraparound sunglasses in shrill colors long to be worn by some new wave band.

The great sweep of the Cardin empire would not have been possible without the contribution of Henry Berghauer, who first met Cardin in the late 1950s. At the time, Berghauer was a young man with a law degree who hated practicing law. He was enamored with the film industry and for a time lived in New York, where he worked at CBS. When he returned to Paris after several years, he found the television market there lackluster by comparison and began a search for his next adventure.

During an afternoon stroll down the rue du Faubourg Saint-Honoré, Berghauer happened across Cardin's shop. The Cardin name was still new and it didn't resonate with Berghauer, who knew little about fashion. "He put in his window: We are looking for an assistant commercial I-don't-know-what. I didn't know the meaning of that. But I called a friend of mine. She had a couture house. What is the meaning of that? And she said, 'Cardin is very, very talented. Why don't you see him?'"[46]

Taking his friend's advice, he applied for the job on the commercial side of the business and was called to Cardin's office to interview with the company's manager. It did not go well. As Berghauer was leaving the office with a sense of disappointment, he met a woman in the stairwell. She mistook him for a model or one of the many young men who would arrive at the atelier to meet their model girlfriends after a day of fittings.

She buttonholed him and guided him into a room filled with tailors, seamstresses, and Cardin himself, who was preparing a couture collection. If Cardin, with his square jaw and high cheekbones, was startled by Berghauer's sudden appearance, he didn't indicate it. Instead, he just asked what the young man wanted.

Berghauer, surrounded by models in white peignoirs, could only marvel at the scene: from the nonchalant goddesses to the couture dresses. The silence started to become uncomfortable. When Berghauer finally regained his composure, he explained that he'd been interviewing for a job. Cardin asked Berghauer a bit about himself. Where was he from? What had he been doing? And then he turned his attention to the frocks.

"Which one do you like?" Cardin asked.

There was a fantastic white wedding dress. It looked like something from Berghauer's beloved Hollywood movies. He was amazed by it.

"You like this wedding dress," Cardin said when he saw the young man eyeing it.

"It's unbelievable," Berghauer replied.

"Are you married?"

"Not yet."

"Would you choose this dress for your bride?" Cardin asked.

Berghauer explained that he would not. It wasn't the expense, but rather, the ostentation. "In my religion, the dress must be very, very simple," Berghauer said.

"You're Jewish?" Cardin pressed.

"Yes." Berghauer was from an observant Jewish family, and tradition dictated a more modest wedding gown.

"In that case, I hire you for tomorrow," Cardin announced. "If you're Jewish, you make a success."[47]

Berghauer wasn't offended. The exchange was emblematic of the era—a time when people made assumptions without worrying about political correctness, the history books, or fair play.

And as it happens, Cardin's collaboration with Berghauer was wildly successful, even if the initial reasoning was askew. Berghauer arrived just as Cardin was finding his footing. "Step by step I had the responsibility for the development of the company. It was very easy because I didn't have to ring the bell. People came to us," Berghauer recalls. "I didn't have a teacher. But I had a friend who was president of Dior. So I call him sometimes: 'What I'm going to do is that and that.' And he says, 'I'm not anxious that you compete with Dior. But if I'm you, you could do that.' So his relationship and experience was very helpful. I listen to him and I study."[48]

Berghauer helped Cardin to spread his gospel of the modern. Cardin's bright, sleek, structured clothes hinted at the future but appealed to clients who had a deep appreciation for the history of couture.

Berghauer stayed with Cardin until 1968. And then, in 1970, he met Emanuel Ungaro. Born in Aix-en-Provence to Italian parents, Ungaro, like Givenchy, had been tutored by Balenciaga. He worked in the master's atelier and eventually rose to chief assistant. While there, Ungaro became friendly with André Courrèges, another young designer in the backroom. Soon Courrèges went out on his own, proving himself to be a futurist fascinated by the practicality and versatility of the male wardrobe. He sought to bring that sensibility to his women's clothes, and it made him a star.

Ungaro left Balenciaga and went to work with Courrèges, more as a matter of courtesy than desire. But after only a few months, and to Courrèges's dismay, Ungaro was on the move again, itching to express his own point of view. He opened an atelier on Avenue Mac Mahon, in Paris's seventeenth arrondissement, near the Arc de Triomphe. With his impressive résumé, the fashion press eagerly awaited his 1965 debut, aching to crown a new prince of fashion.

Ungaro had the sexy, bohemian looks for the part. He wasn't tall. He wasn't matinee idol handsome. But he dressed almost entirely in black and had an air of sensuality, thanks to his thick, dark hair, deep-set eyes, strong nose, and ability to lock onto a woman with a gaze of intensity and admiration. Ungaro was a romantic who created his collections for a woman of his imagination. His clothes were sexual and tantalizing—notable for their raucous mix of patterns. But, by his own declaration, they were not revolutionary.

He launched his collection of minidresses and pastel coats to enthusiastic reviews. The clothes mixed Balenciaga rigor with Courrèges pizzazz. *Vogue* was first in line to celebrate him, and the clients soon followed.[49]

"Emanuel Ungaro came on the scene with bold, gutsy clothes and models who looked . . . like harbingers of a new heroic age," Grace Mirabella, the editor in chief of *Vogue* from 1971 to 1989, wrote in her memoir. "Emanuel's clothes spoke of courage: his fabrics were beautiful and strange and he broke all the rules of fashion convention by layering them pattern on pattern."[50]

Within two years, he'd moved his studio to the fashionable Avenue Montaigne, just down the street from Christian Dior. Guests entered the atelier through a small boutique. He would present his collections on athletic, size 10 models to editors and private customers who sat tightly packed together, knees pressed into backs, on tiny white stools.[51]

Ungaro cultivated a top-notch clientele and the adoration of the press. For a story in the *Washington Post* in the spring of 1973, his clothes were photographed on Valérie-Anne Giscard d'Estaing, daughter of then–French finance minister Valéry Giscard d'Estaing, who went on to serve as president from 1974 to 1981. She wore one of his rust and cream patterned sweater sets, as well as a box-pleated skirt and a blouson-style jacket that had brought him some acclaim.

In the universe of French fashion stars, Ungaro was the least known of the Versailles designers. But that did not deter him from a tendency toward the pretentious and esoteric remark. In a conversation with writer Nina Hyde, he explained that in order to understand his clothes, one had to be fully versed in his history as a designer—his work at Balenciaga and Courrèges, and his earliest years on his own. "To appreciate a Bertolucci or Visconti film, really understand it, you must start with earlier films. To understand Marcel Proust, you must read his books from the start," he explained, by way of comparison. Ungaro had a particular affinity for Proust. Before designing each season's collection, he would retire to his home in Klosters, Switzerland. "I keep silent for a month," he said. "I do nothing but read, and I read only Proust. It is in the level of Proust, the total submersion into Proust that I get my ideas and come up with a new way."

"The modern way is to understand that less is more," he said. "We must take simple ideas and do them in a way that has not been done before."[52]

Over the years, Ungaro would leave that philosophy behind to adopt a more-is-better, body-conscious, ruched-waist dress obsession that would, for a time, epitomize the uniform of the Park Avenue trophy wife. "There were little dresses for cocktails and dinner and everything started to get bigger and more excessive," Mirabella recalls. "I remember the first time I was aware of that, let's say the early eighties. I thought, Where has our Emanuel gone? The clothes were still good-looking, but they were not interesting."[53]

But in 1973, Ungaro was a burgeoning star.

The fifth French designer asked to show at Versailles was an obvious choice: Yves Saint Laurent was the king of French fashion.

Saint Laurent had triumphed at the venerable house of Dior. Now designing under his own name, he reinterpreted the visual arts, incorporating ideas from the world of painting into his work in ways that had not been seen before. Notably, he was enthralled by the flat geometry of artist Piet Mondrian. In 1965, Saint Laurent created a series of dresses evoking the bold colors and stark lines of the artist's abstract work. His technical wizardry was such that the simple A-line dresses hung almost as flat as the paintings, but still acknowledged the curves of a woman's body.

But it was in 1966 that Saint Laurent created what is perhaps his most enduring contribution to the modern fashion vernacular: *le smoking*. It was a tuxedo cut for a woman. When it was shown to the press, it was a scandal—trousers! androgyny! female virility! *Women's Wear Daily* trumpeted, "Yves Sparks Elegant Reign of Terror" and "Standing on the barricades he sows terror inside its institutions."[54]

Over the course of Saint Laurent's career, he would be inspired by the ballet, Africa and Russia, motorcycle rebels, and country peasants. He created leather motorcycle jackets under the auspices of couture and he made peasant blouses into high fashion. He lived in the thick of contemporary life, with its parties and indulgences, and he was at the center of a group of friends that included the model Betty Catroux, with her screen of platinum-blond hair and androgynous looks, and the carefree sprite Loulou de La Falaise. His grandest client, however, was the legendary film beauty Catherine Deneuve.

F ive years after the May 1968 uprising transformed French society, the Versailles show could have been a celebration of French fashion's future. It could have underscored the modern realities of commerce, popular culture, democracy, and the independent woman. Certainly, the French designers selected to participate had been thinking in those terms.

Instead, under the influence of Rothschild and their own unions and urged to show their couture, the French would make a statement about the legacy, glory, and extravagance of their creativity. Their portion of the show at Versailles would be an affirmation of the past. Enough with tumult. It was time for reassuring nostalgia. The Versailles gala was shaping up to be another fancy party filled with fancy people; it was a charity event with the usual suspects and nothing more. It would celebrate continuity, not change.

The French designers were the ultimate fashion team of rivals. They all knew each other, but they weren't friends. "Ungaro and Bohan were not especially talented. Givenchy was calm. Cardin is nothing. In the 1960s, we had two designers for the future: Courrèges and Cardin. They were [supposed to be] making fashion for 2000. We are in 2000. Let me know, does anyone dress like that?" says Pierre Bergé, who was then the powerful president of Yves Saint Laurent and president of the ready-to-wear trade group, the Chambre Syndicale du Prêt-à-Porter des Couturiers et des Créateurs de Mode.

The designers were highly competitive and individualistic. It was the first time they would be showing together and outside of their own ateliers. Getting them to cooperate with each other would be a staggering challenge.

Jean-Louis Barrault, the theatrical director charged with organizing the French portion of the show, had no intention of trying, deciding instead to let each designer have his own separate and distinctive act in the French portion of the show. "Each *maison couture* would show a whole presentation," Bergé recalls.[55] The French designers spent close to $30,000 each to produce elaborate segments with spectacular backdrops, live music, and nearly nude dancers. The Rothschilds contributed $70,000 and underwrote a gala midnight supper. Lambert, the van der Kemps, and the organizing committees set their sights on raising close to a quarter-million dollars for Versailles.

The French were ready to go. Now Lambert had to get the Americans organized. It was time to start corralling the cats.

Six

Disco Balls and Divas

While there were tensions simmering in France between tradition and progress, in America, the early 1970s convulsed with contradictions. Fashion and culture did not move in tandem. The broader world was in the midst of seismic upheaval, deadly tumult, and a soul-sapping malaise, much of it having to do with the war in Vietnam. Fashion was mostly about escapism.

For the first time, thanks to television and the nightly news, a war was made vivid to the folks back home. Americans were losing faith and trust in the government. The publication of the Pentagon Papers revealed the falsehoods of the war. And the Watergate investigation startled readers with its revelations of the government's lies and cover-ups. The early 1970s saw the birth of American cynicism regarding elected officials, the power of the government to do good, and the possibility of transparency in leadership.

But it wasn't just the Vietnam War and lying politicians that made the 1970s such a tense, stratified decade. The country was in a cultural war over the Equal Rights Amendment. The amendment, which would have affirmed equal application of the Constitution regardless of gender, passed both houses of Congress but ultimately failed, approved by three fewer states than the thirty-eight required for ratification. And in 1973, the Supreme Court issued its opinion in Roe v. Wade, affirming a woman's right to an abortion as a matter of privacy. That landmark decision created a wedge issue that even now threatens the very civility of the country.

Much of the 1970s was defined by anger and melancholy, as life simply became less pleasant and less beautiful, and the vision of the United States as a country of prosperity was challenged. The decade after the publication of Rachel Carson's *The Silent Spring* ushered in a new era of concern about pollution. The recently established Environmental Protection Agency began an unusual form of data collection: it unleashed an army of professional photographers across the country to document pollution. They collected images of thick clouds of smog hovering over cities, oil-slicked rivers, and natural landscapes scarred by thoughtless development. Of the many heartbreaking revelations, one was of an East Boston neighborhood destroyed by the expansion of Logan Airport. The photos showed tarmac butting up against tidy backyards and jumbo jets roaring seemingly only a few feet above the tops of modest homes.

And of course, there was the oil crisis. Long lines of gas-guzzling American cars at filling stations became shorthand for a country—for a world—with a sputtering economic engine.

Amid all this, women found their swagger and started dressing like they meant business, whether in the boardroom or bedroom. They were institutionalizing independence and self-determination. Female participation in the workforce had grown by nearly 50 percent since the 1950s. And the 1970s produced the largest such increase in a single decade.[1] *Ms.* magazine entered its heyday as the voice of female self-actualization. And Hillary Rodham Clinton graduated from Yale Law School.

Fashion became happyland, a snow globe of joy. For much of the era, the industry and the colorful bounty swirling around it were a counterpoint to a society that was becoming more constricted than ever by sexual politics, culture wars, national cynicism, and economic despair. Fashion didn't reflect reality; it was an antidote to a toxic world.

I n 1973, disco balls spun as an electronic thump-thump, thump-thump became the soundtrack for freedom—sexual, racial, personal. Hordes of young men and women were happily and hungrily saying "Yes!" to liquid libations and anything else they could snort, smoke, or slip under their tongue for a journey into a Technicolor Never-Never Land. The gadflies and society stars, white-hot celebrities and fun-seeking teenagers, slid into the era's nightlife, ready to release their inhibitions and exist in the tantalizing, irresistible moment.

Folks met up in one disco and piled into any available limousine for a ride over to the next. And there were *always* limos. For the disco set, riding in a limo was the only way to travel. People spent their freshly minted fortunes and their last dollars on them. Fleets of sleek black cars parked in front of nightclubs, ready to ferry bleary-eyed, overserved revelers on to the next party.

One did not hit the clubs dressed for the factory or the secretarial pool. These nights out required costuming. Women styled themselves in cocktail dresses that plunged to X-rated depths and that flew up high on the dance floor. The underpinnings that created the hourglass figures and the bullet bosoms of the 1950s gave way to . . . nothing. Men became peacocks dressed in madly patterned trousers and colorful shirts that reflected the spotlights and the sweaty glow of testosterone. But disco fashion was more than slinky dresses and crazy colors; it was a refuge. The disco was where people came to party, to laugh, to smile, to forget. No one judged. No one pontificated. Life was lived on whims.

People didn't need fashion to reflect reality—not when reality was one demoralizing news story after another broadcast in the sonorous tones of Walter Cronkite. They needed fashion to take them away from it. The fashion of the 1970s was inexorably linked to decadence: sex, drugs, and disco music.

Style was a distraction and a source of commonality in an increasingly fractured world. It cultivated a naive delusion that the entire decade was one giant acid trip or coked-up party. It was a time when everyone was just one bong hit away from euphoria.

The denizens of the fashion industry who were at their youthful apogee during that period tend to have only the foggiest recollections of the era. Oh yeah, it was great, they say, their voices trailing off.[2] They have vague memories of having had a rip-roaring time, when success just seemed to occur by chance and without corporate interference. And now, well into their senior years, they are thankful to have survived it all pretty much intact.

"I remember the vibe, I don't remember the people," said former model Bethann Hardison about her time partying at the club 12 West in New York. "I could have married someone there and not remember their name. At one point, I remember dancing, closing my eyes, and saying, 'If I die tomorrow, I'd be fine, because I am so happy.'"[3]

Women were ascendant in this frothy world. Little girls no longer grew up wanting to dress like their mothers—seeking validation by being appropriate and following the social codes. The young women of the 1970s bent society's rules to their needs. American fashion was a tool for power, independence, equality, and spectacle.

The culture was shifting from the hippie rebellion of the 1960s to a more glamorous, narcissistic, diverse, and cynical sensibility. The Black Power movement had left a mark on the social psyche with its chant of "black is beautiful" and its emphasis on black pride. Racism and prejudice had not been vanquished, not by a long shot, but they were complicated by a cultural curiosity and fascination with black identity. Basic Black at Bergdorf, that celebration of black designers where chitlins and collards were served up to white New York's power brokers, heralded the arrival of a new decade. "It's 'in' to use me," African American model Naomi Sims said in the early 1970s, during the height of her career, when her yearly earnings were estimated at $40,000. "And maybe some people do it when they don't really like me. But even if they are prejudiced, they have to be tactful if they want a good picture."[4]

American culture was changing, becoming more sophisticated, cosmopolitan, and daring—or at least aspiring toward it. No longer content to merely copy, we wanted to know how our visual arts and cuisine measured up against that of the Old World. To wit, out in California, ambitious winemakers were honing their craft, preparing to challenge France's position as the ne plus ultra in the world of wine. In 1976, a group of respected French oenophiles startled wine aficionados by choosing American wines, vintage 1973, over French ones in a blind tasting. The "Judgment at Paris" remains a landmark event that gave the American wine industry a sense of its own aptitude and forced its reconsideration on the world stage. It was a publicity stunt that transformed an industry. But it wasn't the first. And it wasn't the most dramatic. A similar kind of ambition and daring was already growing in American fashion.

If selecting the designers for the French half of the show was a decision complicated by national history and protocol, organizing the American contingent was a task beset by ferocious egos.

Eleanor Lambert, American fashion's own roadside barker, may have hatched the idea for the show, but she had to cope with the imperial Rothschild, who controlled the guest list and the flow of tickets. Lambert also had to negotiate the prejudices and jealousies of the French fashion trade organizations, which had final approval over who would be included in the show. And she had to step gingerly with the Americans, whose insecurities had been loosed by the prospect of a Paris debut.

To smooth the way, and create at least the appearance of collegiality, each French designer was supposed to "invite" an American counterpart to participate. Of course, the French designers didn't really know the

Americans. They were casually familiar with their work, but this was not a case of one friend inviting another. And as stories about the organizing leaked to the press—mostly through fashion writer Eugenia Sheppard—this gracious idea fell by the wayside thanks to egos and publicity concerns.

"What started out last summer as a simple enough plan to put top French and American fashion together in a single show to benefit the Versailles restoration fund . . . has become a boiling pot of feuds, misunderstandings, hurt feelings, jockeying for position, and rumors," Sheppard reported in a story that ran in the *Los Angeles Times*.[5]

The first Americans confirmed for the show were Lambert's longtime clients Bill Blass and Oscar de la Renta. Lambert had worked with Blass since his days as a hired hand at Maurice Rentner. And she'd included de la Renta in her 1968 fashion show at the White House. When she asked them to participate, there was little hesitation. They trusted her. She'd never let them down.

Halston was the next inevitable choice. He had become an iconic figure in American fashion. He'd deconstructed the confining tailoring of the past, embraced the new microfiber known as Ultrasuede, and wrapped his company in the gloss of celebrity. He was the most famous American designer of the day, with access to a multitude of stars from Liza Minnelli to Andy Warhol.

However, from the beginning, Halston was difficult. His Seventh Avenue company had recently been purchased by Norton Simon Inc. The deal transformed him; the designer became a multimillionaire overnight and was suddenly enjoying the perks of wealth, such as a chauffeur, a showroom filled with orchids, and a sense of entitlement. He returned triumphantly to Bergdorf Goodman, where he'd launched his career as the house milliner, with his own in-store fashion boutique. Halston's life was in the midst of a glittering transformation, and all of his energy was focused on exploiting and enjoying that ride. He was too busy for Paris.

He didn't want to do the show. Why? Because it would be a bother. Because he wanted to be the star. Because. Because. Because. Because he was rocketing to the zenith of his career and along the way had picked up the habit of referring to himself in the third person. And who doesn't find that aggravating? "We all handle fame in different ways," remarks de la Renta.[6]

But with all the reporting and the marquee list of names on the organizing committees, the Versailles show had started to give off the irresistible scent of glamour, and that meant publicity. Halston was a bloodhound for both. He relented and told Lambert he'd do it, explaining his change of heart by noting, "November was such a busy time for me. However, it's turned into such a big deal that of course I'll go."[7]

He brought his big personality, the deep pockets of his new corporate parent (which also owned cosmetics giant Max Factor), and his famous buddies. He wasn't worried or intimidated by the prospect of showing against the greats of French fashion.

"He asked friends and personalities to do [Versailles]," says Frances Patiky Stein, who worked with Halston as he was starting his business. "It was all of his pals. We all laughed and roared: 'We're going to have a show in Versailles!' We weren't worried. It was nothing like, 'Oh, my gosh.' Not in the slightest."[8]

With Halston on board, Givenchy suggested inviting James Galanos, who was a bit of an outlier. He'd built a successful career in Los Angeles, establishing his own version of a couture business and luring large numbers of high-profile clients. But Galanos declined the invitation. He had disengaged from the psychological undertow of Paris. He had no desire or need to prove himself in that venue. He came to New York to present his collection at the Plaza Hotel and he did quite well; he did not need Paris. Lambert had asked each designer to contribute $5,000 to the cost of the production, and it was an expense Galanos saw no need to undertake. And he did not want to endure the inevitable backbiting that would occur when a group of designers were forced to all share a stage.

Following Galanos's refusal, Lambert invited Geoffrey Beene, but he got wind of who had been asked to participate and in what order. Beene, who could be both stubborn and thin-skinned, did not want to play second fiddle to anyone. He declined. Other designers considered for the occasion include long-forgotten names such as Donald Brooks and Chester Weinberg, as well as the Paris-born American designer Pauline Trigère.

Lambert wanted to include a woman in the show. She was intent on inviting her client Anne Klein, but no one else wanted her to. Lambert believed that Klein's intelligent ready-to-wear style was a robust representation of American fashion at its essence. She described Klein as being concerned "not with what clothes *might* be, but what they *must* be to the vital women of our time."[9]

Klein was engaged in her own distinctive business. Traditionally, when a woman shopped, she bought a coordinated ensemble: jacket, skirt, and blouse. And she bought it in one size, even if her torso was a 10 and her hips were a 12. Klein disrupted the status quo. She sold women separates. They could buy a jacket in one size and a skirt in another, and they could skip the blouse if they already had one at home. It's pure common sense today, and it's hard to imagine a time when this was revolutionary. But before Klein and her ilk came along, fashion was not about choice.

Klein was selling women their future stitched up in wool and silk. She wasn't focused on offering women subversive fashion that would release them from convention; she was giving them a new set of conventions. She was preparing them for a future of professional careers and personal independence, along with the high-class problem of trying to "have it all"—whatever that may be.

The French were stubbornly opposed to her. Klein's ready-to-wear was solidly practical, wearable, commercial, and, in the vernacular of fashion, boring. The French didn't believe it should be considered in the same breath as haute couture. It wasn't like comparing apples and oranges: Klein's work wasn't fashion; it was just clothes.

But Lambert had a long history of celebrating American style. Her master plan was to have the Americans appear as closely connected to contemporary times as possible, hinting that the French were woefully out of date and out of step. Klein was the most logical choice. She was a working woman dressing other working women. She was in step with the changing demographics of the American workplace. Klein was at the forefront of the shift that would put Diane von Furstenberg on the cover of *Newsweek* in 1976 as the purveyor of the ubiquitous feminine work uniform: the wrap dress. By 1973, Klein had become one of Lambert's clients. And Lambert was determined that Klein would be part of Versailles.

It took diplomatic outreach before the French would agree to include her, and that negotiation fell to de la Renta. His wife, Françoise, who had been editor of French *Vogue* until 1967, knew all the French designers and was friends with Marie-Hélène de Rothschild. De la Renta was Saint Laurent's invited guest designer. He had worked in Paris and had recently replaced Norman Norell as the president of the Council of Fashion Designers of America, the organization founded by Lambert to bring cohesion and prestige to Seventh Avenue. It was up to him to make a case for Klein to Bergé.

"Pierre Bergé said, 'We don't want Anne Klein,'" recalls de la Renta. "I think it was for the very simple reason that she was very successful in something that he was launching a line in: very expensive ready-to-wear. I tell Bergé: We're *all* ready-to-wear. We're not couture designers. She's an important part of our industry."[10]

Bergé finally sent a telegram relenting: in deference to Oscar and his wife, the French would accept Klein.

Klein never knew about the negotiations made on her behalf—at least, de la Renta never told her. But as the excitement surrounding the Versailles show began to build, she remained calm and collected. She had no doubts about her participation. She believed she deserved to be there.

Lambert's final choice was a bit of a wild card. When she called the rising young talent Stephen Burrows with an invitation to participate in the Versailles show, he was just a kid who liked making clothes with his friends. He didn't know enough about anything to be intimidated.

"It wasn't like a task; it was just a benefit," Burrows remembers.

"It didn't impact me at all. I wasn't into the history of Paris at the time. I just wanted to do everything they said you couldn't."[11]

Burrows was living in his own little fashion universe. He and Halston were the wunderkinds of the 1970s. They were both devoted to the visceral, pleasure-seeking aspects of the decade. They reveled in a loose-limbed, simplified aesthetic. They both tapped into the spirit of dance and movement that was such a significant part of the era's escapism. But where Halston's style was sophisticated and urbane, Burrows's was carefree and energetic. Halston made things tidy and muted for an uptown crowd. Burrows left it raw.

Burrows was the hot newcomer. In modern terms, he was Alexander Wang, Hedi Slimane, and Nicolas Ghesquière all rolled into one. Burrows *was* the 1970s. He had bubbled up from New York's downtown hemisphere, from a community of artists and social butterflies. He had studied at the Fashion Institute of Technology, but his real training as a designer came from weekends lived among the sexual free spirits of Fire Island, the mambo dance parties in Manhattan, and the late nights huddled around tables at Max's Kansas City, a restaurant and bar that attracted denizens of the art and music worlds.

He designed dresses in nearly sheer jersey that slithered over the body like a thin layer of sweat. He was influenced by the rhythms of dance and the exploding colors that flowed impressionistically from his imagination. But aesthetically, there was little that overtly identified him as African American.

Burrows also brought a publicist's most beloved commodity to the event: buzz.

Seven

Stephen Burrows's World

Burrows was among a handful of American designers who stood in contrast to an older generation that had been deeply influenced by the French fashion establishment. Men like Oscar de la Renta and Bill Blass had been under the thumb of their French counterparts. They not only traveled to Paris to get their marching orders on the coming season's silhouette, but they also modeled themselves after the Old World in which moneyed clients led an insular social life, jetting from New York to Palm Beach to Paris and back again, chasing one social season after another. They had an American sensibility—an easy, casual way of dressing that included cashmere twinsets, gray flannel trousers, and crisp white shirts—but it was built on the European notion of social rank, propriety, and gentleman walkers.

More than twenty years younger than Blass, Burrows had made his professional connections by spending summers on Fire Island. His list of friends included jewelry designer Elsa Peretti, who would be an enduring source of financial support; model Marina Schiano, who served as his French-English translator at Versailles; illustrator Joe Eula; Naomi Sims, who modeled some of his earliest creations in the pages of *Vogue;* Joel Schumacher, his first contact at Henri Bendel; and most important, Halston.

Burrows was a naturally quiet young man who thrived on artistic expression, hated confrontation, couldn't countenance labels, and needed the support of friends in order to flourish. The freewheeling community of Fire Island was predominantly white but seemed unperturbed by any antagonism over race. It was heavily gay but believed sexual identity existed on a continuum. That quiet acceptance was a deep comfort to Burrows.

But even with such an open and welcoming community around him, Burrows was never comfortable discussing his sexuality publicly—in terms either personal or political. As society grew more tolerant, Burrows was freed from talking about his identity, sexual or otherwise, because no one was forcing him to take on a label. "If you liked them, you liked them," Burrows recalls. "But that was indicative of the time and the 'love the one you're with' attitude."[1]

He had boyfriends but never a long-term partner. "Back then, there were lots of people," he reflects with a chuckle.[2]

Burrows always says race doesn't matter. But racial stereotypes influenced how he was judged. Racial bias shaped his public persona. Radical chic helped thrust him into the spotlight. Critics have always referred to him as a black designer, not just a designer. They would infer that his dynamic use of color was drawn from "what used to be called the joyful side of the 'black experience.'" Instead, he says he gorged on color because his mother would use an entire box of crayons to color a single page when she was teaching him how to draw as a little boy.[3]

Burrows never tried to wield influence. Philosophically, he gave little thought to what it meant to be black in the fashion industry or even in an America alive with activists and Black Panthers. He was not given to protests or rallies. He had avoided Vietnam because of his asthma. The civil rights movement that defined the 1960s was something that happened outside his world.

Because his family had lineage going back to Trinidad, to a large degree it meant that his experience growing up as a black man in New Jersey was not rooted in African American slave history, but in the immigrant story of striving and entrepreneurship. Burrows had a belief in his individuality and a desire to assimilate.

"You do what you can for the movement, in your way. And that's how I think I approached it," Burrows recalls. "I just thought achieving fame would help propel the movement toward nondiscrimination."[4] He wanted the accouterments of success—the fancy lifestyle, the parties, the freedom. But he did not like ruffling feathers.

B urrows lived in and symbolized the dream of good race relations. And it held him in good stead. After finishing FIT, he and his friend Roz Rubenstein recruited an investor and in 1968 opened one of the most intriguing shops in New York: O Boutique, which was a meeting spot, clothing store, and art space situated on Park Avenue South, near Nineteenth Street, a stone's throw from Max's Kansas City. O Boutique was a commune of creativity. The energy and eccentricities of the street flooded through its doorway and drenched everything in its wake.

The center of the O Boutique hive was a little workshop situated in the basement. Bobby Breslau, a package designer who met Burrows on Fire Island, evolved from fan and customer to the group's leatherwear designer. A friend from FIT, William Hill, was the patternmaker. Hector Torres worked on fabric design. And Rubenstein kept the business, if not quite humming along, at least sputtering. The three men and Burrows shared a tenement apartment near Second Avenue and East Seventh Street for about $150 a month. Rubenstein had her own place on the Upper West Side.[5]

There were myriad others in Burrows's circle who inspired him, protected him, or simply made entertaining dance partners. Breslau connected Burrows with Charles Tracy, a talented young photographer whose spirit of artistic experimentation energized everyone. Vy Higginsen lent support and her merchandising eye. Everyone believed in Burrows. He was their fashion Pied Piper, and they were there to speak for him when he couldn't articulate things for himself. They were his sounding board and his bridge to the outside world. This band of friends—black and white, Latin and Jewish—seemed to just be floating happily above the cultural fray. And the result was electrifying.

"There's turmoil everywhere. And here's this little group that looks like they're all getting along quite fine. It was something to point to, in a way. So when O Boutique opened up, it had the sense of being just a little bit on the cutting edge," Higginsen, who is black, remarked. "People were pulling up in limousines for these clothes. They came from everywhere. This was like, *the* spot, *the* crowd, *the* group, and plus it had this whole sense of unisex," Higginsen said. "Everybody wore whatever."[6] The store attracted the hipsters, musicians, and actresses of the day: Miles Davis, Jane Fonda, Roger Vadim, Carol Channing, Faye Dunaway, Nina Simone.

The O Boutique team worked together and partied together. They'd go out to Max's on a Saturday night, moving en masse. Writers started referring to them as a "family." "We hated it," Charles Tracy remembers.[7]

They partied unabated. They'd go out at 1 a.m. and come home at 7 a.m., as lesser mortals were heading to work. Through Burrows, Tracy found himself thrust into Halston's world as well. "I was introduced to society at Halston's. There were always some society dames at his place. I met Diana Vreeland there. I used to get so overwhelmed by this. I'd have to go to another room and take a deep breath."[8]

The boutique attracted the attention of the glossy fashion magazines. Soon *Vogue*'s influential fashion editor Carrie Donovan came calling to write about Burrows. Diana Vreeland was the editor in chief of *Vogue* at the time, and while she was a Francophile at heart, she knew the time had come to give American designers their due. Donovan wanted to photograph Burrows and his clothes for a section called "*Vogue*'s Own Boutique of Suggestions, Finds and Observations." Burrows was the magazine's new discovery. Donovan asked Burrows's friend Charles Tracy to do the shoot on Fire Island, and it became his debut as a fashion photographer.

"Stephen and I were by the dock and out come Carrie Donovan and a model—and it was Naomi Sims. We were crouching down and we literally fell over," Tracy laughs. "She had lashes out to here and legs up to here."[9]

Tracy's photographs were loose, with a bohemian sensibility. In one of them, a long-haired young woman hangs from a tire swing wearing a pair of leather-fringed trousers and a cream-colored jersey peasant blouse. A male model wears a navy and red jersey tunic; another woman wears a beige tunic with side stripes in navy and green. Each outfit was priced at about $80. And Burrows himself, with his modest afro, is pictured straddling a wooden walkway wearing tweed trousers cropped to midcalf ($30) and a belted tricolored jersey shirt ($60).[10]

Later, Donovan introduced Burrows to the model Pat Cleveland, who became his most enduring muse. Cleveland inspired Burrows more than any other model, with her honey-colored complexion, mass of chocolate brown, springlike curls, and waif physique, elongated to Modigliani proportions. Her patter is otherworldly and she moves without inhibition. On the runway, she would spin like she was caught in a windstorm, unpredictable and bursting with violent energy.

Even today Burrows is still enamored of her, saying, "She's full of life, with a great sense of humor and a beautiful mind. And she was very spiritual, which after taking acid, you know, you're really into that kind of thing."[11]

Despite all the press attention, O Boutique was a money pit. Burrows was not a businessman, nor were any of his friends. And if there was any lesson that he might have learned from the experience, it was that he would need a savvy financial guru if he were to find long-term success. So it was more than good fortune when, in 1970, Geraldine Stutz, the dynamic president of Henri Bendel, became a fan of Burrows's. At the time, Joel Schumacher, now a film director, was working in window display at Bendel's and was also a regular on Fire Island. He admired Burrows's work and introduced him to Stutz. Burrows arrived for his appointment carrying a single melton wool bathrobe coat that was intended as menswear—or the closest thing to it that Burrows designed. Stutz slipped it on and twirled in front of a mirror. She loved it.[12]

"The way he dressed himself and his family was like a traveling show-case," Stutz said before her death in 2005. "He has a marvelous sense of color and way of using color as part of the design. Even the patches, which at first seem visual, are a technical tool in shaping the clothes."[13]

Stutz invited Burrows to move his entire operation uptown to her specialty store. She had established a "Street of Shops," the precursor to today's shop-in-shop displays, and she was prepared to give him his own space in the most adventurous store of the day.

Stutz was a "visionary who thought outside the box. She was a big catalyst for retailing," says Joan Kaner, a retired retail executive who worked at Henri Bendel from 1967 to 1976.

There was no store quite like Bendel's during its heyday. Its twenty-five thousand square feet were filled with progressive merchandise tightly edited based on Stutz's point of view. Until the store was sold to The Limited Inc. in 1985, Stutz sought out the most unique designers bubbling up from the industry and nurtured them in the luxurious confines of 9 West Fifty-seventh Street. (Bendel's later moved to Fifth Avenue.) Like most retailers, Stutz favored European brands—and over the course of her career, she debuted designers such as London's Jean Muir and Paris's Left Bank star Sonia Rykiel—but she also looked for up-and-coming Americans. When Ralph Lauren launched his women's wear in 1971, Stutz embraced it. A young Joan Vass once came in with a shopping bag of little knit hats and Stutz told her to go make a few sweaters for the store, a decision that put the iconoclastic designer on the map.

Stutz called Bendel's sensibility "dog whistle" fashion: clothes with an aesthetic pitch so high and particular that only an extremely sophisticated—and supremely thin, thin, thin—woman could hear their call.[14] Indeed, Stutz's very presence evoked the Henri Bendel customer. She was five foot six and 110 pounds, a slender size 6.[15]

"We carried nothing larger than a size 12, even a French size 12," Kaner says. "I could barely squeeze my arm into it."[16]

Everything in the store was selected to appeal to a petite, chic, rich customer. Its clientele included Babe Paley, Amanda Burden, Diana Ross, Lauren Bacall, and Candice Bergen. It also drew a host of fashion magazine editors. These were women whose natural habitat was the Upper East Side of Manhattan but who would also migrate to other glittery enclaves. When assembled under one roof, they could be intimidating to those who were not of their kind. But Bendel's was devoted to them.

"No one thought Bendel's did any business, but we absolutely did," recalls fashion publicist Marion Greenberg, who began her career as a buyer at the store.[17]

The Henri Bendel imprimatur was invaluable to a designer. It was where any newcomer wanted to be. Indeed, the store would host a weekly open house during which designers could bring in their work in hopes of a nod of approval—and an order—from one of the store's buyers.

Burrows arrived at Bendel's like some beacon from another planet. Stutz named his shop "Stephen Burrows' World," because he truly lived in his own universe. American retailers and designers were fretful about what was going on in Europe, but not Burrows. Before Burrows, women wore a hat and gloves to work. With his move uptown, Burrows convinced the ladies of Park Avenue to get rid of their bras.

Stephen Burrows' World was painted black and filled with music—tapes that Burrows's disc jockey friends made. Its atmosphere was thick with the smell of musk. The whole salon reeked of it. Musk was Burrows's favorite scent and thus the favorite scent of all his friends.

The shop attracted all sorts of characters. A lapsed nun once showed up, with no makeup and a hairnet, dressed in black and accessorized with silver studs. Gay guys would come in to try on the tops and trousers even though Bendel's designated them women's wear. Burrows had brought his philosophy of unisex dressing uptown.

Burrows arrived at Bendel's as part of a group, including Rubenstein and Breslau. Stutz found jobs for them all. She understood how the creative dynamic worked. It was Burrows she wanted, but he needed his supporting cast in order to shine.

"He was surrounded by this group. This group made him work. They idolized him and they gave him a sense of security. I think they all fed on what was happening at the time: the gayness, the freedom, the daring to be different. They were all gifted and talented—that was the common thread," Kaner remembers. "It was an explosive time. It was his time."[18]

It was an enormous business coup for Burrows, as well as a personal one. It changed his mother's view of his budding career in fashion. "She thought [fashion] was gay. She was fine with my being an art teacher. When I decided to switch she was upset," Burrows recalls of leaving art school for FIT. "She came around after Bendel's. Then she loved it. She'd say, 'Where's my next dress?'"[19]

Burrows found success at Bendel's because the store protected him. It controlled the manufacturing and production side of his business, which Burrows never gave a second thought. He was a paid employee making about $500 a week. "Bendel's treated [Burrows] like a little infant boy," remembers Stan Herman, who was an in-house designer alongside Burrows. But the store also gave Burrows "his freedom, and that's when he's at his best."[20]

By 1973, thin little jersey dresses with contrasting stitching rippling along the hemline had become Burrows's signature. These were not constructed out of the heavy, figure-shaping jersey used today. Today's jersey can hide a multitude of sins; its heft smoothes bumps and ripples and even minimizes jiggle. Burrows used a featherweight Jasco-brand jersey, a material typically used in lingerie. Wearing one of those dresses was as close as one could come to being publicly naked. Indeed, it was the difficulty of sewing such insubstantial fabric that led to the wave effect along the hem. Burrows pulled the stitching too tightly as he was hemming one of his jersey dresses and the fabric curled. He liked the effect so much that he began using it not only along the hem but also along the cuff and at the neckline. During a meeting with Diana Vreeland, she referred to one of his undulating dresses, which was green, as "lettuce." And the term "lettucing" stuck as a way of describing Burrows's fortuitous accident.

Burrows was selling a half-million dollars in merchandise at Bendel's.[21] No small amount considering that his dresses were about $49 and $59 wholesale. By comparison, at the time, one of Oscar de la Renta's dresses would wholesale for $375.[22]

Everything seemed perfect. He was in a store helmed by an independent, creative-minded president who took care of all the exasperating business aspects of producing a collection. Burrows was left simply to create, surrounded and inspired by his friends.

"We loved being together," Rubenstein said. "It was kind of like this big force just moving together."[23]

On June 21, 1973, Burrows became the first black designer to win a Coty Award. He won for his women's wear, alongside Calvin Klein—another newcomer who had started his business in 1969 by peddling pea coats.

Bernadine Morris, the *New York Times* fashion writer, chaired the Coty Award selection committee, which was made up of the country's fashion editors. At the awards presentation, Morris stated, "A fine designer's work is as recognizable by its unique 'brush strokes' and color palette as that of a top painter. The committee decided to make this year's awards to designers who have established their own school of fashion."[24]

Morris asked Audrey Smaltz, who was the fashion editor of *Ebony* magazine, to organize the fashion show for the awards program, which was held at Alice Tully Hall at Lincoln Center. Smaltz had only been working at *Ebony* a few years, but she regularly traveled to Europe with Eunice Johnson, the magazine's cofounder, who shopped the haute couture salons for the company's fashion extravaganza, *Ebony* Fashion Fair, which traversed the country by bus.

The *Ebony* Fashion Fair was a fashion road show that mixed racial uplift with glamour and theatrics. Johnson bought glorious clothes from top design houses, which were then given a workout by the *Ebony* Fashion Fair models. Those girls would whip capes and stoles above their head, allowing them to float out around them like magic carpets. They were adept at slipping out of jackets with the speed of a cyclone. And they understood the power of the big reveal.

Smaltz also had stage presence to spare. She was a statuesque woman standing six feet tall, with a regal posture. Onstage for the Coty Awards, she didn't stand behind the lectern; she stood in front of it. "So you could see me!" she laughs.[25] There was a lot to see. She wore a long chocolate brown Halston gown made out of Jasco jersey—the same fabric that Burrows used for his signature, barely-there dresses. "Girl, there was nothing underneath that gown but me and a pair of Hanes panty hose," Smaltz recalls with a satisfied chuckle.[26]

When she introduced Burrows, she did so in *Ebony* Fashion Fair patois: "SB stands for Soul Brother. And here is Soul Brother Stephen Burrows." Earlier, Smaltz had bottles of Dom Perignon champagne delivered backstage so the models could have a little something fizzy and inspiring. Burrows's models exploded onto the stage wearing Technicolor dresses and dancing to the music. Calvin Klein's segment had been mostly gray, white, and beige. Oscar de la Renta, who also received an award that year, dabbled in color. But like the pictures he grew up coloring with his mother, Burrows's collection displayed the entire box of Crayolas. "It was so exciting, I cried,"[27] Smaltz says.

"That's when Eleanor realized she had to invite this little black boy [to Versailles]. She asked him at the last minute. She didn't know nothing about Stephen Burrows until she saw him that night."[28]

That's a bit of Smaltz's signature hyperbole. But it is without question that the summer of 1973 was when Burrows took center stage in the American fashion industry.

It was also when Burrows moved on from Bendel's.

Encouraged by Halston and with support from garmento investors, Burrows established his own studio in the Garment District. He was actively seeking a larger audience, more money, and more fame, with the help of Ben Shaw and Guido de Natale, the kings of Seventh Avenue. The designer wanted to "dress the world." Critics predicted that his first year's gross would hit $5 million.[29]

Burrows's move to Seventh Avenue, over the summer of 1973, was an unpleasant, toxic, and unprofessional mess. His departure from Bendel's was less a decisive act than it was muddled, ill-mannered happenstance. "They wouldn't give me a raise," Burrows complains. "I had a million-dollar business there. They wouldn't give me a raise."

"It was vacation time," he continues. "We were in negotiations to renew my contract with Bendel's. We couldn't come to terms. And, well, I couldn't go back. I just didn't come back from vacation. After they wouldn't give me a raise, I didn't come back.

"I couldn't understand why, after three years, I was still making $500 a week."[30]

Geraldine Stutz learned Burrows was leaving by reading the news in *Women's Wear Daily*. Burrows didn't alert her to his decision to walk or explain himself. He said nothing. He simply didn't return from his vacation and blamed the entire episode on lawyers.

"I was shocked," Stutz remembered. "We had a good relationship, a marvelous relationship. He had been a great plus for us and I know we had been great for him. It was 'even-Steven': he owed us nothing and we owed him nothing. But not to have told us or given us some idea . . . What could we have done but wish him luck?"[31]

Burrows was not prepared for the toughness that Seventh Avenue required. Designers had to be ready to fight. Burrows had always hung back, content in his own space. His new partners were pure businessmen; they were not the hand-holding, reassuring, paternal types. Stutz was a savvy merchant, but she was also a bit of a therapist. She knew there had been a particular chemistry of personalities fueling Burrows's creativity at O Boutique. Rather than risk disturbing that, she simply picked up the entire package and moved it uptown.

On Seventh Avenue, Burrows was essentially alone. Shaw and de Natale were investing in Burrows, not some funky downtown collective. Friends who had been loyal to him, who had spoken up for him, said he failed to do the same for them—not because he didn't care but because he didn't want to deal with the ugliness. The "family" soon disbanded, at least professionally.

Burrows had strong opinions about the aesthetics of his brand, but couldn't seem to win any of his arguments. The new manufacturers didn't understand the subtleties of working with his signature lightweight lingerie jersey; it took them months to perfect his lettuce hems.

"They didn't know how to make knit clothes," Burrows says of his new partners. "It became a big problem. I'd tell them you have to put a fabric tape—today it's called jelly tape—into the neckline and shoulders to keep them from stretching. There has to be tape in there, otherwise it just turns into string. It became a big problem with them cost cutting. Everything got returned."

"Halston said, 'You should be on Seventh Avenue.' I was listening to him," Burrows says. "In hindsight, I should have investigated: Did they know how to do knits? But they had a good reputation; they were doing everybody."[32]

When Lambert approached him about participating in the show at Versailles, Burrows had not yet been deflated by the harsh realities of Seventh Avenue. He does not remember the exact day Lambert called, but it was when he was riding high, when he reflected the devil-may-care ethos of the times. Burrows gave off the aura of a man who had nothing to lose because everything that he had gained had merely washed ashore in front of him. He'd kicked up the tide, but he'd done it with no definitive strategy. He had no psychic investment in the international stature of the American fashion industry.

Burrows had been to Paris once before, in 1969, when he was thinking about producing a line of shoes. He returned without a shoe line but with admiration for Yves Saint Laurent. Still, it was as if he'd shut down his fashion receptors while he was on foreign soil. Nothing about Paris seeped into his work. Fire Island was his geographic inspiration. It was the key ingredient in his artistic identity. So when Lambert invited him to Versailles, Burrows accepted just because he wanted to go to France. He wasn't out to prove himself to the kings of couture, he just wanted to put on a show in a new place, to try something he'd never tried before. And he wouldn't have to go alone. He'd be surrounded by friends: Roz Rubenstein, Charles Tracy, Joe Eula, and Halston. Lambert assured him he'd be able to bring his favorite mannequins: his house model Bethann Hardison, along with Alva Chinn, Pat Cleveland, Karen Bjornson, and Jennifer Brice, who had a terrible crush on him.

Burrows's reasons for accepting the invitation were as uncomplicated and uncalculating as the man himself. Of all the American designers, Burrows was the one whose motives were the least fraught with emotional and professional baggage. For the others, their insecurities and ambitions were writ large. Almost immediately, they began taking their frustrations out on each other.

Eight

Insecurity and Egos

The Americans' first organizational meeting took place at the de la Renta apartment. The designers arrived, each with a small entourage, except for Burrows, who came alone. Chip Rubenstein, Anne Klein's husband, would serve as the treasurer of the group. The relationships were friendly but competitive.

Halston and Burrows were chums from Fire Island. De la Renta and Blass had known each other for years from Seventh Avenue. Blass's right-hand man, Tom Fallon, had met Burrows while they were students at FIT. De la Renta had a working relationship with Halston. "When I first came to Seventh Avenue, he did hats for my shows," de la Renta recalls. "When I first knew Halston, he was a really nice guy, good looking. Then he started his own business. . . . He really was *it*. No question about it."[1]

Lambert was there, of course, as was the fashion illustrator Joe Eula, a slight man with thick-rimmed glasses and the ability to create characters and convey emotions with only a few deft strokes of his pen. Eula, who died in 2004, was a magnificent, in-demand talent whose sketches appeared alongside Eugenia Sheppard's column in the *New York Herald*

Tribune. He also provided illustrations for Saks Fifth Avenue, magazines, and album covers, and worked closely with Halston. And as a result, Eula knew virtually everyone. He'd agreed to create the Americans' set.

"We talked about the project and what it would be," Burrows remembers of the first meeting. "There was a lot of competition between the other guys. And Joe would spark little fights and incidents. I was amazed how he could get everyone going. There was bickering already about the order [of the show].

"I didn't care," Burrows shrugs. "It wasn't like a big thing to me if I went last or first."[2]

In that initial meeting, the designers made a few key decisions. Their tiny finance committee would consist of Lambert, de la Renta, and Chip Rubenstein. They would keep count of the expenses and make sure each designer paid his or her fair share. They envisioned each designer having about twenty minutes to present a collection. Today, that much time allotted to each designer would be obscene. A runway show now lasts little more than ten minutes—and that's for a designer presenting an entire season's collection all on his own, not a few well-chosen highlights. But back then a typical runway show lasted forty or forty-five minutes, so twenty didn't seem so terribly long, especially for a special charity event where the audience was looking to be entertained, not to shop.

The Americans were ready-to-wear designers, and that was what they would show. But they also decided they would make a few special pieces for the occasion.

To be frugal, they created a pool of money to cover model fees. But that meant that at least three designers had to approve a model before she could be added to the master list. A designer could still bring a favorite mannequin or two, but he alone would have to bear the cost. Again, this would be unheard of today. Designers are barely willing to share models over the course of a day of shows during fashion week, let alone for one event. In the 1970s, each of the half-dozen or so models in a designer's show would regularly navigate eight or nine quick changes. Today, a

---

designer like Marc Jacobs will hire fifty models, one for each look, to eliminate quick changes and allow for more elaborate styling.

Each of the designers agreed to share models and their costs, except for Halston. In 1973, things were different for him. Up to his neck in Norton Simon money and with an address book of famous friends, he used only a few favorite professional models. Otherwise, he would invite demi-celebrities such as actress Baby Jane Holzer and model Marisa Berenson to walk his runway. And he proposed inviting Liza Minnelli.

Fresh from an Academy Award win for her performance in *Cabaret*, Minnelli agreed to perform at Versailles. For Halston. For his segment alone. This did not sit well with other designers, most notably de la Renta.

"There was going to be an opening number and closing number with all the designers and one number for each designer. But Halston was being very mysterious about his segment. Every time we talked about it, he'd say, 'Oh, we can talk about that later.' And then, uh, I heard that Liza Minnelli is going to be in Halston's show. Liza Minnelli was a great, great friend of Halston.

"Well, when I heard Liza would walk for Halston, I knew Raquel Welch was in Spain doing *Three Musketeers*. So I called her up and I said to her, 'Would you please do me a huge, big favor. We're doing this show in Versailles; it's very important for me. Will you come and do one dress of mine?'

"When Liza Minnelli heard about it, she said, 'If Raquel is in the show, I'm not going to do it. I'm going to be singing my heart out and Raquel is going to walk out and get all the accolades.' So at that moment, it was decided Liza would be the needle that would thread all the way through for everyone. She'd be the only star in the show."[3]

Minnelli agreed to work for free, but the designers paid $1,000 for two male dancers to accompany her and another $1,000 for a sound and lighting technician. Minnelli's contract also stipulated that she could not do television gratis, so there could be no TV coverage of her performance.

Eula designed the set for free, too, with only his expenses covered. The designers received other financial breaks as well, the first from a very unlikely source. The chemical company Monsanto, which manufactured artificial hair for its Elura wigs, agreed to kick in $15,000, along with the expertise of the hairstylist Kenneth Battelle. Better known simply as Kenneth, he was the hairstylist to social swans, most famously creating Jacqueline Kennedy's famous bouffant. Of course, Monsanto wanted more than a little in return. The company wanted the rights to a three-to-six-minute promotional film that would be put together from the dress rehearsal. And it demanded that at least one-third of the American designers incorporated Elura wigs in their part of the production.

At the time, Monsanto was in need of positive publicity. The company was one of the leading producers of Agent Orange, a defoliant that was used extensively in Vietnam, as well as the pesticide DDT. The latter was banned in the United States in 1972, and by 1973, Vietnam veterans were pointing to a link between Agent Orange exposure and certain cancers and birth defects.

Lambert balked at Monsanto's wig request. She didn't want the Versailles show to become a spectacle of corporate sponsorship that risked overshadowing the designers themselves. She responded with shock and bewilderment and a not-so-gentle rebuke.

"This totally violates the spontaneous, cooperative spirit of the show, which is to help American fashion in general," she wrote in a memo. "It's not a publicity stunt or a hard-sell promotion of Monsanto and its various departments in my opinion—unless there has been a serious miscommunication."[4] Monsanto backed down. The designers used Elura wigs at will and Monsanto received a credit in the program.

Max Factor chipped in $25,000 to be the beauty company of record. Most of its money went to pay for the production costs and the models' expenses, including their flight on Olympic Airways.

The biggest value, however, came in the form of the models. There were thirty-six of them: blondes, brunettes; black girls and white. They were at various stages in their careers—some who had been working regularly for years and others who were just beginners. They were from a generation for whom modeling was a glamorous job, but not a road to immense wealth.

For their services, each received a flat fee of $300 plus a $25 per diem. That covered their rehearsals in New York, as well as four days in Paris. It was a ridiculously low payday. One of them, a black woman named Charlene Dash, who was represented by Ford Models, already had credits in *Vogue* and had been photographed by Richard Avedon. She was regularly earning $50 for only a couple of hours of modeling at the Plaza Hotel.

Yet when Lambert asked her to do the Versailles show, Dash agreed. Eileen Ford, who ran her agency, was aghast. "Are you crazy?"

"I'd been to Paris before," Dash explains, "but I hadn't flown over just for the weekend!"[5]

A lot of the models felt that way. "I was excited about going to Paris and being part of another culture," says Billie Blair, who had never been to the fashion capital before. "I respected the French and the name they'd made and the path they'd made for designers. But to be there with them actually? The Eiffel Tower! The Champs-Élysées! In my naive mind, there were going to be artists wearing berets and painting, and poodles with pink ribbons! This is the mind of a twenty-three-year-old."[6]

As the plans started coming together, the designers held occasional meetings at Eula's studio on West Fifty-sixth Street. Every gathering was a blend of creative kibitzing, growing anxiety, and barely contained self-doubt. Each designer contributed between $5,000 and $10,000 for the show—although Burrows doesn't remember putting in much of anything. In all likelihood, a significant portion of his assigned contribution came from Halston, a personal friend, enthusiastic supporter, and newly minted millionaire.

The stakes were especially high for Halston. "Some people are calling it American week in Paris and others the Versailles Follies, or according to columnist Hebe Dorsey, 'A giant promotion for Halston, the golden boy of American fashion,'" wrote Sheppard, whose work appeared in dozens of newspapers, most notably the *New York Herald Tribune*.[7] David Mahoney, Norton Simon's president, was planning an extravagant dinner party in the days before the show at a famous Paris restaurant, the art nouveau masterpiece Maxim's. "Halston had more invested in the show," says Karen Bjornson, who started her career as Halston's house model when she was fresh from her high school graduation. She remained one of his favorites throughout her career. "He had more responsibility."[8]

Halston knew he had to pull off something remarkable in order to live up to the hype he was doggedly generating. He decided the group needed a choreographer. Kay Thompson, best remembered as the author of the *Eloise* children's books and for her role in the 1957 Stanley Donen film *Funny Face,* was an experienced choreographer and also happened to be Minnelli's godmother. Her retainer, plus the cost of an assistant, was $10,000. It was the American's single largest expense, but it would turn out to be money exceptionally well spent. The designers agreed that when it came to the production, Eula and Thompson would have the last word, which was a quaint idea that dissipated on the wind almost as soon as it was uttered.

The gist of the American plan was to re-create scenes from *Funny Face,* opening with Minnelli, her two dancers, and all the models performing a version of "Bonjour, Paris," the number Audrey Hepburn sang in the film about an ingénue introduced to fashion in the big city. Having settled on a theme, and agreeing on how the expenses would be covered, the designers were left to anxiously and thoughtfully determine what styles they would present to the world's elite.

Since Eula was in charge of the set, the designers came to a consensus that he should be dispatched to Versailles to do advance work. Eula took Françoise de la Renta along because of her familiarity with Paris and the French fashion establishment.

The Palace of Versailles is about an hour's train ride west of Paris. The town of Versailles that exists beyond the palace walls is little more than a well-preserved little suburb with modest businesses, unmemorable restaurants, and a grand city hall that will forever lie in the shadow of the palace's gold-encrusted splendor. Eula and Françoise were the first among the American contingent to walk across the expansive gray-stoned Courtyard of Honor, and there inscribed high above their heads on the south wing of the palace—just before the ornate gates leading to the Royal Courtyard—was an inscription they worried would set the tone of the show: A TOUTES LES GLOIRES DE LA FRANCE—To all the glories of France.

They had arrived in the belly of the beast.

The Royal Opera House at Versailles, known as the Théâtre Gabriel, was designed by Ange-Jacques Gabriel—France's most prominent architect of the eighteenth century—and was completed in 1770. It is an expression of noble wealth and extravagance that can only exist under a monarchy. It is a place of pomp and circumstance and intimidation by lavishness.

Four carved golden pillars flanked the theater's proscenium stage. A heavy pale blue curtain decorated with fleurs-de-lis served as the backdrop. The walls were adorned with lush renderings of celestial creatures, reclining semi-nudes, and other flashes of bacchanalian indulgence. Seven chandeliers glittered from the ceiling and a large central chandelier served as an overhead focal point and hung above the king's loge.

The theater walls looked as though they were hewn from marble but instead were the result of a trompe l'oeil effect on wood. This aesthetic trickery made the walls light enough to be shifted to suit any production. The gold and the crystals that dangled from the chandeliers, however, were real. Originally lit with two thousand candles, the chandeliers made the theater an enormous fire hazard, which helps explain why in its first twenty years it was used fewer than forty times. The theater was inaugurated in 1770 with a lavish production of *Persée,* an opera based on the Greek myth of Perseus, to celebrate the marriage of Marie Antoinette to Louis XVI.

Rows of blue velvet benches lined the wooden floor and three tiers of balconies rose up toward the ceiling. While the theater itself was far and away more extravagant than anything that might be constructed today, it was also an uncomfortable place to watch a show. The main floor seats were glorified bleachers, nothing like the deep-cushioned stadium seating complete with cupholders in today's film theaters.

The theater presented clear challenges for a fashion show. First, it was enormous; it would easily dwarf the models. The wings soared forty-five feet high. And it featured a classic proscenium stage. There was no runway and there were no plans to extend a catwalk into the audience. So the presentation would essentially be a theatrical production, with side-to-side movement rather than the back and forth promenade of a typical fashion show. The clothes would have to hold their own in a theater built and embellished for a king.

During the trip, Eula met with the unionized technicians at Versailles to go over lighting requests and measurements for the set design. The Americans wanted to use colored lights and chiaroscuro effect to create a sense of drama and mystery on stage. The lights would shift in a geometric sequence in shades of blue, primrose, and magenta to bring the production to life.

The sets for the American designers were fairly plain. Eula's freehand sketches of Paris landmarks painted on a scrim would serve as the backdrop. The unadorned aesthetic of the Americans stood in stark contrast to what the French were planning. They had hired the director Jean-Louis Barrault, who proposed a modern version of the sort of spectacle that would have been presented during the time of the monarchy. If they were going to celebrate couture, they would do so in its regal, stupefying tradition.

Barrault assigned each designer a particular float that was inspired by history or the designer himself.

The French planned to use a live orchestra. The Americans were using recorded, contemporary music. The French were sparing no expense. The Americans, due to their need for frugality, the complications of organizing an event from across the Atlantic, and a desire to reflect their modern sensibility, kept things simple.

A fter a few days in Paris, Françoise de la Renta and Eula returned to New York for a final meeting with the group at Eula's studio. It was time to settle the fine details, which meant that Halston and Oscar de la Renta had yet another opportunity to butt heads.

"I needed to call Paris to give them the order of the program," de la Renta explains. "Who will be first, second, you know. I'm the one who is supposed to call Marie-Hélène to give her the order."[9]

God forbid that this decision be simple and free of subterfuge.

De la Renta and Blass left their respective showrooms at 550 Seventh Avenue and shared a cab for the short ride to Eula's studio. As they made their way through midtown traffic, they discussed the running order. De la Renta suspected that Halston would be gunning for the grand finale slot, and he did not want him to have it. He was tired of Halston's shadowy shenanigans, his attempt to hog Liza Minnelli's talents, and his haughty attitude. Everyone was.

Yet de la Renta knew he couldn't suggest that the designers show in alphabetical order, because that would mean he would go last. The other designers would see it as a transparent attempt to gain an advantage. It would certainly rile Halston and a fight would ensue.

So de la Renta told Blass that he planned to suggest they all draw straws from a bag to determine the order; that way, no one could complain. It would be a matter of luck—and if luck were on de la Renta's side, Halston would not get to show last. Blass nodded his approval.[10]

For that final meeting, all the designers turned up except Klein. Chip Rubenstein was there, though, representing her interests and dutifully keeping track of the group's expenses. Kay Thompson was on hand, too, as was Eula. The debate over the order of the show began with an unconvincing display of magnanimity: the designers all respected Thompson's résumé and her skill, so they asked for her opinion. She suggested opening with Klein, because she was the only female designer and her clothes were the least formal. Thompson wanted Burrows to show next because he was the young rebel, and while his clothes evoked seventies nightlife, they had an ease and lightness that was more appetizer than main course.

Blass was an established ready-to-wear brand. He designed for an American ideal—a sporty, sophisticated dame. He should go third.

Thompson suggested de la Renta show fourth because his work was more formal than Blass's but was still mostly daywear. Halston, she said, should be the finale. Uh-oh.

"How did you come to this conclusion?" demanded de la Renta.

"Because Halston makes evening clothes," Thompson explained.

In exasperation, de la Renta exclaimed: "So do I!"

Before Thompson could respond and de la Renta could embark on a full-throated argument, Blass spoke up. "Sounds great!" he chirped.

"I could have shot him," de la Renta recalls.

After the meeting wrapped up, Blass, de la Renta, and Rubenstein commiserated on the street. "You really disappointed me today," Rubenstein told de la Renta. "You let Halston get away with what we were worried about."

The next morning, de la Renta called Rothschild in Paris to give her the order of the American segment of the Versailles show. He said it would be as follows: Anne Klein, Stephen Burrows, Bill Blass . . . Halston, and, finally, Oscar de la Renta.

When Thompson's assistant checked in with de la Renta to make sure the show's order had been transmitted to Paris, de la Renta told him what he'd done. He also said that if Halston had any questions about the order, he could call him. De la Renta was ready for a fight.

Halston never called.[11]

With the order of the show established, the sets settled, Thompson scheduled to choreograph each segment, and the cost of the show underwritten by corporate donors, all that was left was to build anticipation and sell tickets. The proceeds from ticket sales would go directly into Versailles's coffers. *Women's Wear Daily*, which in the 1960s had done so much to turn American designers into personalities, worked overtime to transform the charity event into an international "battle" between French and American fashion. Indeed, it was *WWD* that promised a showdown. The trade publication planted the seed that the winner—as determined by *WWD*, of course—would claim some sort of moral victory.

But while *Women's Wear Daily* fanned the flames, the French press remained characteristically blasé. The fashion editor Eugenia Sheppard— tiny, blond, and feisty—captured the exaggerated French malaise, reporting: " 'One thing I can tell you for sure,' says a certain French prince who doesn't want to be mentioned by name. 'No Frenchman would ever pay around $500 to go to this kind of evening. Everyone I know has had a free ticket given to him, usually by an American.' "[12] He exaggerated the $235 ticket price for effect.

The general-interest media wavered between dismissal—it was just another charity event for the usual cluster of social butterflies—and complaints that the show was a frivolous endeavor by the American fashion industry in the middle of an energy crisis caused by the OPEC oil embargo. "Not only should any charity money have gone to Israel, some tongues wagged, but such conspicuous consumption hardly fitted into the trials and tribulations of a Western world shivering through the Arab oil squeeze (though for the time being it has not affected France)," wrote Jonathan Randal in the *Washington Post*.[13]

But most everyone gave it high approbation in advance, as it promised to be a splendid source of fizzy gossip.

"I went from New York, from the women's department, to cover it," recalls Enid Nemy, who spent forty years as a writer for the *New York Times*. "They wanted a feature story, not fashion. They wanted the party atmosphere, not just a show review."

The Paris and New York social worlds overlapped, and the wealthy regularly crossed the Atlantic for the promise of a good time. No one was about to miss out on a good party. But one had to be invited to spend $235 per ticket. In France, getting on the list could be accomplished with the right family name. In New York, family name was important, but money could make up for having had the misfortune of being born a Jane or John Doe.[14]

It was useful to know someone, to be someone of modest fame, or to fabricate some convincing story about precisely why one simply had to be included. The whole experience was a bit like the annual Costume Institute gala at the Metropolitan Museum of Art, a similarly curated extravaganza that takes on outlandish importance among those who traffic in social currency. In 1973, the breathlessness was palpable in the telegrams and letters sent to Eleanor Lambert's office. Lambert was put in the exasperating position of navigating conflicting international schedules and whiny demands.

The John Barry Ryans made a last-minute decision to go, according to a rushed cable communication: *"Could the tickets be sent to the Plaza Athénée and paid for upon their arrival?"* Stuart Kline of Philadelphia added incorrectly and only sent $900 for four tickets. He had to be contacted to make good on the missing forty dollars. *"Please pardon me for writing rather than having the letter typed, but my secretary has been out. . . ."* For her part, Lambert barely concealed her impatience in her own memos: *"I have simply forwarded your check to Paris. If your cancelled check isn't receipt enough, I suggest you request one in Paris."*[15]

Guests made out checks to the Versailles Foundation and Lambert forwarded them to Rothschild at her Paris office in the eighth arrondissement. For her part, Rothschild had assembled an all-star list of attendees.

She invited Princess Grace of Monaco to be her special guest. The celebration was now under the patronage of French prime minister Pierre Messmer and the U.S. ambassador to France, John N. Irwin II—whose name was misspelled as "Irwing" on the official invitation. It was a hectic few weeks. But with the wealthy placated and designer egos tamed—for the time being, at least—everything had come together.

Nine

Muses, Marijuana, and Mayhem

T he planning for the entire extravaganza happened in only a few months. Indeed, the models were not confirmed until a fortnight before the show. But once all the decisions had been made, it turned out that the Versailles runway would host one of the largest contingents of African American models to ever walk in a major, multiracial fashion show—a show that did not use them as a gimmick, an overt aesthetic statement, or a political flourish. Of the thirty-six American models hired for Versailles, ten were black.

The American designers didn't have much money for models, and many of the biggest names in the business, such as Lauren Hutton, were out of their price range.

"A lot of the models were turning it down because they weren't being paid enough," recalls Tom Fallon, who worked with Bill Blass. The black models en masse were just starting to find acceptance, and, as Fallon says, "You could get them at a bargain price. They were willing to go for a reduced salary."[1]

None of the models hired were getting rich at their craft. Even on their best-paying days, their salaries were meager by today's standards.

Models did their own makeup and were often responsible for their own hairstyling. Some of them would later run into serious financial troubles. No one was taking taxes out of their paychecks, because they were independent contractors, and no one was offering them advice on investments or retirement accounts. None of these girls were snagging million-dollar advertising contracts of the sort that exist today.

Still, modeling had its glamorous perks: travel, clothes, parties. And for many of the black women, modeling was far more lucrative than the jobs they'd left or those that might have been in their future.

Fashion in 1973 was a much smaller and more insular world than it is today. Everyone knew each other, and designers had their favorite models with whom they worked regularly. These women epitomized the designers' ideals in proportions and aesthetics or were simply their friends. Blass, for instance, was typically drawn to a Mayflower beauty with an athletic body. Halston liked a lithe physique and a certain sophisticated, jet-setting mystery. He was famous for his Halstonettes, several of whom modeled for him at Versailles, including Pat Cleveland and Karen Bjornson. Burrows preferred his models rail thin. He had a preference for black models, but not to the exclusion of others. He, too, adored Cleveland, as well as Alva Chinn.

In 1973, the modeling world was divided into print girls and runway walkers. There was little crossover; that came later, in the 1980s. Print models were classic beauties who were photographed for advertising campaigns and magazine editorials. Runway models brought clothes to life on the catwalk. They needed stage presence and grace. The American designers who went to Versailles hired exclusively runway girls.

But even for models accustomed to commanding a stage, Versailles presented a unique challenge. Because most of them were modeling for more than one designer, and because Thompson was choreographing a presentation that was more Broadway-style performance than traditional runway show, Versailles required long rehearsals, plus it came with all the stresses associated with a high-profile performance. By hiring so many black models, the American designers got themselves a deal.

S ince the designers had decided to pool their money and share models, each woman had to be approved by at least three designers before her fee could be paid out of the kitty. Billie Blair was a shoe-in.

Of the group of gifted girls asked to come to Versailles, Blair was the runway queen. She was simply called "Billie" and known for her nearly shaved head. Over her career, she worked with all the greats, traveling to Europe, Asia, and all around the world. The styles of the day were perfectly crafted for her dramatic gestures and big personality—these clothes needed to be seen in motion, because at rest, they looked like large, sad sacks.

Blair didn't epitomize the 1970s culture of indulgence, although she definitely waded in it and ultimately managed, through luck and prayer, to survive it. And despite her successes, she did not emerge as a "supermodel." Over the years, she was featured in a host of advertising campaigns, but she was never a Cover Girl or much of a household name. As modeling began to take on the more damaging contours of flesh-peddling capitalism, she was winding down her career and listening to a new calling. She managed to avoid the subjugation that came to afflict so many drug-addicted, lost young women who were swept onto the runway and then into rehab—or the grave. Blair's career was born when modeling still had the fresh aroma of liberation.

She was not the most glamorous, the most accomplished, or the best-connected of the young women who would bring the American designers' work to life at Versailles. "She was not a pretty girl," says Barbara Summers, author of *Skin Deep*, a history of black models. "She had a long, horse face and no hair."[2]

But that didn't matter. Blair could move in a manner that was magical.

She was transformed on the runway; she didn't come to life, she became a new person—a dramatic catwalk creature who made Oscar de la Renta swoon. Her astonishing drama and poise made Bill Blass turn away, if only briefly, from his obsession with Mayflower beauties. She made Halston's gaggle of celebrity friends look banal and flat.

Blair was meticulous in showing off clothes. She could spin, but she also had grace and dignity. Her every gesture exemplified nuance. Blair morphed from a gawy kid into a smoldering, haughty queen. Folks in the fashion industry knew she was talented, but at Versailles, she was a revelation.

Blair was a tall, skinny, sweet-faced girl with a medium-brown complexion. She had enormous eyes, a generous smile, a well-balanced face, and the delicate legs of a yearling.

She was born in Arkansas, where her parents, Hattie and William, met. Her father was so certain that she was going to be a boy that he never considered any names except William Junior. When Blair entered this world as a girl, the family was stunned. No one could think of an unabashedly feminine name, so she became Billie, after her father's diminutive.

Her parents moved to Flint, Michigan, where William had a job at General Motors. In the 1950s, Flint was in its glory days. It was a prosperous city that revolved around the auto industry, which helped boost generations of bootstrapping, striving black southerners into the middle class.

By the time Billie Blair came of age, Flint's glory days had passed and the city was beginning to feel the effects of a declining auto business. Blair grew up as a rust-belt girl. As a teenager, she loved fashion. She'd sit in school with a fashion magazine tucked behind her textbook. She fantasized about being photographed for the pages of *Vogue* or *Life*, posing confidently in an advertisement for Virginia Slims, or looking cherubic in a Noxzema ad. She had the body to be a model; it was long and angular, the perfect hanger—but no one in her circle ever suggested she pursue it. Modeling simply didn't seem like a realistic prospect for a black kid from Flint.

By the early 1960s, only a few women in shades of brown had made significant inroads on the fashion runways. Some were so fair-skinned that they often couldn't immediately be identified as black. And if no one asked about their race, they didn't tell. "Everyone was playing a racial charade. If you identified too strongly as African American, you were not getting anywhere," Summers explains. "When they did shows for the department stores, they were in the afternoon and open to the public. Black people always recognize black people. Blacks in the audience knew the black models. Others in the audience probably didn't know."[3]

The impossible began to seem possible when Blair started seeing pictures of Naomi Sims and other black models in all the magazines. "High fashion is taking a silky little step toward equality," wrote Judith Martin in the *Washington Post* in 1968. "Turn the glossy pages of *Vogue* or *Harper's Bazaar* and suddenly, looking marvelously at home, there is The Black Model. Magazine officials will say that she's been there for years. But to the reader—and to the model herself—she is startlingly, conspicuously new."[4]

There was even a story about Sims in the *Detroit Free Press,* the local paper from the nearby Motor City. "A new look was developing, the real Afro-American model. Designers weren't going to try and make her look white or Mexican," Blair remembers. "No, we were going all the way to the other end. I looked at her and thought, She's really Afro-American. That made me feel like there's really a place there for me."[5]

Blair started going down to Detroit and picking up work through the local modeling agencies, which mostly booked young women for the big auto shows at Cobo Hall, a cavernous convention center with the romance of a cellblock. The models in the early days of the consumer trade show, which lives on as the North American International Auto Show, didn't have to know very much about the cars. Their technical savvy wasn't what got them hired. Their job was to be pretty and pert while caressing the latest feat of American engineering.

For all of her early insecurity, as far as Blair can recall, being black was neither an issue nor a hindrance. It may even have been something of an advantage.

"When I came in, I didn't have to kick open the door," she says. White designers "appreciated my facial features. The coloring, they adored. They just loved the brown skin. The door had been opened and I could pretty much do what I wanted to do."[6]

In an odd way, Blair's timing couldn't have been better. In the same way that Burrows's debut as a designer happened to capitalize on the feelings of hope and do-goodism that had been stirred in the wake of the 1967 race riots and the release of the Kerner Report, Blair began modeling at a time when people were looking to fashion and the media to pave the way toward racial harmony.

One day, Marji Kunz, fashion editor of the *Detroit Free Press*, saw Blair draped over a Buick concept car at the Detroit auto show. Blair was wearing silver go-go boots and hot pants. "I looked ready to take off to Mars," Blair remembers.[7]

"Marji discovered me," Blair states frankly. "They'd take a local model to New York and do a color supplement for the *Detroit Free Press*."[8]

Like Dorothy arriving in Oz, Blair arrived in New York in 1973, under the auspices of the *Free Press*. She was twenty-two, mature for a model who was just establishing herself in the big league, but she was terribly young in temperament and worldliness. Her head was shaved because she'd been putting all sorts of chemicals in her hair—most recently to create blond streaks—and her locks had given up and started to fall out.

Blair stayed with Kunz at the Plaza Hotel, where most of the fashion press set up shop and where Eleanor Lambert regularly held court with her American designers. "This little girl from Flint, Michigan. The Plaza! It was just such a transition," Blair says. "But God knew what He was doing. I didn't."[9]

Designers were showing their fall collections. Blair posed in Central Park wearing a body suit that fit like it was an anatomy lesson. She loved it. The trip was supposed to last three days. Blair signed with the Ellen Harth agency and ended up staying in New York almost twenty years.

Her first big job was with designer Clovis Ruffin. Blair arrived at his studio clutching her meager portfolio and wearing a pageboy wig and a little cloche-style hat. As Ruffin paged through the photographs she had accumulated from working the local market, he was confused. The young woman in front of him looked insecure, mundane, and desperately bourgeois. But the girl in the pictures, the one with the micro Afro, spoke to the times. She was authentic—at least in the way it was increasingly being defined.

"Is this how you look now?" Ruffin asked, pointing to her portfolio. "If you present like this, I'll hire you for my show."

Blair immediately whipped off her wig. And the job was hers.

As a model, Blair experienced more than she ever imagined possible. In addition to the travel, she met celebrities and dignitaries and was part of the 1970s nightclub scene, with all of its music, drugs, and glitter. "You didn't have a lot of time to spend in the clubs if you were working, but every chance I got, I made every minute count! I'd go with the boys.

"There was one place called the Loft down in the Village. You had a little membership card and it had Spanky and Our Gang on it. You could bring one guest or two. It was people like Halston, the models. It was another kind of Studio 54. . . . They put a stamp on your hand, you couldn't fake anything; it was very, very private. You passed coat check. And you were in. You walked up one flight of stairs and it was like dirty, dirty.

"There were three areas, one with long tables and high-back chairs with pillows on the floor, another area with bathrooms, and then there was a big, huge room where you danced. Danced. Danced. Danced."[10]

Blair's love affair with New York was in its giddy honeymoon period when she was hired for the Versailles gala. And by inviting her to France, the American designers would be bringing a rising star with them.

Tom Fallon, Bill Blass's right-hand man and a friend of Halston's, was handsome, charismatic, and garrulous. He was a born storyteller with a flair for dramatic interjection. But as every great storyteller knows, the art of weaving a splendid yarn lies in having exquisite powers of observation. Fallon knew when to stand back, watch, and listen. These skills also made him a terrific party guest who knew how to handle himself in the presence of the fanciest folks, those accustomed to being the center of attention and being tended to.

Fallon grew up in Pittsburgh and spent a year at Georgetown Law School in Washington, D.C., avoiding the Vietnam War. But he hated law school more than he loathed the war. He dropped out and spent a year studying at Parsons before he was drafted. He managed to get himself assigned to a Defense Department post in New York and was soon taking night classes at the Fashion Institute of Technology. "This is 1966 and I'm the only person coming to class in an army uniform," Fallon says.[11]

Fallon met Halston at one of the myriad fashion parties he attended while he was at FIT. Halston was fascinated by Fallon's double life—a soldier by day and an aspiring designer by night. When Halston made the decision to start his own custom clothing collection within his salon at Bergdorf Goodman, he asked Fallon to join him, promising to teach him everything he needed to know about fashion. Fallon was twenty-six and Halston was eight years his senior when the former army lieutenant took the designer up on his offer. By 1967, Fallon was by Halston's side as the designer finalized plans to hang out his own shingle.

"Everyone assumed I was Halston's boyfriend," Fallon says.[12] And Halston made no effort to correct them. During a trip to Paris with Halston, Fallon had a chance encounter at a Balmain couture show during which he received an invitation to a ball in honor of the Duchess of Windsor. At the party, he was drawn into a conversation with guests Bill Blass and Jerry Zipkin. Zipkin was described in the *New York Times* upon his death in 1995 as a "social moth" and was believed to have been the catalyst for the term "walker," which *Women's Wear Daily* first used to describe his role as a male going-out buddy to married women whose husbands were disinclined to accompany them to parties and dinners.[13]

"You look like you're hiding," Zipkin teased Fallon. "Oh my God, Bill, we've got to protect his virginity!" Fallon spent the evening under the thrall of Blass, and the two forged an invaluable friendship.

Returning to New York and anticipating Halston's imminent departure from Bergdorf Goodman, Fallon began to look for a new opportunity. He called Blass, reminded him of their meeting in Paris, and wondered if he might have a job opening.

Blass invited him around to his studio on Seventh Avenue at ten the next morning, where his first words after "Hello" were: "You still hanging on to your virginity? The night I met you in Paris, I knew we were going to work together. What the hell took you so long?"[14]

Fallon spent more than twenty years working alongside Blass, eventually overseeing the designer's licensees, as well as developing his own side projects, which included creating the costumes for a particularly ill-fated off-Broadway tap-dance musical about the movie business called *Sweet Feet*. "It lasted about four nights," Fallon says of the 1972 disaster.[15]

When Blass got the call to go to Versailles, he immediately turned to Fallon because he knew of the young man's love of theater. Versailles was shaping up to be more Broadway musical than catwalk production. Blass's all-American style would be juxtaposed with France's historic races at Longchamps and the accompanying music would be by Cole Porter.

"We needed clothes that would read well onstage," notes Fallon. The wheels of his imagination began to turn: There should be dazzlingly tight black dresses dripping in beaded fringe. Perhaps he and Blass could choreograph the show so that the fringe would sway in unison as the models walked, like waves lapping against the seashore under a night sky? Blass was just starting to do menswear, so there should be male models, too.

The designers had decided to edit their presentations down to six minutes each, reduced from the original twenty minutes. Blass argued that short and punchy was better than interminable. But with only six minutes, every detail counted, every second had to be dramatic.

Fallon worked closely with Blass on the collection for Versailles. The friends spent no small amount of time arguing about the theatrics, the props, and the clothes. But out of the continual fussing, a sophisticated collection grew.

With all but the final details settled, Blass dispatched Fallon to Philadelphia. Blass had promised to participate in a fashion show at the city's Museum of Art. He wanted Fallon to represent him at the event and to take along an evening dress for the presentation. Blass had just finished his finale gown for Versailles and he wanted to give it a tryout. It was a pale gray slip of a dress stitched from matte jersey—God how the Americans loved jersey!—and adorned with clear sequins. The hem was trimmed in sable. It was paired with a sable coat with a sweeping train. The model would be wearing chandelier earrings and clutching a long, dramatic cigarette holder. (Blass was a prodigious smoker, and he smoked with such suave panache that he almost made one forget the health hazards.)

As Fallon left for the train station, Blass barked a single order in his gravelly, smoke-infused voice with its Noël Coward pacing: *Put the gown on a Grace Kelly type!*

On the train and running late, Fallon bumped into Renauld White, the male model whose career blossomed during the 1970s—culminating with his becoming the first African American model on the cover of *GQ* magazine in November 1979.

The two were chatting when Billie Blair walked into their car. White introduced Fallon to this "long, tall, skinny black girl wearing a chrome-yellow, fake fur chubby and yellow disc earrings. She was adorable. But she was the goofiest-looking kid," Fallon remembers. "She was like an Olive Oyl cartoon."[16]

Fallon didn't think much about the character he'd just met. By the time the train pulled into Thirtieth Street Station, he was making a mad dash for a taxi. He had no idea Blair was only a few steps behind him. By the time he arrived at the museum, an hour late, the fittings for the show had ended and all the models had headed home for a few hours of rest. Except one: Olive Oyl.

"We put this dress on Billie Blair. She's a little rattled as we hand her all this shit. Here are your earrings! The cigarette holder! Then they whisked her away." Fallon remembers thinking, "I'm in deep doo-doo."

That evening, Fallon returned for the show wearing his tuxedo and settled into the audience. "Let's get this over with," he thought. He was prepared for a disaster: a gangly black kid, who looked nothing like Grace Kelly, stumbling out in the gown his boss had designed for his grand finale at Versailles. She'd probably trip over the sable. Fallon was woozy with dread.

Then he got a look at Blair. She was standing at the top of a staircase. Her short hair had been molded into marcel waves and she bore a striking resemblance to Josephine Baker. She was dripping with attitude—a head-back, haughty, and confident demeanor the likes of which did not regularly appear on the streets of Philadelphia or Detroit, let alone Flint. She was a young girl moving with the sway and the cool of her own fantasies.

"She had one hand on her forehead. And she's got the cigarette holder in her other hand and it's shooting straight up," Fallon says admiringly. "My jaw hits the floor. You've never seen anything like it in your life." Blair moved with a grace and strength beyond her years. "This kid, where could she have learned this? When I finally got backstage to her, she's standing there looking at me and laughing like a goofball."[17]

When Fallon returned to New York, Blass was eager to hear how things had gone, how the crowd reacted to the dress. "How'd you do last night?" he asked. Fallon told Blass he'd brought the house down. The designer was thrilled. "You found Grace Kelly?" Fallon admitted that he had not. "I found a black girl who channeled Josephine Baker. She's one of the girls coming to Paris. And we've got to put this dress on her in Paris."

Blass thought Fallon had gone bonkers; he'd been adamant about his vision of a classic blonde wearing the dress. As the two launched into one of their battles, the telephone rang. It was Oscar de la Renta. Blass picked up the line and his argument with Fallon spilled into a grumbled greeting: "Fallon has lost his mind. So, are you ready for Versailles?"

De la Renta was. In fact, he was especially excited because he had sketched out a plan for his six-minute segment. "I found the girl I want to be the centerpiece of my show. She's a kid from Detroit." Billie Blair. She was, de la Renta coos, "extraordinary." Blass quickly pronounced her the star of his show as well.[18]

For Blair, the attention was overwhelming. She wasn't terribly sure of exactly what she had done. She just knew that the dress, the hair, the attention, had all made her feel wonderful. She felt like she was emerging from a cocoon right there on the runway.

"When you're young, nothing's right. You're too this; you're too that. Those guys really encouraged me and helped me to develop," Blair says. "They saw this butterfly before it came out of the little cocoon."[19]

The modern model doesn't have to work so terribly hard on the runway—not compared to her predecessors. Today, models just walk. Or stomp. And stare unblinkingly into a bay of photographers all aiming long lenses at them like a pack of hunters in a shooting gallery. If a contemporary model displays even a slight hip wiggle or an errant arm flutter, she stands out as being flamboyant, a throwback. Yet these sleepwalkers can build far more lucrative careers than women like Blair and others of her generation ever imagined. For women lucky enough to be genetically blessed with the right look and attitude at the right time, and the chutzpah and nerve necessary to navigate the emotional, economic, and cultural land mines of a volatile industry, an individual model can become a brand. The only similarity between the modeling world of the early 1970s and now is the path to that first job. The first opportunity to pose in front of an established photographer still comes the same way it did nearly forty years ago. Models were and are discovered through contests, chance meetings, cold calls, and the eagle eyes of fashion editors working inside and outside the New York market.

Most of the models invited to Versailles had not yet made big names for themselves—after all, the designers were looking for bargains. Today, the names of many of the models resonate only within the industry itself or among the most ardent fashion nerds. The group of professional models booked for Versailles was notably integrated. Billie Blair, Bethann Hardison, Pat Cleveland, Amina Warsuma, Charlene Dash, Ramona Saunders, Norma Jean Darden, Barbara Jackson, Alva Chinn, and Jennifer Brice were black. Together they comprised nearly 30 percent of the American roster. But all the women, whether black or white, were runway models. They all understood that their role was not merely to wear the clothes, but to bring them to life.

The typewritten final list, as memorialized by Eleanor Lambert, misspells several of the models' names and lists others only by their first names.

Wednesday November 7, 1973

Models Definitely Booked for Versailles

Virginia Hubbard	Charlene Dash
Marion York	Stephanie Vail
Carol Brandt	Lynn Yaeger
Fran Healy	Tanya Dennis
Tasha	Bruena
Susan Pelland	Carla La Manta
Jac Dubelle	Kit Gill
Jennifer Brice	Hilery Beane
Karen Bjornson	Heidi Goldman
Beth Anne	Peggy Butler
Nancy North	Anna Lindt
Carla Araque	Norma Jean
Basha	Alva Chen
Chris Royer	Anina
Barbara Jackson	Billy Blair
Ramona Saunders	Stephanie McDonald
Pat Cleveland	Diana Lambert
Jennifer Hauser	Claudia Clarke

The three dozen female models were joined by a pair of male dancers who accompanied Liza Minnelli and a duo of male models who worked with Bill Blass. Several of the Halstonettes were in the model pool: Pat Cleveland, Alva Chinn, Carla Araque, Chris Royer, and Karen Bjornson. Halston sponsored other models such as Shirley Ferro and Heidi Lieberfarb.

Halston also brought along model Marisa Berenson, fashion editor China Machado, jewelry designer Elsa Peretti, cult actress Baby Jane Holzer—women drawn from his circle of friends who would only walk in his segment of the production.

"Except there was one thing: in Paris, nobody had any idea who [most of] these girls were," recalls Oscar de la Renta. "Halston made more beautiful clothes than anyone at that point. [But] he misjudged the impact of what he could do."[20]

Halston loved models, and was even ready to step in to make sure Stephen Burrows could bring his house model to Versailles, but he failed to realize that they would even outshine celebrities.

Burrows was intent on bringing Bethann Hardison, his house model, to Paris, but she hadn't gotten the minimum three votes from the designers. And Burrows couldn't afford to pay her way.

Hardison was, in several ways, a bit of an odd duck in circumstances, background, and looks. "I had a full-time job while I was modeling. I couldn't afford to be a model full-time; I had a child," Hardison says. "Most people didn't even know it. I didn't try to hide it, but I didn't mention it. I didn't take him anywhere. I didn't take him on vacations with me."[21] That child, Kadeem Hardison, grew up to become known to the public as the actor who portrayed Dwayne Wayne, the left-brained smart aleck, on *A Different World*.

While the other models had come from households that were either nonpolitical or calmly ameliorative in their activism, Hardison was schooled in disruption and revolution. As a young woman growing up in Bedford-Stuyvesant and Crown Heights, Brooklyn, she learned about cultural awareness, rebellion, and discipline at the knee of her father, Lee Hardison. A Muslim, he took on the name Ameer Hasaan, made the hajj, and became an imam who welcomed Malcolm X into the family home. He taught his daughter that the civil rights movement, with its sit-ins, marches, and legal battles, aimed to change the structure of society, codifying equality and outlawing racist acts. The Black Power movement "was more about interior thought. It was about emotional, psychological empowerment," Hardison says. "It was a social movement. When you say 'black is beautiful' . . . it encouraged people to feel pride in their blackness."[22]

By the time Hardison began working in the fashion industry in the late 1960s, she had spent her adolescence listening to treatises about social responsibility, conversations about current events, and the rumbling sounds of a revolution. Her father had taught her about propaganda. He refined her bullshit meter. She was political.

"It was hip to be. Like, you know, it was intellectual. Of course you were up with Fidel [Castro]. That was just common sense to me," she explains.[23]

As a model, Hardison was neither a classic beauty nor a sweet-faced gamine. She had dark skin, a short Afro, and no waist. "I was an interesting girl; I was like a boy. [Stephen] was very nervous. He said to Halston, 'I'm worried Bethann might not go.' Halston told him, 'Don't worry. She's going to go even if I have to vote for her.' At the last minute, Oscar said yes. And Anne Klein needed me because she was doing this African-inspired thing."[24]

Halston's house model, Karen Bjornson, a wispy blonde with delicate features—a true Grace Kelly type—arrived in New York in 1970 from Cincinnati, eager to make her way in the industry. She'd won a contest sponsored by *Ingenue* magazine, which promoted itself as the premiere glossy for sophisticated teens, a kind of predecessor to *Teen Vogue*. The contestants received a trip to New York, and Bjornson stuck around for an extra week to visit the agencies. Because she was still in high school, the booker at Wilhelmina told her to go back to Ohio, finish school, and go to prom. She also told her to stop wearing such garish false eyelashes.

After graduation, Bjornson moved to New York and settled into an apartment with her cousin. She called Wilhelmina and occasionally landed go-sees, but nothing was really happening for her. Finally, after her cousin told her she really needed to find a job, *any* job, and get her own apartment, Bjornson got work at Bloomingdale's, where she met another model who told her that Halston needed a house mannequin. It was the go-see that would change her life.

"He liked me because I was from the Midwest," Bjornson says. "He taught me how to wear clothes and respect clothes. He taught me how to work the runway—how to take off your coat and how to put your hand in a pocket."[25]

By 1973, Bjornson was twenty-one years old and a full-time model booking jobs across the industry. But whenever Halston needed her, she was there.

Nancy North was another of Halston's mannequins, as models were sometimes called. She came to Manhattan looking for glamour and to escape Fairfield, Connecticut, where she'd grown up. She was studying design at Pratt Institute where she met Bill Dugan, another student. Soon they were part of a group of friends who hung out at Max's Kansas City listening to music. And in that very 1970s way, North began to meet the artists who called Max's their clubhouse: Andy Warhol, Robert Rauschenberg, Brice Marden. She met Halston, who invited her and Dugan to a fashion show at his studio on East Sixty-eighth Street.

North was a tall girl with an ivory complexion and all-American good looks, but with a hint of aloof sophistication. It was the slight haughtiness in her demeanor that made her perfect for the runway. Halston asked her to model and invited Dugan to work in his studio. And with that, North had a career.

Cleveland, with her fair skin and wild curls, was a well-known beauty. She grew up in New York and started modeling at sixteen, when she toured with *Ebony* Fashion Fair, her mother tagging along as her chaperone. She was beloved for her stuttering, spinning, back-stepping antics on the runway, a style she developed by watching dancers, particularly those in the Katherine Dunham Dance Company, in which her aunt performed.

"I was a mascot. I just sort of watched and absorbed what was around me," Cleveland says of her time hanging around the dance troupe. "As a young girl, you like to show off. Every time you got from behind the [stage] curtain you could do what you wanted. . . . You just break the egg and get out there."[26]

Cleveland has a childish, treble clef voice and speaks in terms both thoughtful and esoteric. She has a dramatic personality, prone to large gestures and theatrical sighs, which blossomed in the spotlight. She built an enviable career in Europe and returned to New York from Paris, where she had been working, for rehearsals of the Versailles show.

"Modeling, artistically, she can just carry on. She's fabulous to watch," Blair says of Cleveland's signature runway style. "She's a character to me."[27]

Most important for a model, Cleveland was an ethnic chameleon, able to be whatever was required or preferred in the moment. "I didn't consider Pat black," shrugs model Amina Warsuma. "She was whatever. In France she was French. In Italy, she was Italian."[28]

Amina Warsuma was a big-city girl. She was born in the Bronx and grew up in Harlem. Her father was from Somalia; her mother was American. They met at the United Nations, where Warsuma's mother worked as a secretary. After they split up, Warsuma's father returned to Somalia. Her mother stayed in New York and she gave up the raising of her daughter to her intimates in the neighborhood.

"I'd see her every five years or so. Some women shouldn't be mothers," Warsuma says with a tone of resignation. "She was educated and black and that was really hard. She typed ninety words a minute, knew her math, and spoke well. In the end, [the limitations] just got to her. She did the best she could."[29]

Warsuma was not sure what she wanted to do, but she liked nice things, fancy things. She would sew her own clothes and when she got a bit of change, she'd go over to 125th Street, Harlem's main drag, and buy the most expensive dress or pair of shoes she could afford. She was five foot eleven by the time she was seventeen, but she didn't consider modeling because models weren't the women she admired. Warsuma lived five blocks from the Apollo Theater, a neoclassical showplace for black entertainers, and her idols were performers. (She even took classes at the Phil Black Dance Studio.) While there were all sorts of happenings downtown, Warsuma was living life uptown. It was the 1960s and her world was composed of a handful of blocks on the island of Manhattan.

"I'd go get a Simplicity or Vogue pattern and get dressed up and run behind the Temptations! Motown was my life. That's what I looked up to," she says. "You didn't really have black people on TV. You had *Julia* and Bill Cosby on *I Spy*. So the singers were the role models."[30]

Warsuma's high school English teacher worked part-time modeling and suggested Warsuma give it a try. She took a few pictures of her fifteen-year-old student, with her deep ebony skin and wide-set eyes, and took her down to meet Eileen Ford. "Not yet," said Ford. Warsuma had a look, but fashion wasn't ready for it. "Give it a couple years."

So Warsuma continued to make her own clothes and chase after music. Even though she was only sixteen, she started going to a gay bar called Andre's. She'd put on false eyelashes and lots of makeup and her hand-sewn glamour kit and off she'd go—no identification required. The uptown club attracted Broadway performers, and although Warsuma had grown up less than four miles from the heart of the Theater District, she'd never been to a Broadway show. The performers invited her to see them in action, and at their shows she met designers, and the designers invited her to their studios at FIT and on Seventh Avenue.

Before she knew it, designer Scott Barrie asked her to model in one of his shows "because he knew the people I knew uptown," Warsuma explains. Barrie was a young African American designer from Apalachicola, Florida, celebrated for his draped jersey dresses. Like Stephen Burrows, he studied briefly at the Philadelphia Museum College of Art and then came to New York, where he built a business out of his apartment and did odd jobs around Seventh Avenue to make ends meet. Bloomingdale's and Henri Bendel launched his career when they bought his designs.[31] Warsuma worked for him gratis.

At seventeen, Warsuma was clerking at Henri Bendel. She'd wear a little brown dress uniform and stand by the fitting room opening the door for customers. Just upstairs, Stephen Burrows was making his own little bit of history. The two would occasionally see each other in the lunchroom, and one day Burrows suggested Warsuma come up to his boutique and try on some of his clothes. And when she did, he was impressed enough that he booked her for a show he was having at the store, which was a bit ironic because that very day Warsuma was fired. A white man, with his Texas lady friend on his arm, had swatted her on the tush. When she complained, she was fired. It was, she says, her first real encounter with racism.

Nonetheless, Warsuma was on her way. Burrows took her to a party Halston hosted to mark the opening of the film *Love Story*. Warsuma met the celebrated designer as well as artist Andy Warhol and fashion editors Diana Vreeland and Carrie Donovan. One party led to another, and in 1970, Warsuma signed at Wilhelmina.

"At that point I really loved [modeling]. I didn't think, 'Oh, the white girl is getting more than me.' I was from a poor background. I was happy to be getting!" she says.[32]

The world was in turmoil around her—Vietnam, the assassinations of Martin Luther King Jr. and Robert Kennedy, the riots, the Black Power movement. "I didn't think about it," she says. "I was just glad to have the life I had." She was making $50, even $100 an hour doing advertising. She was working a lot. Her cost of living was low. And Burrows was giving her clothes.

Then, one day, in 1973, he called her with news: "You're going to be in my segment at Versailles. It's all paid for."

Warsuma had been to Europe the year before, in search of a more lucrative work environment. Antonio Lopez, the fashion illustrator, had introduced her to Karl Lagerfeld, who was designing for Chloé. She walked the runway for him and dined at La Coupole, where everyone ate, with the designer and his entourage. In Paris, she played with the glamorous set.

She was never closely associated with a single designer; she wasn't part of a *cabine*—a designer's regular troupe of models. While Yves Saint Laurent had long been enamored with black models, there were few with Warsuma's deep-brown complexion on the runways. And sometimes, she had to beg—even cry—to get paid.[33] Her career always felt tenuous.

Versailles was different. Bigger. It might lead to something else. A psychic had read her cards and had a vision of Warsuma's name up in lights. "I'd been modeling since 1967," she says. "I wanted to start thinking about my future."[34]

In the late 1960s, Charlene Dash, a classic beauty with large eyes, an angular nose, and a regal stance, was a student at Hunter College in New York and working at Shell Oil Company. Although her responsibilities included little more than filing, she had her own office at Shell and was feeling fairly grown-up. But she wasn't having much fun.

Dash recalled only one other black woman working at the company during her tenure. And when Dash would pass her in the hallway, she would barely say hello. Her name was Ramona Saunders, a striking woman with almond-shaped eyes and a full nose and lips. One day Saunders arrived for her job in the key-punch department at Shell wearing a pantsuit—something that wasn't done in the 1960s. Saunders had just given notice. She was leaving her nine-to-five to become a model.

"I forgot about her, and then about a month later I looked at the Sunday [*New York*] *Times* and there was her picture. And I thought, Oh my God! If she can do it, I can do it," Dash says.[35]

Saunders was born in Brazil and spoke with a vaguely Continental accent. Publicly she could be aloof and distant; privately she was a spiritual soul. She was exceptionally tall—around six feet—and lean. She made a habit of floating around Manhattan with an endlessly long silk scarf wrapped around her neck and blowing in the wind behind her.

On the runway, Saunders had a dramatic flair that could be too much for some designers, who avoided hiring her. Her gestures could be broad and distracting. But she gained her footing in modeling when, after signing with Wilhelmina, she found a fan in Stephen Burrows, in whose circle of friends she regularly traveled. It was Burrows who insisted she go to Versailles.

Inspired by Saunders, Dash did a bit of research and found contact information for Wilhelmina Models, which had opened its doors in 1967. She went on a cold call. The agency took a pass. So Dash took her two little fuzzy portraits to Ford Models. She was accepted. It was August 1968.

Dash started doing Eleanor Lambert's designer shows at the Plaza Hotel for $50 a day. One of the editors in the audience was Baron Nicolas de Gunzburg, from *Vogue*. "He took me in to meet Diana Vreeland. And she said, 'What are you doing tomorrow? Be at this address.' The next thing I knew, I had six pages in *Vogue*!" exclaims Dash.[36]

In short order, Dash was a working model doing photo shoots with Richard Avedon and Bert Stern. She was still living at home, but her pictures were appearing in *Vogue*. While she had been making $78 a week at Shell, as a model she was making almost that much in a single day.

And now, she was flying to Paris. For the weekend. For a fashion show at Versailles.

Norma Jean Darden was a Sarah Lawrence student who grew up in

Montclair, New Jersey, in a politically conscious black family that was active in the NAACP. Her father, Dr. Walter T. Darden, sat on the life membership committee. While Bethann Hardison had been grounded in the radical politics of black power, Darden was rooted in the social justice of the civil rights movement.

The NAACP occasionally hosted fund-raising fashion shows, which attracted celebrities such as Sammy Davis Jr. At one of those shows Darden met Dorothea Towles Church, arguably the first successful black model in Paris, who worked for couture houses such as Christian Dior, Elsa Schiaparelli, and Pierre Balmain in the 1950s. Darden was captivated by Church, and by fashion.[37] But her middle-class parents were not so enthralled with the industry. One afternoon, Darden was having lunch with her mother at Macy's and models strolled through the restaurant showing off the latest trends. Her mother harrumphed, "Who would put on a dress and parade around like that?"

Me! Me! Me! thought Darden, who with her deep-set eyes and wide forehead had a look of refinement and elegance.[38]

While Darden was at Sarah Lawrence in the late 1950s, *Mademoiselle* magazine put out the word to campuses that it was looking for students to model in an upcoming issue. The school sent Darden as its representative. She arrived at the magazine's New York offices wearing a natty red coat with a matching capelet, a gray suit, pillbox hat, and patent leather pumps. She explained to the receptionist that she'd been sent by Sarah Lawrence. She was directed to the service entrance. And then she was dismissed outright. "They told me the magazine was for white women," Darden says. "That was my first rejection. And it was powerful."[39]

A few years after she graduated from Sarah Lawrence, as she was beginning her fashion career, Audrey Smaltz called. The two had met on the occasion of one of those NAACP shows. Smaltz was working as a model and she was frustrated. She wanted to picket *Harper's Bazaar* because the magazine wasn't using black models. So Darden, the daughter of the NAACP activist, and Smaltz, who had grown up in Harlem mingling with

Bob Moses—one of the organizers of the 1964 Freedom Summer voter registration drive in Mississippi—went to make their case to the fashion magazine.

The protest didn't get either woman a job, even though a few months later, *Harper's Bazaar* produced a photo spread around the theme of Black Power. But slowly, things began to turn Darden's way. In the course of countless "go-sees"—the modeling equivalent of interviews—designers such as Scott Barrie booked Darden for shows. So did Burrows. She found work with Clovis Ruffin, who'd given Billie Blair her break. And then Darden began traveling to Paris, where she worked for Dorothée Bis and Hubert de Givenchy.

When Darden returned to the States, her agent told her about the Versailles show. "I wasn't thrilled, but I said, 'Yes, I'll go.' They weren't paying very much, but I wasn't doing anything for the weekend. So I thought I might as well go."[40]

Alva Chinn was from Boston. A fair-skinned young woman of Chinese, English, Indian, and African American lineage, she had light brown hair and classic bone structure. She was a conservative girl from a conservative town. She grew up in Boston's South End neighborhood, which at that time was a working-class enclave with a large African American population. After her parents separated when she was three years old, Chinn lived with an overprotective father who insisted she steer clear of the neighborhood kids.

"I became a loner, extremely shy. I didn't want to be closed. I didn't want to be closed in. I made a very big effort to come out of my shell. I had a great desire for freedom," Chinn says. "One day, I decided I didn't want a conventional life. I was at the University of Massachusetts. I had a friend who worked in the art department of *Mademoiselle* magazine. They were putting out the college issue. She thought I could model. So she arranged an interview. And I was accepted. This was the beginning."[41] It was the late '60s. *Mademoiselle*, which had almost ended Darden's career before it began, helped launch Chinn's.

In 1972, Chinn left college, two years shy of graduation, and fled to New York, where she waited tables and modeled whenever she could find work. Initially, it was tough going. Chinn had the body of a skinny teenager but the sophisticated face of a woman—one of indeterminate ethnic origin. "I thought I'd never work [in New York] because I wasn't a junior or a miss," she says of those early days. "People were on all the 'black is beautiful' stuff and people were telling me that I wasn't black enough. I found it bizarre."[42]

But eventually, Chinn was championed by Halston, Burrows, and Oscar de la Renta. They were also the reason she was booked for Versailles. She was twenty-two years old and she'd studied French in school. The Versailles trip "was like a dream come true," Chinn says. "I felt like a fly on the wall. It was quite the eye-opener."[43]

Barbara Jackson was another *Ebony* Fashion Fair alum. She was discovered when she went backstage in 1967 after one of the troupe's shows hoping to get the models' autographs.

Jackson grew up in Charleston, West Virginia, the youngest of nine children. When Fashion Fair came to town, she and a girlfriend made sure to get tickets. It was, after all, the most glamorous thing going. Jackson was only sixteen when she went backstage, wowed by the show she'd just seen. The show's commentator at the time, Carol DiPasalegne,[44] took one look at Jackson's large eyes, strong jawline, button nose, and high forehead, and asked: "Child, have you ever modeled before?"

Jackson was taken aback, because she'd never even daydreamed about modeling: "I thought, Wow, people just say anything!" DiPasalegne handed her a business card and told her to call if she ever came to New York.

"The following year, after graduating high school, I was visiting an aunt in New York. I had a summer job in an office typing and I thought, Oh, God! I couldn't type. I was supposed to go back to Charleston, but I called DiPasalegne at her office at Johnson Publishing and asked her if she remembered me. Of course, she didn't remember me, but she told me to come down and see her anyway."

"I was working on Lexington Avenue, and Johnson Publishing wasn't far. I flew. I was literally running down Lexington to get to their office. When I got in there, she said, 'Let me see you walk.' She liked the way I walked. She said, 'Can you be in Chicago tomorrow?' My heart started pounding so hard. I had to call my mother. But I said yes.

"We walked right downstairs to American Airlines, which was in the same building, and she got me a ticket. I was on a plane the next day at 6 a.m. I'd never been on a plane in my life."[45]

Jackson was booked for that year's show, called Fashion Rebellion '67, and was even the subject of a short squib in *Jet* magazine, along with Richard Roundtree, highlighting the models making their debut. She spent a year traveling around the country learning how to twirl, strut, and entertain.

By the time of the Versailles show, Jackson had been modeling for nearly five years. She had taken dance lessons as part of her Fashion Fair training and was represented by the Ellen Harth agency in New York, from which she'd been booked to work Eleanor Lambert's shows at the Plaza Hotel and to walk the runway for Stephen Burrows and Anne Klein.

"I would have done [Versailles] for free," Jackson recalls with a laugh. "I was from West Virginia and I was getting a paid trip to Paris, where I'd never been."[46]

Washington Post fashion editor Nina Hyde plucked Jennifer Brice from near obscurity. Hyde was part of a group of influential newspaper fashion editors that included Bernadine Morris of the *New York Times*, Marylou Luther of the *Los Angeles Times*, Genevieve Buck of the *Chicago Tribune*, and Patricia Shelton of the *Chicago Sun-Times*, who established the fashion beat as a significant part of American newspaper journalism. If Eugenia Sheppard, who died in 1984 after spending much of her career at the *New York Herald Tribune*, nursed modern fashion reportage through its infancy in the 1950s and '60s with her emphasis on personalities and trends, then these women brought the beat to its adulthood with a focus on business, society, and culture.[47]

Hyde and Brice met backstage after a fashion show at the U.S. State Department. Brice was eighteen and freshly married. She had graduated from Sears charm school, a multiweek course that taught young girls proper table manners and good posture and culminated with a fashion show. Afterward, she started doing some modeling in Washington, D.C.

After the State Department presentation, Hyde needed one of the models to slip into some of the clothes so they could be photographed. Brice obliged. Hyde was impressed enough that she told the young model to call her at the *Post*. When Brice failed to follow through, Hyde telephoned her a month later. She'd come across an advertisement that said Hecht's department store was sponsoring a model-of-the-year contest. She thought Brice should enter.

Brice demurred. She'd seen the poster featuring Cybill Shepherd, a blond, blue-eyed beauty. "I'm too black for that," Brice, whose flawless skin is the color of dark chocolate, remembers telling Hyde. Like all models, Brice was a genetic anomaly: tall, reed thin, and with the face of a doll. She didn't have a sultry look or an aloof demeanor. She was cute. Hyde admonished her not to think that way. "Every area will have different winners," she said.[48]

Brice won the local competition, and the day after her victory, Hyde ran a photograph of her in the *Washington Post*. She went on to New York to compete in the national competition at the Ed Sullivan Theater. Brice didn't win, but she did get a taste of the big city and the possibilities it offered. When the model agencies started calling, Brice answered, despite a husband who would have preferred she ignored them. She quit her job as a charm school teacher for the District of Columbia Department of Parks and Recreation and her husband stopped work as an appraiser for a car dealership.[49]

Brice had been living in New Jersey and working in New York for about six weeks when Hyde came into Manhattan on business. She was well connected within the industry and had close relationships with most every established and up-and-coming designer on Seventh Avenue.

Brice was walking along Seventh Avenue, heading to a casting call for models, when she spotted Hyde coming toward her. Brice began bouncing up and down on her feet, excited to see not just a familiar face, but her benefactor. Hyde was on her way to meet with Oscar de la Renta and Stephen Burrows and insisted that Brice accompany her.

"I don't know if they loved me or it was just because of her," Brice says, "but I ended up in both of their shows."[50]

Brice also developed a schoolgirl's crush on Burrows, who loved her beanpole body and called her "a pencil." Endearingly, of course. "I was butt naked [in the showroom]. He was gay as a jaybird and looking at me as an art piece. After he saw me nude, my heart got soft for him. I couldn't believe he didn't like girls," Brice recalls. "He was in love with a little Cuban guy named Victor."[51]

Two months after Hyde ushered Brice around Seventh Avenue, she was booked for Versailles. "I was the youngest and the shyest" of all the models, Brice says. She'd hoped the other, more experienced women might take her under their wing, but no one was feeling sisterly.

To the other models, Brice was a curiosity. She had not been working very long and they wondered who the "tall, chocolate girl with the curly hair" was. Brice thought Billie Blair "was the craziest woman in the world. She was so experienced. The designers loved her. She was a fully blossomed woman. She'd throw those titties out there," Brice laughs. "She could really work the runway."[52]

Pat Cleveland was "one I thought had fallen from another planet," Brice says.[53] She was eccentric and was constantly posing. Even if she was simply seated on the arm of a chair, it was as though she could see cameras off in the middle distance and was always giving them her best side.

Brice did not think Hardison liked her and so steered clear of her. She was intimidating. She thought Warsuma was a tough city girl—"a little bit too ghetto for me," Brice says. "She was a cusser and too unladylike." Cleveland, Saunders, and Chinn moved in a pack. They were confident, focused, and, at times, it seemed, vain.[54]

Saunders was stunned to find Charlene Dash part of the Versailles group. After all, this was the kid from the file room at the Shell Oil Company, the one Saunders had left behind as she set out for an adventure. "She was not thrilled to see me," Dash remembers. "She was really quite nasty because I was doing better than her."[55]

Karen Bjornson felt like all the personality politics was going over her head. Versailles was going to be her first trip to Europe and she was thinking about logistics, about having to do her own hair and makeup. Besides, she had a bit of a bladder infection and was not feeling her best. Norma Jean Darden remembers Blair praying a lot. The group certainly needed it.

With the models finally confirmed, rehearsals began in New York a few days prior to leaving for Europe. Most of the women remember two meetings with choreographer Kay Thompson. "It was crazy," Warsuma says. "I felt like I was doing a Broadway show."[56]

The staging required the models to perform a bit of modest choreography. And Warsuma, who had always wanted to act, was thrilled to be putting her limited experience at the Phil Black Dance Studio to use. She had terrific jazz hands.

The New York rehearsals focused primarily on the opening number, which was based on a song from *Funny Face*, which Thompson had starred in alongside Audrey Hepburn and Fred Astaire. Her connection to *Funny Face*, and its swashbuckling depiction of the fashion industry, made Thompson attractive to the Versailles designers. Her signature number from that film, "Think Pink," showcased Thompson at her imperial best: a gray-suited editor with a physique honed by denial, a face like chiseled granite, and a modest voice bolstered by her own certitude, twisting about with yards of pink fabric.

Thompson, who died in 1998, has been described as a "skeleton key to mid-century Broadway and Hollywood." She was a "creative survivor."[57] She was born in St. Louis to an immigrant father and a midwestern mother. She studied music and voice as a child and made it her mission to get out of St. Louis as fast as possible. "I had an inferiority complex," she said in 1936, recalling her childhood. "I always felt, when I was little, that I was ugly. My sisters and my mother were so gorgeously beautiful. If people asked my mother what she thought the children would grow up to be, she used to say that [Blanche and Marian] would probably be a writer and an artist—they were so talented—that her son might be President. Then she would add: *and Kitty has a lovely personality.* All this must have awakened the determination in me to do something outstanding."[58]

Thompson was part of that generation that understood beauty as a form of currency, invaluable to a young woman's future. Without it, Thompson had to make do. She willed herself into a Hollywood career by force of personality, as well as multiple rhinoplasties and capped teeth.[59]

Thompson found success in radio, onstage, and in film, particularly backstage, where she worked as a musical arranger and vocal coach. Her long friendship with Judy Garland—Thompson ultimately planned Garland's funeral—led to her being chosen as godmother to Liza Minnelli. "She was this funny, serene force," Minnelli said. "I remember once we were walking around in New York, I was about four, and she had a big wolf coat, gray, just heavenly looking—she was so tall and thin. She stopped by the Stork Club. This very nice black gentleman opened the door, and she asked for Mr. So-and-So, and the man wasn't in. And she said, 'Yeah, well, just tell him that Miss Thompson and Miss Minnelli stopped by.' And my world changed! I was *Miss Minnelli*."[60]

Thompson was sixty-four years old when Halston asked her to

choreograph the American half of the Versailles fashion show. She was not aging well, her body disintegrating after numerous plastic surgeries and regular visits to Dr. Max Jacobson—known as Dr. Feelgood—who regularly injected his high-society clients with a pick-me-up solution of vitamins and methamphetamines. Her deep-set eyes were heavily hooded; her nose was a narrow ski slope, and she was little more than bone covered in a thin layer of skin.[61]

"She looked horrible: wrinkled and old," recalls Norma Jean Darden. "But she had such fire and dedication."[62]

Thompson was charged with teaching the models the song "Bonjour, Paris!" But Thompson altered the lyrics for the occasion of Versailles.

What a lovely night.
I'm feeling so fresh and alive.
And I'm so glad to arrive.
It's all so grand.
You see who's here to see.

I'm at home in a palace.
I feel like I live in Wonderland.
Allo, allo, mes amis.
Allo, allo, je suis ici.
C'est merveilleux to be back in Paree.

In Paris, it's always spring.
Makes you want to sing
And sing and sing and sing. . . . [63]

Thompson, who survived on cigarettes and Coca-Cola, offered encouragement and support. "The choreography wasn't tough and she was kind and patient," Brice recalls.[64] She peppered her stage directions with inscrutable commands, a strange blend of impressionistic motivation, fortune cookie encouragement, and gibberish.

"Walk like praying mantises!"

"Elocution with your arms; vocabulary with your fingers."

"Walk like you have ice water in your brassiere."[65]

B y the time the models boarded Olympic Airways flight 401 to Paris on Saturday, November 24, their simmering excitement had escalated to a roiling boil. The young women were booked in the coach section of the plane. And while it was not a charter flight, they soon took it over. In an era that predated the Transportation Security Administration, before flight crews called police at the sight of passengers loitering in groups, before smoking was banned, and when booze was still free, the models clustered about the airplane, chattering about their upcoming adventure and basking in their own success. Some of them danced in the aisles. Clouds of marijuana smoke wafted throughout the tourist-class cabin.[66] The flight attendants stood down. They were outnumbered.

"I thought it was horrible, just awful," Dash says. "I was so embarrassed because some of the black models were showing their asses. There were other passengers on the flight! But they wanted to be famous and make a name for themselves."

"It was a party atmosphere to the extreme."[67]

The models' flight landed at Paris Orly Airport on Sunday morning, three days before the Versailles show was scheduled to take place. The weather was gray, the sky spitting an icy rain. The women disembarked, a rainbow flock of young starlings full of twitchy enthusiasm who had done themselves up in their finest plumage to take on the city.

The thirty-six models represented the American mosaic: ivory-skinned redheads, blue-eyed blondes, honey-toned and ebony-skinned African Americans, and sun-kissed brunettes. It was a perfectly optimistic picture—a portrait of American beauty that had been forged out of riots, cultural soul-searching, friendships, politics, and a subtle subtext of racial fearfulness that ran through American life.

Billie Blair vividly remembers standing outside baggage claim, an enormous grin stretching across her face. "Girl you were happy, happy, happy!" she says, describing herself. She was wrapped in a grand fur coat. "Clovis [Ruffin] let me borrow that. I don't know what that is, a raccoon?"[68]

Nancy North also arrived in Paris draped in fur. Pat Cleveland wore a regal turban with sunglasses.

Amina Warsuma landed in Paris only a few days after her birthday and she considered the trip a continuation of the celebration. Her basketball player boyfriend had dropped her off at John F. Kennedy International Airport in his Mercedes-Benz. She was feeling especially grand. For her arrival, she pulled on her red fox coat and hat, feeling like a cabaret performer from *Lady Sings the Blues*. She had been to Paris before, but this time, the trip felt like pure Hollywood.[69]

The designers all flew separately. Stephen Burrows and Joe Eula had been on an Olympic flight that arrived on Saturday. Oscar and Françoise de la Renta flew together on a Pan Am flight. And Halston flew in with Liza Minnelli and Kay Thompson on a flight that was briefly diverted to Marseilles due to bad weather.[70]

That Halston was even flying commercial was a bit of a compromise brought on by world events: the oil crisis. Just weeks earlier, Egypt and Syria had attacked Israel in what became known as the Yom Kippur War. The United States' support of Israel sparked the Arab oil embargo, which, by November was in full swing: the results included gas lines, reduced speed limits on highways, and thermostats set low enough to require long johns indoors. Critics repeatedly alluded to the impropriety of heating and lighting the Palace of Versailles for a fashion show. It was simply unseemly, they thought. Fashion had the capacity to change minds and move hearts, but this was beyond the pale. David Mahoney, chairman of Norton Simon, the company that had acquired Halston's brand, was an American businessman with a public relations crisis.

"Only Mahoney seems to have worried about saving fuel—and the corporate image," wrote Jonathan Randal in the *Washington Post*.[71] Mahoney decided against fueling up the corporate plane, a BAC-111 jetliner, at an estimated cost of more than $8,000 (about $42,000 in 2013) for the jump across the pond. Instead, he flew his guests over commercially—albeit in first class.[72]

Each designer was assigned a private car with a chauffeur to ferry them to their hotels. Most stayed at the Plaza Athénée. Situated in the center of Paris on the glamorous Avenue Montaigne, the storied hotel is not far from the Seine and only a few steps from the headquarters of Christian Dior. It exudes luxurious privilege with its marble pillars that are the color of a winter sunset and its lobby filled with scented candles.

The hotel opened in 1913, and by the 1930s, along with its restaurant Le Relais-Plaza, it had become a favorite of the powerful, wealthy, and famous. The hallway leading to the restaurant is lined with photographs, most of them signed, by the many familiar names to have stayed or visited there: Sophia Loren in 1963, Jacqueline Kennedy in 1970. In 1971, Elizabeth Taylor and Richard Burton spent more than six months in the hotel's Royal Suite.

The hotel attracted the top of the fashion set. Just outside Le Relais-Plaza, tucked into the old telephone closet—a red-brocade-lined sitting room where public telephones could be accessed—there is a black-and-white photograph of Pierre Cardin, Yves Saint Laurent, Jean-Louis Scherrer, Guy Laroche, Pierre Balmain, and Eugenia Sheppard dated 1973. In it, Cardin gazes off toward his right, his angular face with its high cheekbones reflecting the light. Saint Laurent's thick hair is nearly at pompadour height and he bears a faint smile below his dark-rimmed glasses. Sherrer, too, dons a half smile. Laroche, the smallest of the designers, is the only one looking directly at the camera, with his head tilted slightly to the right. Balmain is nearly in profile, decked out in a vest with a small pocket watch. And Sheppard, the influential fashion editor, gently embraced by both Cardin and Laroche, wears a big, delighted grin.

The restaurant has not changed much since then, with its elaborate art deco stained glass and a glorious chandelier with wedge-shaped crystals surrounding a central sphere. A bas-relief in gold and silver called *Diana, the Huntress* is installed behind the bar.

A small but mighty contingent of American guests stayed at the Athénée, as well. Lyn and Charles Revson of Revlon called it home for the four-day extravaganza of parties that surrounded the Versailles show. Charles was especially pleased with himself for having arranged with Marie-Hélène de Rothschild to have gilded boxes of Revlon perfume given away, even though Max Factor was the official cosmetics sponsor of the event.

The Plaza Athénée was also where Libyan leader Muammar el-Qaddafi happened to be staying on his concurrent visit to Paris and where his security clogged up the entrance, which did not sit well with guests who deemed themselves just as important as the dictator. Qaddafi did not attend the Versailles show.

Fashion editor Carrie Donovan, who'd help put Burrows on the map, stayed there, along with investment banker John Barry Ryan III and his wife, Didi, who'd made a last-minute decision to attend. Eugenia Sheppard was tucked into the Hôtel de Crillon.

Unlike the show's attendees, its stars—the models—were not given private cars with drivers. A chartered bus shuttled them from the airport to their hotel, which was not the Plaza Athénée or the Crillon or the Meurice. Their hotel was not even in Paris proper. It was in a *banlieue*, in the gray suburban blur between Paris and the town of Versailles.

"It was like a Holiday Inn," recalls Dash. "It wasn't very French and the rooms were small." And there were two models assigned to each of those rooms.[73]

As guests poured into Paris, Pierre Cardin sent arrangements of orchids to welcome the American designers. Hubert de Givenchy sent word that his atelier was available to any of the visitors who might need a workroom. And Blass returned the graciousness with a telegram to the French, cooing: "How nice of you to invite us."[74]

To paraphrase Al Green's 1972 recording, it was nothing but "love and happiness." Or at least it seemed that way.

As American swells arrived, assorted French socialites and businessmen, such as Edmond Bory, the owner of the Paris gourmet shop Fauchon, hosted dinners for them, Minnelli, and Thompson.

"The extravaganza has everyone in the fashion and social whirl in what might mildly be called a tizzy," wrote Enid Nemy in the *New York Times*. "There is little else of interest or discussion. The 720 seats of the blue and gold theater . . . are sold out ($235 each). And those who are not on the guest lists for the pre-divertissement series of parties can scarcely look one in the eye as they insist that although they have been invited, the whole thing is too much."[75]

The elaborate meals included everything from pureed fish molded into the shape of fish tails to an ice cream sculpture decorated with chocolate quills to resemble a large porcupine, and, as the media of the day lovingly described it, "pheasant shot by aristocratic guns."[76]

Guests ate, drank, and partied, but the models remember no such fun. They quickly negotiated roommates at their meager hotel. Rehearsals and fittings, as they recall, began at the palace a few hours after their arrival. Darden's roommate, Billie Blair, said an especially fervent version of the Lord's Prayer.

Ten

Waiting

Early on Sunday morning, November 25, jet lag and adrenaline
playing a tug-of-war with everyone's bodies, the designers and
models, who had not even been to their hotel, made their way to
Versailles.

While the models were forced onto a bus for the thirty-minute drive,
the designers all had private cars and chauffeurs. Liza Minnelli, the star
of the Americans' production, had a driver too, but she opted to meet the
models at their hotel and ride with them. The models were thrilled by the
display of camaraderie and impressed that Minnelli was so approachable.
They were all one big show biz gang.

Upon arrival at the palace, the Americans were duly awestruck. Rings
of balconies rose up around the Théâtre Gabriel's massive proscenium
stage. The ceiling soared 118 feet above their heads. This was three di-
mensions of unwieldy, challenging space. Who could appreciate the stitching or details on a dress from a balcony seat? What could compete with
chandeliers that created a galaxy of twinkling crystals? The theater was
majestic, regal, and . . . as cold as an icebox.

Over the next two and a half days, the Americans did not settle in.

The models and designers never got comfortable. They navigated the theater swaddled in overcoats, scarves, and hats. They quickly discovered that the bathrooms had not been stocked with toilet paper, their hosts had not provided food or water, and the French crews that ran the theater's lights and other backstage operations adhered to their union contracts ruthlessly. Like American Teamsters on a loading dock, they came and went as their labor rules dictated—not a minute earlier, not a minute later.

The Americans had expected logistics to unfold smoothly. After all, the tough decisions had already been made, such as the order of the show and the amount of time each designer would have onstage. The designers had planned that the first day and a half at Versailles would be spent making a few last-minute fixes on garments, working with choreographer Kay Thompson to block out each segment, and going through a technical rehearsal on stage.

Then there was the big Norton Simon party for Minnelli and Halston on Monday night at Maxim's. Of the other designers, only Burrows had been invited, along with Halston's favorite models. It was Halston's coming out at Maxim's, not America's. On Tuesday, the day before the show, the American designers would have their dress rehearsal.

It did not work out that way.

The Americans' commitment to arguing with each other was impressive. Resentments over the order of the presentation lingered; they bickered over who was to be the biggest dog in the pound. They were aggravated with the French because of their inhospitableness, but instead of directly confronting them, which the American designers were too insecure to do, they squabbled with each other.

The garments came together, but the music nearly didn't. The sets were sized all wrong for the stage and had to be remade. Thompson didn't have enough time to give each designer his or her fair share of attention. And on Tuesday, the French hogged the stage, causing the Americans' dress rehearsal to be little more than a cursory run-through.

The squabbling was all minor, except on one topic: the disdain for Anne Klein. None of the other designers—not the French, not the Americans—wanted her there. Their scorn for her was obvious. She was shunted aside. Her opinions went unrecognized. She was belittled. She was forced into a work space in the basement, which was akin to being banished from the fridge and tossed into the freezer. Oscar de la Renta never told Klein how, at the insistence of Eleanor Lambert, he'd lobbied the French to accept her. But he didn't have to; she knew she was the outsider. She had worried about being the only woman and the only straightforward sportswear designer. When she arrived at Versailles, her fears were realized.

"Being a woman designer, it was very, very tough. She was treated so rudely—beyond rude. How angry was I at the way they treated Anne? She was so ignored," recalls Donna Karan, Klein's assistant at the time. "Everybody was doing what they were doing and I was sitting and watching. It wasn't spoken, but you know when you aren't really wanted. They did not like Anne.

"I was the pregnant [assistant] looking on and thinking: Is this the business I'm getting into?"[1]

The low opinion of Klein was apparent to the models as well.

"She was crying," recalls Amina Warsuma. "People thought they could push her around and walk all over her."[2]

The French had been against Klein's inclusion because they believed her work was pure commodity that lacked finesse. They didn't think it belonged on the same stage as haute couture. And in a sense, they were right. The complicated, labor-intensive finery that the French designers created in their ateliers was an entirely different entity from the down-to-earth, pragmatic attire on which Klein had built her reputation. In today's fashion environment, it would be akin to putting Chanel alongside J. Crew and asking critics to judge which is better. It is an impossible task: the two brands are attempting to do wholly different things.

Today, consumers allow that sportswear and couture can coexist, even side by side, in the closet of a single woman. But in 1973, the thinking within the fashion world was that one had to choose. The Americans worried that Klein would be an albatross; they thought her subdued work would drag down a show that already had them on edge.

Beyond aesthetic integrity, however, jealousy was surely at work. Klein's company was arguably more successful than the others. Her brand and its licenses were generating about $50 million a year in sales, and she'd just sold a quarter of her company to Takihyo, an offshoot of a centuries-old Japanese apparel and textile company. Klein was a savvy businesswoman in other ways as well. She had built a path to security for her brand's future and had been grooming Karan to follow in her footsteps. Every indication was that her way of designing and merchandising was the future of fashion. And she'd realized that before all of these sniping, backbiting men.

Klein might have shed a few tears, but she never stopped working. She was tough.[3] She was "leaning in" before that became a new feminist rallying cry. She was secretive and paranoid, but determined. She had her husband, Chip Rubenstein, there to support her, and she had Karan, who was unsophisticated in the world of international fashion but deeply loyal. Klein was relying on the element of surprise to give her an advantage. The other Americans had discussed their collections with each other, but Klein hadn't told anyone what she was planning.

She'd decided to create a collection inspired by Africa, including an "elephant walk" print.[4] Dashikis, after all, were the rage. The collection was sexy, with low-rise skirts and bra tops that called to mind something that African dancers might wear. "It had an ethnic appeal," Karan recalls. "It was sort of tribal."[5] Klein had never designed anything with such overt and exotic subtext.

She wasn't known for using black models either, but for Versailles, she wanted to work with them to give her work cultural legitimacy. Before leaving New York, Klein had talked about her plan with model Bethann Hardison. She asked her opinion about using black models; she didn't want it to seem like a cliché. "Her theme was Africa," Hardison says. "I told her it made sense."[6]

Klein relied heavily on Karan. The assistant helped with fittings and walked the models through the details of the clothes. Klein was not the sort of designer who believed in creating the illusion that she was a perfectionist who did everything herself. She gave Karan a great deal of credit and made sure the press understood her contributions to the business. Businesses, after all, can go on forever. People die.

And Klein knew all was not well with her health. "I knew something was up, but not that she had cancer," Karan says.[7]

Klein hadn't gotten the official diagnosis, but she knew the breast cancer she thought she'd vanquished was back. It was Klein's silent agony. Cancer was still not something that was readily discussed in public. This was before First Lady Betty Ford underwent a radical mastectomy due to breast cancer and then discussed it forthrightly. Klein was a steely, veteran garment industry woman. She did not want sympathy. Yet, if the other designers had known of her dire circumstances, perhaps they would have reined in their mean-spiritedness.

Instead, pettiness was just one of the ways in which the American designers expressed their fear and nervousness. Being in the position of an underdog can reveal a good deal about a person's character. Klein was not prone to treating others as poorly as she was being treated.

"Anne Klein was so nice to me," recalls model Jennifer Brice, who was new to the runway. During rehearsals, "I was sitting out in the audience and she came up to me and took my khaki baseball cap off. She said, 'You're so beautiful. You don't need to hide your beauty.'"[8]

Halston expressed his own stress through his imperious behavior—he managed to exacerbate almost everyone's anxiety. He had taken to referring to himself in the third person and acted as if the entire enterprise would collapse without him. With his recent financial windfall, Halston saw himself, in Wall Street's modern-day macho parlance, as the "big swinging dick." If he didn't get the attention he felt he deserved, he balked.

"He walked out and sat in a car by the sidewalk," said Eleanor Lambert, who hovered during rehearsals like a doting mother ready to dish out tough love. "He wanted the models to retire with him but Liza said, 'Listen, girls. Don't you dare go out. This is show business. We're committed to it.' And so they all turned around and came back."[9]

"He behaved like a monster," Bill Blass recalled. "One day, we shared a ride back into Paris from Versailles. I pushed him into the car and told him to shut up."[10]

Although Karen Bjornson, his friend and former house model, attributed Halstson's terrible behavior to his wanting to make sure the Americans had what they needed to put together a successful show, other models remember him acting like a spoiled, overly tired child.

Burrows was the most relaxed of the designers. He, after all, was poised in that sweet moment of anticipation, satisfaction, and disbelief before reaching a summit. Every switchback along the way had revealed an ever more spectacular view. He was now Lambert's client. He had moved from the protective cloister of Henri Bendel, where his aesthetic had evolved, becoming more sophisticated and mature, to Seventh Avenue. He had also moved up from the East Village apartment he had shared with friends into his own flat in a town house at Irving Place and East Seventeenth Street, which he rented for $350 a month.

At Versailles, Burrows simply didn't care about what was happening around him. He was excited about an adventure he had never thought he'd have. He'd heard about the French and what they had accomplished in the world of fashion. He was curious to see their work up close. But he didn't feel the competitive tension that designers such as Bill Blass and Oscar de la Renta did. "You design what you come from," Burrows says. And he came from Newark, the dance clubs of New York, the free-spirited beaches of Fire Island, and the black community, which had its own rules about style.[11]

While the other designers were having a verbal slugging match, Burrows quietly focused on his work. The American collections were mostly finished. But rare is the fashion show, even today, for which every garment is complete well in advance of a presentation. Fabric is delivered late. Samples take longer than expected to construct. Designers procrastinate and deliberate. Fashion is in a constant state of self-inflicted urgency. There is always one difficult dress that holds everything up. At Versailles, Burrows was obsessed with a single long gown.

"As an homage to the event being in Paris, I lined something," Burrows says with a laugh. "I had to line it because you could see right through it. It was a wrap top and a long skirt with a long, long train. It was almost to the back of the stage. It was my duck dress because it was yellow. I used to think in those terms back then. Olive Oyl, ducks. It was silk, almost a silk faille."[12]

His calm was admirable. His only competition was with himself.

Burrows's fit model, Bethann Hardison, worked in his studio as a kind of living dress form. His clothes were constructed based on her body's proportions. "Stephen was more of a knit guy; this dress was in a woven fabric. He was really trying to make it like a couture dress would be made. It would fit this way and snap that way, like underwear attached to the dress. It was so detailed and he'd never made anything like it. I had to fit it two days before [the show]. I fainted twice. It was so late. He was constantly pinning and fitting. He'd say, 'Oh Beth!' I'd fallen out again."

But Hardison never worried about whether he could make the dress work. "He was a very talented guy in terms of his technical skill. He could make a pattern, grade it," Hardison says. "I never thought he *couldn't* pull it off.

"I knew it was my dress; I was going to wear it in the show," she says. "I wasn't happy about the dress, to be honest with you. I felt like it was so different from the others. Everything else was so typical Burrows: the matte jersey, the colors. And here was this canary-yellow, woven dress.

"But I couldn't say that. It was an ode."[13]

On Monday, the squabbling continued at a dull roar. Halston, who had been instrumental in booking Minnelli, was panicking, worried that he'd lured his famous friend into the middle of a train wreck. Klein's nerves were raw, as she was constantly on guard against slights and imbalances. De la Renta, competitive and blunt, had let Halston's behavior get under his skin . . . again. Blass wasn't in the thick of it; he was a horrified bystander, but one who wasn't hesitant to weigh in when necessary. And Burrows was sitting astride a velvet settee in one of the many ornate rooms off the theater that had become a makeshift atelier. He was fighting with his canary-yellow dress.

Every Super Bowl has its pre-parties, and Versailles was no different. The big pregame event, the one everyone talked about, was Monday night. The A-list social event was a dinner at Maxim's hosted by David Mahoney, the head of Norton Simon. The party was being thrown in honor of Liza Minnelli and, of course, Halston himself at a cost of $20,000, causing the French media to dub Mahoney "Monsieur Money, Money, Money." In 2013 dollars, the price tag would be just under $105,000.[14] It was reported that the event was the first time the entire bistro had been bought out by a single person in its eighty-year history.

"You can't believe the pressure we've had from people who wanted to be invited," Mahoney told the New York Times. "There was nothing we could do. The restaurant only holds 220 people."[15]

The setting alone was worth a million bucks. Maxim's, at 3 rue Royale, sits just off the Place de la Concorde in the center of Paris. Over the years, it has been favored by everyone from Marcel Proust to Maria Callas and Brigitte Bardot. From the exterior, it's a relatively modest building with a facade of warm wood, but the interior is a spectacle of art nouveau overabundance. The eye has nowhere to rest in Maxim's; every surface is carved, mirrored, or gilded. Entering off the rue Royal, through a pair of narrow French doors, guests are greeted by their own reflection in an oversized mirror. The dark-paneled walls are decorated with swirling vines and flowers. Sconces shaped like angular palm leaves gently illuminate the dining room. Flanking the main floor bar, gold sculpted maidens hold glass lampshades that curve earthward like wilting flowers. Translucent glass panels line the ceiling and glow with a rose-colored light that casts everyone in flattering warmth. The tables and booths are almost all framed by mirrors, creating the illusion that every guest is part of an elaborate tableau vivant and every gesture is a theatrical cue.

The location might have been art nouveau, but the guest list was overwhelmingly old, old money, and aristocracy. "It was very, very *ancienne* French," says writer Enid Nemy.[16] The high-wattage evening included appearances by various princesses, baronesses, and duchesses, including the Duchess of Windsor, making one of her first public outings since the death of the Duke of Windsor in the spring of 1972. She arrived wearing a turquoise silk Christian Dior gown. Socialite Gloria Guinness, who'd married into the beer dynasty, wore Yves Saint Laurent. The van der Kemps were there, with Florence dressed in a pink and black printed dress from Christian Dior, her favorite design house.

International Best-Dressed List favorite Vicomtesse Jacqueline de Ribes, who had helped Oscar de la Renta establish himself in New York, arrived in a turquoise, hand-painted Dior gown. Paloma Picasso partied with this ultra-haute crowd, and the journalist William Safire gathered string for his 1973 essay comparing Stephen Burrows to John Lindsay "of eight years ago, the comer."[17]

Marie-Hélène de Rothschild, wearing black Yves Saint Laurent haute couture, was in attendance, of course, and was reportedly in such a snit about not being seated in a place of honor next to Mahoney that she departed early.

"The seating was like planning the Normandy invasion: scenes of high drama and hissy fits with all those personalities involved," reflected David Moriarty, Mahoney's assistant at the time.[18] Indeed, while guests were quaffing drinks upstairs, Moriarty spied Françoise de la Renta downstairs rearranging the seating cards.

The American designers and models came ready to party—*to rage*—and to dull their nerves. The rail-thin Kay Thompson had slipped into a

Halston pantsuit. Little Joe Eula was there in his thick-framed Mr. Magoo glasses. Pat Cleveland arrived dressed as brightly as a peacock in a cobalt-blue-and-green-feathered coat from Burrows. Model Nancy North was draped in mint-green Halston sequins with a flower tucked into her not-so-discreet décolletage. Marisa Berenson wore one of Halston's long, sleeveless gowns, but the real star of her ensemble was the elaborate horsehair hat that sat atop her head like a Henry Moore sculpture. Halston and Minnelli arrived together, dramatically late. She had on the designer's white sequined coat over a low-cut sequined dress that one might describe as the precursor to the infamous Versace scarf dress that entertainer Jennifer Lopez would wear to the 2000 Grammy Awards, twenty-seven years later. Minnelli's dress plunged to navel-grazing depths, and at one point over the course of the long evening, she popped out of it, her bare breast eliciting only a slight shrug.

"It was just as well that France's pro-Arab oil policy so far has spared the country any fuel cutback or even much soul searching. Otherwise Minnelli and Berenson doubtless would have come down with pneumonia because their décolletes were beyond beyond," sniped the *Washington Post*.[19]

After a nearly two-hour cocktail "hour," which, according to media reports, had the French guests beside themselves with impatience because they apparently do not like to dawdle that long over drinks, the guests moved downstairs into the red velvet jewel box that was Maxim's main room. There, they found a meal of roasted poussin, shrimp mousse, watercress salad, and raspberry sorbet. They washed it all down with Pommery champagne, a Sancerre from the Loire region, and a 1964 Château Siran red Bordeaux that the hard-to-please crowd described as a *"cru bourgeois."*[20]

The celebration lasted until past three in the morning, thanks to multiple bands and free-flowing drinks. Minnelli did not sing for her supper, but models North and Cleveland climbed onstage to sing and dance. Before the night ended, Cleveland performed an emphatic solo version of "I've

Got You Under My Skin," after countless dance partners had thrown in the towel from exhaustion.[21]

The French guests found fault with the evening's pacing. They hated the seating. They were dismissive of the wine choices. But the Americans partied like it was the last hours of the *Titanic*.

On Tuesday, as Tom Fallon, Blass's aide-de-camp, recalls it, the American designers sat in the theater, stewing and fighting for what seemed like an eternity while they waited for the French to finish their rehearsals and relinquish the stage. But the French were living their own Gallic nightmare.

When the planning began that fall, they'd concocted an elaborate production that required complicated blocking, lighting, and musical cues. They were working with a forty-piece orchestra and five different stage sets, which were still under construction and which designers were only just getting to see. Each set was meant to evoke the designer's work as well as recall theatrical performances of the era of Marie Antoinette.

The French weren't the least bit mindful of the Americans' needs. The French portion of the show would be first, so they rehearsed first. And they went on and on and on.

Their production was directed by Jean-Louis Barrault, a highly regarded actor, director, and (that very French avocation) *mime*. In the 1940s, he had been a star of the Comédie Française, essentially the state theater of France. In 1947, he left to create his own troupe alongside his actress wife. The two were the pride of the French government, happily ensconced in the state-supported Théâtre de l'Odéon, on Paris's Left Bank, where they produced new dramas by Samuel Beckett, Eugène Ionesco, and Jean Genet.[22]

In 1968, however, during the Paris uprising that had university students and blue-collar workers rioting in the streets, Barrault gave solace to the students, allowing them to gather in the Odéon. They turned it into their headquarters. The French establishment was furious with Barrault, and after the mayhem subsided, President Charles de Gaulle had the theater company cast out of the Odéon. Barrault was dismissed from his position as its director. While he wandered in the cultural wilderness, without state financing, he mounted productions of his own adaptations of works by Voltaire (*Zadig or The Book of Fate*) and Friedrich Nietzsche (*Thus Spake Zarathustra*).[23] Eventually he was forgiven, and by the time planning began for the Versailles show, thanks to President Georges Pompidou, Barrault was back in the warm embrace of the French elite. But he had little experience in directing the kind of effervescent, contemporary production that 1970s fashion increasingly demanded.

Barrault's aesthetic philosophy was maximalism, and that took time. The orchestra had to warm up and rehearse its musical cues. The bawdy dancers from the Crazy Horse cabaret needed to get their bearings and their G-strings just right. And Rudolf Nureyev, thirty-four, who was dancing a pas de deux from *Sleeping Beauty*, needed time to run through his choreography with a new dance partner because the original French ballerina had mentioned, in public, that the famed, but aging, ballet star had stepped on her foot and he'd had her tossed out. He decided to dance instead with the Royal Ballet's Merle Park.

Barrault rounded up various international performers from high culture and kitsch—including a few who were teetering toward the great beyond. The French were atwitter about the appearance of Zizi Jeanmaire, a gamine of a woman who was a ballet dancer and the wife of choreographer Roland Petit as well as a friend of Saint Laurent's. A veteran performer, Jeanmaire, forty-eight, famously crooned a song called "Mon Truc en Plumes," which she regularly performed as a kind of coquettish vaudeville while male dancers fanned out behind her holding giant plumed fans. The effect was that of a woman, who looked vaguely like Audrey Hepburn, shaking her tail feathers. She was hired to sing during Yves Saint Laurent's segment.

And finally, the French invited Josephine Baker, sixty-seven, to perform. It was a rather brutal slap that the American entertainer, who lived as an expatriate in Paris because of the oppressiveness of her own country's racism, would be performing in this Franco-American extravaganza for her adopted country and not her homeland.

Baker still looked every bit the sexy dancer despite her advanced years. She was long and lean with the waist of a teenager, and she had lost none of her nerve for provocation. Still, in 1973, Baker was more of a historical icon—an early civil rights advocate and fierce integrationist—than a lively, contemporary star. She died less than two years after her performance at Versailles.

When the Americans first spotted her on Tuesday, the day of dress rehearsals, she was wearing her costume for the show, a crystal-studded bodysuit that gave the illusion of nudity. Burrows practically purred with delight, and photographer Charles Tracy nearly hyperventilated. "We were in the open backstage of the theater," Tracy recalls. "Josephine Baker came out and Alva started crying. All the girls were just in awe."[24]

The appearance of this glamorous black woman, who had defied American racism to find fame abroad, was particularly overwhelming to the young black models who were still coming into their own beauty and their own maturity. Baker's life story had inspired Amina Warsuma, in particular, to come to Europe to pursue her dream. France might allow her to have all the things that the States would not. Perhaps in Europe, like Baker, she would not feel as though she had to work twice as hard as her white counterparts for the same level of applause; she would not have to be impossibly perfect in order to succeed. "Here I had to be my best self and more," Warsuma says about working in New York. In Europe, "I was just being myself and they loved me. That was new and different."[25]

Baker had a reputation for generosity, as well as a keen recognition of what she symbolized and her own clout. She adopted her Rainbow Tribe of multicultural children. She refused to play to segregated audiences. She used her glittering persona as both armor and cudgel.

"I never in my life had met Josephine Baker," says Oscar de la Renta. Nonetheless he decided to approach her during a break in the French rehearsals. "I went to Josephine Baker and said, 'Would you do me a favor? There are about ten black girls just dying to meet you. Would you come and have lunch with us in a little restaurant across from the court? I'm going to take these girls to have a bite to eat. Would you come?' She was fantastic. She was marvelous."[26]

The lunch, Warsuma says, "was the highlight of my life."[27]

After lunch, as the Americans continued to sit and watch the French rehearse, waiting for their time onstage, the designers were dumbfounded by the elaborateness of the French spectacle. The young models, some of them seasoned travelers, others fresh from the Midwest, were agog.

Marc Bohan of Christian Dior had been assigned a backdrop of a fairytale pumpkin. "What the hell am I going to do with a pumpkin?" Bohan asked no one in particular.[28] Barrault had given Hubert de Givenchy a woodland set dominated by butterflies and a romantic flower basket that was lowered from the ceiling. A rocket—which de la Renta remembers as a "*Spoot-nik* sort of thing"—fittingly underscored Pierre Cardin's futuristic sensibility. Emanuel Ungaro ended up with a circus/gypsy theme with actor Louis Jourdan—of *Gigi* fame—gallivanting onstage wearing rhinoceros ears. And Yves Saint Laurent oozed urbane glamour against the backdrop of a 1930s Rolls-Royce, along with Jeanmaire and a chorus line of drag queens.

Jean-François Daigre was hired to design the floats, as the thematic sets were called, with a bit of input from each atelier. Daigre was a curly-haired, mustachioed Frenchman with a hot temper whose place on the international social circuit had been solidified thanks to his relationship with Marie-Hélène de Rothschild, the event's chairwoman. Daigre had gotten his start in the mid-fifties at Christian Dior, where he worked on store displays. Dior himself recruited Daigre, who was only nineteen at the time. Daigre stayed on to work with Dior's successor, Saint Laurent, after Dior's death in 1957. By the late sixties, Daigre and his partner, a fellow named

Valerian Rybar, had opened an interior design enterprise that serviced a high-society clientele, including Rothschild. In fact, Daigre had worked closely with Rothschild on her famous Proust Ball of 1971.

Daigre was known for his flamboyant and luxurious aesthetic, both professionally and personally. Long after his death in 1992, when the contents of the Rue de Bac home he shared with Rybar were put up for auction at Christie's Paris, items for sale included military trophies in gilded wood that had belonged to novelist Somerset Maugham, a statue of the Roman god Mercury, and dozens of pairs of cuff links by Tiffany, Verdura, and Jean Schlumberger.[29]

The duo's flashy and extravagant decorating style was on particularly bold display in December 1969, when they created the set for the Oriental Ball, another one of the era's bacchanalian parties attended by social swells. It was hosted by Alexis von Rosenberg, known as Baron de Redé, a snooty and pretentious fellow who proudly declared that he spent his time busily "doing nothing."[30]

For his Oriental Ball, Baron de Redé invited four hundred guests to his home in the Hôtel Lambert. The festivities began at 10 p.m. and went on until sunrise. The main set consisted of two life-size white papier-mâché elephants upon which costumed handlers perched under golden canopies. The baron was dressed as a prince in a fur hat and embroidered coat with a dagger slipped into his belt, an ensemble created for him by Pierre Cardin. Marie-Hélène de Rothschild arrived as a "Siamese" dancer. A countess turned up dressed like a golden pagoda; the costume was constructed of metal and she'd arrived on the back of a truck, as it was impossible for her to sit.[31] Oscar de la Renta was there, too, wearing a feathered headdress, jeweled medallions, and a Fu Manchu mustache.[32]

As guests climbed the staircase to the main apartment, sixteen half-naked men holding torches lit the way. They'd been plucked from Paris gymnasiums and hired to dress as "Nubian slaves."[33] It was as distasteful as the chitlins and dashikis at Bergdorf that same year. The Americans loved radical chic. The French loved the exotic.

This was the manner in which the French social elite was accustomed to partying: with opulence, formality, hauteur, and a hard-to-digest cocktail of cultural insensitivity and fascination with the "other." In this context, the floats Daigre designed for Versailles made perfect sense. His French audience would have expected nothing less. Marie-Hélène de Rothschild would have had nothing less.

When Rothschild secured permission from the French political establishment to host a gala at Versailles, she promised a spectacle, not some basic, middling fashion show. While she remarked that under the stress of organizing Versailles she had lost eight pounds and more than a month off her life, Rothschild was also appalled that the Americans were planning to use prerecorded music. What was a gala if it were not fraught with hand-wringing, five million loose ends, belabored decisions, enough let-them-eat-cake opulence to make the hoi polloi want to riot, and enough political incorrectness to make a lefty gag?

The Americans were bemused and intimidated by the French confections. The French designers spent close to $30,000 on each segment, and private donors—including Baron de Redé, São Schlumberger, and Hélène Rochas, the widow of designer Marcel Rochas—contributed some $80,000.[34]

The entire American budget was only about $50,000. Joe Eula, the illustrator in charge of the American stage, had managed to fit their entire set into a single duffel bag. The backdrop was always meant to be modest. The Americans were planning to hang lengths of fabric featuring Eula's drawings from the ceiling of the theater. He'd worked on them in New York, often spreading the fabric out on the floor of photographer Charles Tracy's studio.

On arrival, however, Eula realized there'd been a miscommunication. The fabric, measured out in feet instead of meters, was much too short. The sets were not going to work. So Eula went out to buy a bolt of white paper.

He unrolled it down the Hall of Mirrors and, working freestyle, sketched a bare-bones depiction of the Eiffel Tower in his evocative but minimalist style. That would have to do.

Even though their production was more streamlined, both by intention and default, the Americans still had plenty to fret about. The gods were giving them a hard time. Rodney Pearson, the twenty-seven-year-old sound engineer who'd begun his career at the British Broadcasting Corporation and who had been sent ahead to organize the technical aspects of the American production, ended up in Athens rather than Paris. His Olympic Airways flight had run into bad weather and was diverted to Greece. It was Friday—five days before the Versailles extravaganza.

Pearson had been working as Liza Minnelli's sound engineer during her concert performances. The week before the Versailles event, Minnelli's secretary had called to abruptly inform him that they were going to Paris. That was it. He wasn't particularly surprised by the lack of detail. He'd become accustomed to the casual disarray that defined a Minnelli event. But he was not expecting to land in the wrong country.

He had no equipment with him. He had been planning to rent it all in Paris. And now he feared he'd be stuck staring at the Parthenon through the weekend and he'd have nothing when the models and designers arrived to rehearse. "I was really ticked off," Pearson says.[35]

Because flight schedules were more limited in 1973, one fellow passenger, who was on his way to Africa, couldn't get another plane until the following week. That was air travel back then. But as luck had it, Pearson was able to rebook on a flight later that afternoon. So with his own inconvenience put into perspective, Pearson spent the morning at the Acropolis and arrived in Paris later that same day. He checked into his hotel, the PLM St. Jacques, a new, ultramodern business hotel in the fourteenth arrondissement. It was slick 1970s efficiency bumping up against artful, seamy old Montparnasse. The hotel is now a Marriott with an adjoining conference center.

Pearson remembers stepping into his room to find it freezing. When he went down to the front desk to see if something could be done to warm up the space, "The clerk said, 'Are you alone? Perhaps we can arrange something.' "[36] Pearson informed the clerk that he just needed extra blankets and a thermostat adjustment, not a courtesan. Then he set out to rent the necessary tape players, speakers, and other equipment for the American performance. He had less than two days to organize it all before the first day of rehearsals, and he barely knew what was planned. Of the designers, he'd only really ever heard of Halston, because he and Minnelli were friends. He had the vague sense that Oscar de la Renta and Bill Blass exuded a certain class. No one had told him about the proposed sets, the clothes, or the choreography. Everything was a blur.

All he knew was that the Americans wanted their prerecorded music to be loud. *Really* loud. Dance club loud. Once the tape started, there would be no stopping. Each model would have to hit her marks, every performer would have to master their choreography perfectly, and every quick change would have to be executed flawlessly. There was even prerecorded silence as one designer's set transitioned to another. There was no room for even a few seconds' delay.

By the time the Americans claimed the stage for the rehearsal, having shooed the French brigade out of the theater, it was nearly 10 p.m. Everyone was annoyed, impatient, hungry, and, of course, cold. Kay Thompson felt the brunt of their wrath as she tried to organize each segment. She was still sorting out the choreography.

She paced back and forth, one pant leg pulled up to her knee and one hanging around her ankle, a bandanna wrapped around her head. First, she plotted out Minnelli's performance. Then she spent significant time reassuring Klein that her straightforward daywear wouldn't be lost on such an enormous stage. "Everyone was mad that Kay gave Anne all this time," Karan recalls.[37]

Although there is no evidence that this was true, the other designers gossiped that Chip Rubenstein had bribed Thompson into giving his wife more attention. "Anne had cancer then, though none of us knew it at the time," Lambert recalled. "She was ill and nervous that her casual designs would pale beside these elaborate evening dresses of the others. So she kept asking Kay how to make her segment shine. The others were annoyed that this was eating into their precious rehearsal time."[38]

The attention Thompson was giving Klein, coupled with the long wait, pushed Halston over the edge. And he took Thompson with him. "Halston had a major screaming shout-down with Anne Klein," remembers Fallon. "It got so vicious that Kay Thompson quit—right on the spot."[39] But not before she yelled at Halston, "Shut up! It's guys like you who give fags a bad name!" Halston, not to be outdone, declared: "Halston is leaving!" And he stomped out of the theater. Enid Nemy, the *New York Times* writer, sat through the entire dress rehearsal; she witnessed Halston's wretched behavior as well as his close attention to his public image. "He said to me, 'If you report that, I'll never invite you to another show.' And I said, 'Halston, you never invite me to your shows as it is.'"[40]

Minnelli, impatient with her impertinent friend, convinced the models to stay, noting that this was how show business works. Not everyone gets the same attention; there's plenty of waiting around; and there are an endless array of glitches and hurdles. Halston returned. Thompson didn't quit. But it quickly became apparent to Oscar de la Renta, Bill Blass, and Stephen Burrows that they were going to have to punt. The fighting had wasted too much time. Thompson would not get to them.

For Halston's segment, Thompson went for the dramatic. A single spotlight would illuminate each model, who would own the massive proscenium stage for just a few seconds. It meant that everything had "to be bigger and more dramatic," model Karen Bjornson says. At Versailles, she'd have to spin like a top to bring Halston's big, bias-cut dresses to life. "I'd never spin like that on the runway because there wouldn't be space."[41]

Bjornson would do what the models of that day were taught to do: sell the clothes, give them energy. But the extreme drama and grand flourishes needed at Versailles weren't part of her usual style. Everyone ramped up their energy. The designers requested it, the clothes inspired it, and the venue demanded it.

Pat Cleveland, the queen of runway antics, energized Bjornson. Cleveland would spin around in the vast backstage wings, figuring out just how much speed she needed for maximum effect. For Versailles, nothing less than a whirling dervish would suffice.

As Halston's group was finishing its rehearsal, Burrows was still working backstage, a solitary guy sporting ivory wool trousers with a fun-loving three-dimensional billiard ball print, a striped shirt, and sailor hat. As he hunched over the last few stitches of his collection, including his beloved yellow dress, his troupe of girls gathered around him—a mix of black and white women as thin as toothpicks—looking to him for direction.

Burrows had been expecting Thompson to choreograph his segment. But it had become clear that he was going to have to tell the models what to do. And he had no idea. Charles Tracy was sitting in the audience with Halston and Joe Eula waiting to see what would unfold when the model Ramona Saunders walked onstage with a long feather in her hair. The light picked up the feather and created a dramatic, exaggerated silhouette on the backdrop. It looked like a praying mantis.

"I got off my seat and ran backstage and told Stephen what had just happened," says Tracy. "He and I put [the segment] together in two seconds. We decided the girls would come out one at a time and then go and stand in the back.

"At the end, they all walked forward with the color, the trains, the light, and the posing. Stephen egged them on to express themselves," Tracy says. "When some girls like Karen Bjornson saw them doing all these things, they started doing it."[42]

De la Renta also plotted out his own segment. "I had never in my life choreographed a show to the sound of music. We're already doing shows in New York where you have music in the background, but when you have to synchronize a show—where the music begins and ends with your presentation—it's more difficult," de la Renta says. "I had an idea on how I wanted the segment to be, so I said, 'Is there a room where I can go with the girls?' I took all the girls: Alva, Pat. I lock the doors at this room in Versailles." And he went to work.[43]

Bill Blass turned to Tom Fallon, the erstwhile Broadway maven. "We're going to have to do our own directing on the stage," Blass told Fallon. "You're going to have to do all that stuff we talked about and make it happen."[44]

Fallon found Billie Blair and told her that he needed her to do for him what she had done that night in Philadelphia. She would move into place onstage in the dark and then a white spotlight would slam onto her in thrilling fashion. She was to move forward and open her coat to reveal her glittering gray evening gown. And then, in what Fallon described as a "bold, sultry way, with your head back," she was to stop and spin until the accompanying coat was at her feet in a puddle.

The Blass team had been onstage for about fifteen minutes and Fallon was just starting to block things out when suddenly one of the workmen told him that his time was up. "I was furious," Fallon remembers. "But I just said, 'Yes, sir.' I could not get involved in the viciousness of what was happening."[45]

He pulled the models to the side, found a quiet corner, and continued to explain the choreography. But the electricians were starting to pack up and turn off the lights for the night. The Americans weren't close to finishing. Chip Rubenstein called Versailles curator Gérald van der Kemp, who was hosting a black-tie dinner party in celebration of the show. (Eleanor Lambert was already there.) Rubenstein implored him to keep the lights on in the theater. His demands were punctuated by thuds and minor crashes as the Americans began to grope around in the dark.

Because so much of the panic unfolded on Tuesday, the night before the big show, it all felt very dramatic—like a coordinated plot against the Americans. But in reality, much of what occurred was the result of unsympathetic work rules and a French contingent that had its own enormously complicated performance to sort out. Van der Kemp got the lights turned back on. The Americans finished rehearsing around midnight. And afterward they were last-minute guests at the curator's party. "There was a jitney bus from Versailles to their place across the courtyard," recalls Nemy, who hopped on that same shuttle. "Liza Minnelli got up to sing on the bus—'It's going to be a great day!' It was quite a surreal moment, but it was fun."[46]

> *When you're down and out*
> *Lift up your head and shout*
> *There's gonna be a great day*
> *Angels in the sky*
> *Promise that by and by*
> *There's gonna be a great day*
> *Gabriel will warn you*
> *Some early morn you*
> *Will hear his horn rootin', tootin'*
> *It's not far away*
> *Hold up your hands and say*
> *There's gonna be a great day*[47]

The van der Kemps' Tuesday night buffet in their Versailles apartment was the final coda to the dancing, drinking, and gorging that had been going on in Paris for three days. The designers and their entourages, some dressed casually in plaid work shirts and jeans, arrived to find a buffet spread over three rooms with bumper-to-bumper VIPs, many of whom had been partying since Sunday night. It had been planned as a sit-down black-tie dinner for forty, but it had ballooned to eighty-five thanks to last-minute requests and the addition of friends of friends. The formally attired guests were mostly visiting American socialites and business folks—the van der Kemps knew who their donors were—but a few locals were there, too. It was the usual mix of personally flawed but professionally glossy jet-setters.

Charles Revson, the mercurial founder of Revlon, who had horned in on Max Factor's sponsorship of the Versailles gala, was there with his wife, Lyn. She wore a gold-bedazzled, black tulle ballgown by Norman Norell. Her choice was not without significance. In 1971, Revlon had bought the rights to Norell's fragrance, which had the distinction of being the first American designer perfume, introduced in 1968. Revlon paid nearly $1.25 million for it.[48] In 1972, Norell died from a stroke.

As it happens, these were also the last days of the Revsons as a couple. In February 1974, on their tenth anniversary, Charles Revson gave his wife a tin can—traditionally tin represents durability and flexibility—filled with $30,000 and five jeweled Van Cleef & Arpels bracelets. He kissed Lyn good-bye and left for the office. An hour later, his lawyer called: "Charles wants a divorce."[49]

San Francisco's Denise Hale circulated around the interconnected rooms dressed in black trousers, turtleneck, suede jacket, and a gold and diamond necklace of significant carats.[50] Hale had briefly been Liza Minnelli's step-mother thanks to a short marriage to director Vincente Minnelli; she was now married to the department store entrepreneur Prentis Cobb Hale, with whom she'd been accused of having an affair while married to Minnelli.[51] Prentis's first wife had committed suicide in 1969, shooting herself in the temple in the family home in San Francisco. He and Denise married two years later and swiftly settled into life as a high-flying couple, welcomed into the finest homes without comment.

The great beauties, the best dressed, and the grand hostesses were all there in anticipation of the Versailles gala. Socialite São Schlumberger, who was on the French planning committee, was in attendance; she was well known for her interest in art and fashion. Journalist Pat Shelton re-members taking in the whole scene and being amazed at the glamour of the gowns and jewels, as well as being dismayed by the chilly oblivious-ness of some of the guests. Schlumberger "had on a white satin sleeveless dress with perspiration marks under the arms," Shelton says with a wry chuckle. "She was bumping into everyone around the buffet line. She was so rude."[52]

Van der Kemp issued apologies all around for the fiasco of a dress rehearsal. He calmed the American designers and models. Not having eaten anything for much of the day, they were famished and sprinted to the buffet line to load their plates—a last banquet before the Versailles games.

Eleven

One Night at Versailles

VERSAILLES! It is wonderfully beautiful! You gaze and stare and try to understand that it is real, that it is on the earth, that it is not the Garden of Eden—but your brain grows giddy, stupefied by the world of beauty around you, and you half believe you are the dupe of an exquisite dream. —MARK TWAIN[1]

The evening of Wednesday, November 28, 1973, as guests began arriving at Versailles, the palace glowed under a full moon and through a scrim of light snow—the first dusting of the season. Red-uniformed, saber-wielding gendarmes flanked the gilded palace gates, along with some one hundred footmen in eighteenth-century white powdered wigs and livery. Marie-Hélène de Rothschild, dressed in a green, ostrich-trimmed gown by Yves Saint Laurent and with solitary diamonds pinned in her thick hair, greeted guests: brushing kisses on the cheeks of the French and offering handshakes to the Americans.[2]

"You'd never seen anything more beautiful in your life," recalls Tom Fallon.[3]

The pale blue invitations, with gold script, announced that the *Grand Divertissement à Versailles* was to begin promptly at 9 p.m. It also prescribed black tie for men and long gowns for women. Guests expected the Versailles gala to be another in a series of notable parties of the era that they had all attended: Truman Capote's Black and White Ball in New York, the Proust Ball, the Oriental Ball. The Versailles gala was, of course, a charity event, but mostly it was old friends gathering for a deliciously decadent evening.

In the decades since the Versailles event, our culture has become more informal and restrained, even at its poshest moments. In Washington, every four years, the presidential inauguration resonates with history and gravitas, but an inaugural ball is a crowded, unglamorous affair akin to an oversubscribed wedding reception. Washington still has a fair number of black-tie soirees in the ballrooms of embassies and the like, but the level of glamour is moderated by political correctness and diplomatic decorum. The Costume Institute gala at New York's Metropolitan Museum of Art is known for its dazzling display of runway fashion, but it does not have the show of jewels—many owned, not just borrowed—that blinded the eye at Versailles. That November night, the family jewels were proudly displayed; Princess Grace of Monaco, who was a guest of the Rothschilds, even wore a tiara, which she paired with a cream-colored Madame Grès gown.

"There were such jewels!" recalls Donna Karan. "There were jewels on top of jewels, tiaras on top of tiaras."[4] And scattered discreetly through the crowd were security guards keeping a watchful eye over the many millions of dollars' worth of precious gems tucked into glistening cleavages and pinned into skyward bouffants.

"I had my own jewels, but I was also loaded with diamonds from Van Cleef and Arpels," says guest Simone Levitt, whose husband William was considered the father of American suburbia with the creation of Levittown. "We had to have bodyguards, which was a pain in the neck. The bodyguard, wherever I was, there he was."[5]

The Versailles gala was unabashedly, unashamedly jaw-dropping. "The hype of the thing was enough to make your eyeballs go up into your head," recalls guest Lynn Wyatt. "You opened your eyes and you were just blinded by the splendor and beauty."[6]

The *Chicago Tribune* declared the Versailles guests to be "the most superbly turned out crowd seen in one place for a decade. Rivaling the show on stage, hundreds of famous and wealthy women sat in the tiered, basket-shaped marble, velvet, and gold Versailles opera [house] among their black-tuxedoed escorts, looking like flower bouquets in feathered chiffons, or with the glitter of mermaids in sequins."[7]

There was no hint of or desire for discretion. Writer Eugenia Sheppard described "a brilliant, international audience all turned out in couture clothes and proving that made-to-order fashion is alive and well."[8]

Hélène Rochas wore a white chiffon Saint Laurent gown with oversized sleeves and a jeweled bib; her hair, in a single thick braid, wrapped around her head like a crown. São Schlumberger wore a caramel-colored gown by Givenchy to match her hair. Viola Loewy, wife of Raymond Loewy, the industrial designer who had worked for Studebaker, chose a knife-pleated tube dress by Pierre Cardin that was attached to a necklace of ruby-colored stones.

The Duchess of Windsor wore blue crepe Dior and dripped with sapphire jewelry. Gloria Guinness chose black chiffon from Yves Saint Laurent and accessorized the simple V-neck gown with glittering hoop earrings. And Paloma Picasso made a sentimental choice: a draped Madame Grès gown from the 1950s that had belonged to her mother.[9]

Patriotism held little sway in matters of personal style and reputation. Lyn Revson, for instance, wore a gown by Balmain. But a few guests did fly the flag of Seventh Avenue. Lily Auchincloss, a trustee at the Museum of Modern Art, wore a red chiffon Halston toga. And socialite C. Z. Guest chose a yellow Mainbocher open-back gown in chiffon with gold sequins.

"I wore a big, jersey black dress and I wrapped my head in a turban," says Karan, who worked backstage that night. "It was long sleeves, very fitted in the breast, with a huge circular skirt."[10]

Some of the guests had pulled strings to be there. The uninvited called in favors from friends who were already on that elite guest list. Others made their case to publicist Eleanor Lambert, insisting there'd been some terrible oversight; they *clearly* should have been on the list. Everyone relished the moment when they passed down the stone corridor and entered the Théâtre Gabriel. Even the most privileged among them immediately looked up, their eyes drawn skyward by the theater's soaring height and the flashes of light bouncing off the myriad crystal chandeliers. The great French designers sat in private boxes, along with their Seventh Avenue guests and a few VIPs. Artist Andy Warhol, who had come to witness the boozy high-society kaffeeklatsch, sat in a prime box with Saint Laurent and Pierre Bergé. Only the designers' assistants were allowed backstage. That's how Rothschild wanted it.

"*Ooh-la-la,*" says Didier Grumbach. "It was magnificent."[11] He was twenty-six years old in 1973 and his family business held the license for Yves Saint Laurent ready-to-wear.

The guest list at Versailles was not a who's who of boldface names in the way we might think of now. The main-floor seats—benches, really—and boxes were not filled with the famous actors and musicians of the day. This was not like the Academy Awards, where everywhere you look there's an immediately recognizable face. Instead, the pews of Versailles overflowed with the burdens of history, the dignity of the state, the power of provenance and of extraordinarily dusty money. It was a bit like being in the Cathedral of the Holy Order of Social Stratification.

"It wasn't very comfortable," remembers journalist Pat Shelton, "but it was awfully pretty."[12]

For the American designers, walking to their private boxes to watch the show felt like entering the Colosseum to be devoured by the lions. The Grande Divertissement à Versailles had not been organized as a competition, but through the media attention and human nature, it had become just that. The American designers, who'd agreed to the show because it promised to bring them publicity, now just wanted to survive it with their dignity intact. They'd spent days fighting with each other and wrestling with sets, music, and choreography that were still in disarray. They'd booked their models on the cheap. Would the young women have enough stage presence to bring the clothes to life? Their music was canned. Would everyone be able to hit their marks?

The American designers had gotten the gist of what the French had planned. It was going to be big. It was going to be sweeping. It would carry the weight of tradition.

But while the Americans worried they'd be dwarfed by the French spectacle, the French, who'd been expecting to easily dazzle and then gloat, began to worry that they'd overreached.

As the 720 ticketholders and representatives of the French state settled into their seats, Rothschild appeared from behind the royal blue stage curtains, with their gold fleur-de-lis design, to announce that the evening had netted more than $280,000—an amount akin to $1.5 million today.

After polite applause, the curtain opened on the French haute couture presentation. The orchestra began the whispering violin overture from Sergei Prokofiev's *Cinderella*. The main set depicted the lushly painted forests of Versailles with a temple of love in the distance. The Cinderella pumpkin, constructed from cardboard and tinsel, rolled out for the Christian Dior presentation. French actress Danielle Darrieux introduced the segment. She was fifty-six years old but was described in the *Washington Post* as giving off "vibrations despite the inroads of time."[13] Marc Bohan designed the Dior collection, but his name appeared on neither the gilded invitation nor the evening's program, with its advertisements from Revlon and Piaget, which guests were able to purchase for about $23. Bohan was merely a caretaker of the great fashion house. His collection was elegant and relatively austere, and mostly executed in shades of black and beige.

The historical record is slim on the details of the fashions that came down the runway that evening. The press at the time was more enamored with the social aspects of the event and dazzled by the plumage of the female guests; when the show began, reporters were dumbfounded and distracted by the French sets. No one bothered to mention the clothes.

"Marc Bohan's fashions for Dior were completely dwarfed by a giant pumpkin that was rolled in for some reason to symbolize the Cinderella story, of all things," marveled Eugenia Sheppard.[14] The only Dior look anyone seemed to remember after the curtain came down was a black steamer coat, a kind of minimalist trench coat, cinched over skirts and jackets.

The French interspersed each designer's presentation with additional musical performances and dramatic readings that gave the stagehands time to swap out sets. The transitions were jagged and jarring. Spaceships followed Cinderella. Bohemians preceded drag queens.

After the pumpkin rolled off stage, the curtain went up to reveal a two-dimensional cutout rocket ship emblazoned with the Cardin name. It was meant to symbolize the designer's futuristic aesthetic. It wobbled and the sound effects screeched during its faux landing into a set piece choreographed by the South African–born, Paris-based dancer Peter Goss.

The models emerged from the rocket's doorway wearing short, mod dresses with severe angles over dark tights. A black and mustard-colored jersey moon suit was paired with a gleaming, space-age headpiece. They "looked like gorgeous but decidedly earthbound creatures," said the *Washington Post*.[15] Cardin's presentation, which included menswear, caused *Women's Wear Daily* to marvel: "Would you believe a rocket in the forest at Versailles? Would you believe men in sleeveless jersey jumpsuits with vinyl jock straps? Would you believe thrust for takeoff?"[16]

The audience reaction was warm and polite but not particularly enthusiastic. As Pierre Bergé of Yves Saint Laurent watched the French portion of the show from his box seat, he remembers being chagrined that each segment was an event unto itself: "It was one house after another and not very cohesive. There was no blending."[17]

The models, overwhelmingly white and veterans of couture, moved elegantly around the stage—heads high with long limbs in graceful repose. The women were splendid hangers. But not much more.

Emanuel Ungaro went third, which signaled the arrival of entertainers Jane Birkin and Louis Jourdan for a bit of a bohemian, Wild West romp. It was like a mash-up of *Cat Ballou* and *Hair*. Birkin wore a white T-shirt and micro-mini-shorts—panties, really—and Louis Jourdan wore peaked animal ears that left the audience confused as to whether he was meant to be a rhinoceros, cat, or, given the French party ethos of the day, more likely an unfortunate rendition of a Native American.

A wooden cart was rolled onto the stage and Ungaro's models followed dressed in shades of rust, black, and gray. Trim coats were cinched over fluid trousers. A black mink jacket topped a black cashmere dress. He mixed prints and textures in the way that had made him famous, but the press simply lamented the "sawing" of the bass player who accompanied the whole crew on stage. "We were not dancing or anything. We were just moving around. I felt pretty stupid," recalls model Gunilla Lindblad, who worked with Ungaro. "We were standing there and we had to move a little bit but I don't remember the whole point."[18]

Yves Saint Laurent's work was highlighted by Zizi Jeanmaire, dressed in a men's tails and singing "Just a Gigolo" in English. She was backed by plus-size female impersonators, more camp than convincing, wearing feather-adorned robes and jeweled headdresses accented with yet more feathers.

Saint Laurent's segment, which referenced the 1930s, had as its official float an elongated antique car—cardboard, not real. It showed some sophistication, but it harkened back to an old-fashioned cabaret style instead of underscoring the youthful street culture that was informing his work. A floor-length, violet chiffon evening gown was cinched with a sash in tones of green ranging from deep forest to rich emerald. Chiffon dresses with bell sleeves were thickly trimmed in feathers, and cloaks swept the floor with regal grandeur.

Hubert de Givenchy closed the French presentation with a group of translucent evening gowns in floral-hued chiffon. "Shocking pink was the color of Givenchy's long chiffon gown with slim skirt that burst into fullness at the knees," noted the *Chicago Tribune*.[19] Of all the French designers, he was the only one who'd created a wholly separate collection for Versailles. His work was full of romance and he had, perhaps, the least obtrusive of the floats with which to contend. His was a fairly modest basket of flowers that descended from the rafters against a set on which his name was spelled out in paillettes. Givenchy chose the French actress known as Capucine as his runway celebrity. Before going on to act in the *Pink Panther* films, she had modeled for Givenchy, as well as for Dior.[20] After Givenchy's segment, Rudolf Nureyev and Merle Park took to the stage to dance a pas de deux from *Sleeping Beauty*. Nice. But the audience was not wowed.

The French used the least extravagant set for their final two acts. The floats were, at last, gone. No rockets or pumpkins or forested wonderland. Instead, there was a simple backdrop of individual poles—*stripper poles*—for the benefit of fourteen dancers from the Crazy Horse cabaret. Opened in 1951 by Alain Bernardin on Avenue George V, Crazy Horse remains a well-known theater, specializing in burlesque. With its red velvet seating and lacquered wood walls, it has attracted a host of celebrities to its nightly shows.

At Versailles, the Crazy Horse dancers were swaddled in fluffy furs from Revillon, Christian Dior, Emanuel Ungaro, and Yves Saint Laurent. As the dancers wiggled and pranced, the furs slowly fell open to reveal naked bosoms and teasing glimpses of the tops of stockings.

"At the end, there was a long moment of almost complete nudity," wrote Enid Nemy for the *New York Times*. "The coats were flung open to reveal sparkling G-strings, but whether they were couture or not, no one said."[21]

The finale was Josephine Baker, who emerged onstage in her sequined, chocolate-colored catsuit, feather headdress, and fur. Accompanied by dancers choreographed by Dirk Sanders, she belted out an emphatic version of "Mon Pays et Paris." "I have two loves," she sang in French, "my country and Paris." The audience, at last, cheered, "Bravo!"

The French segment ran nearly two hours. The audience received its conclusion with warm applause.

"The entire French half of the evening was built around the glories of the past," declared Eugenia Sheppard. "Not even Nureyev dancing a pas de deux could have made the atmosphere any less than funereal."[22]

With the clock ticking toward midnight, the audience streamed from its seats for intermission, during which they drank champagne and whiskey. The American designers feared how their simple little show would compare to such a spectacle. "My God, they've buried us alive," Bill Blass fretted to his friend Fallon.[23]

But Blass misread the French audience. It was bored. "I knew it was a flop for France," Bergé says.[24]

The French presentation had been elaborate, ostentatious, plodding, and disconnected. "It was beautiful but it was not the point," Grumbach recalls. "What they showed was fabulous, but the spectators were just in a mood to have champagne and look at something."[25]

After the short and blessedly boozy intermission, it was time for the second act.

"By the time the crowd filtered back to their velvet seats they were revved up for the American show," wrote Jonathan Randal in the *Washington Post*.

Entertainers will often talk about the perils of being overrehearsed, that it purges any sense of spontaneity and serendipity from a performance. The Americans had nothing to worry about in that regard. Their dress rehearsal had been cursory at best.

Liza Minnelli, wearing Halston's gray wide-legged trousers and camel turtleneck, with a red sweater draped around her neck and a fedora atop her head, once again pep-talked the models toward confidence for the opening number, the rewritten "Bonjour, Paris."

"I'm going to run out onstage and hit the first note and you run out behind me," Minnelli told the models. "The more natural it looks the better—just like people on the street seeing the Eiffel Tower for the first time. Tap each other on the shoulder; you're not modeling, you're acting. Make it look as natural as possible."[26]

The models trotted out after her in a panoply of quintessential American sportswear contributed by all the participating designers, all in shades of beige: pea coats, trench coats, pleated skirts, pullover sweaters, shirtwaist dresses with their collars popped, easy trousers, and hats—broad brimmed, tipped to the side, pulled snug over their ears. The only backdrop was Joe Eula's last-minute sketch of the Eiffel Tower. As Minnelli hit the final notes, Fallon heard the audience applaud. He heard cheers. Minnelli came racing backstage. "My God," she exclaimed, "we got them."

Now, the trick was not to lose them.

Anne Klein was up first. The designer put model Barbara Jackson in a beige leotard with cap sleeves—little more than a bathing suit, really. "She had me lead the group [of models] downstage. She wanted me to run down toward the audience, and then she said, 'Kick your leg up!' She wanted people to just see all legs," recalls Jackson. "I wasn't as flamboyant as Pat or Billie. I had a little funky quality to my walk. I would come out with a big grin on my face—happy to be there. I was *very* happy to be there. *Ebony* Fashion Fair was my training ground and it was more entertainment and not just showing fashion. . . . You just wanted to walk to the beat of that music and flip your hair."[27]

It was quite a start for the Americans.

Klein's so-called Africa collection included black shirts, pleated skirts with abstracted elephant prints, djellabas, loose-fitting shirtdresses with dropped shoulders, and sexy two-piece dresses in beige with coordinating turbans. While the French models had moved with regal, self-conscious slowness, hands on hips, making precise pivot turns, the Americans were moving to the rhythms of prerecorded contemporary music. Klein used the soundtrack from *Scorpio Rising*, a 1963 cult film about gay, Nazi biker culture that incorporated early rock and roll music to tell its story. The music included songs by Elvis Presley, Martha Reeves and the Vandellas, and Ray Charles, artists embedded in our popular culture.

Kay Thompson had insisted that the models move at top speed. "Zoom, zoom, zoom! One, two, three! It was completely different from any kind of show," says Enid Nemy.[28]

Originally, each designer had planned to show seventy-odd looks, but Blass forcefully argued for ruthless editing, believing a few well-chosen garments would have a bigger impact. Still, even with only about twenty looks each, that was at least 100 entrances. The models had to make whiplash-fast changes with the help of a few assistants—many of them amateurs recruited for the evening. Nicole Fischelis was a twenty-one-year-old French kid working in the Paris buying office of Saks Fifth Avenue when one of the store's executives enlisted her help getting the models dressed. "I couldn't say no," Fischelis remembers. "To be in Versailles and to be backstage and have a view of what was going on—it was a big coup."[29]

The backstage area was expansive, but it was crowded and dark. Between the French and Americans, there were close to three hundred stagehands, models, and assistants passing through. Donna Karan was backstage, too, six months pregnant and so overwhelmed by the stress of overseeing Anne Klein's models that she started having what she described as "pre-labor contractions." In particular, she had to get Billie Blair out of one garment and into the next. Pronto. "She walked off with one arm still onstage and I was dressing the other arm," Karan says.

"Literally half of me was being undressed and half was dressed," Blair says. "Things moved so quickly; when you finished a passage, right offstage they're standing there with the next garment."

"There were no zippers," Karan says. "You pulled the clothes on."[30]

It only worked because the clothes were simple. Unlike the French styles, with elaborate hooks and eyes that practically required a lady-in-waiting to fasten, the American clothes were designed for a quick-moving, independent woman. This was fashion's future in the wings of the Théâtre Gabriel: a woman getting dressed fast and furiously.

Klein got the American segment off to a rousing start. It wasn't the clothes that made everyone snap to attention. Klein didn't design show-stoppers. Grace Mirabella, then the editor of *Vogue*, attended the show and described them as "Any Woman's" kind of clothes. People didn't remember or take note of the look of the garments, but they couldn't forget their attitude—and that of the models. They were snappy.

Burrows was up next. The French, with their couture models, had shown beautiful clothes worn by restrained women. Burrows was about to set those women free.

He and Charles Tracy had choreographed the entire segment in a matter of minutes. Each model walked out individually wearing one of Burrows's wildly colorful, body-conscious matte jersey gowns. There were halter gowns that hung from the neck by little more than a thread. Others were pieced together from a rainbow of colored jersey so that they exploded like fireworks on the models' bodies. The rippling lettuce hems gave the garments a sensual energy. With each successive woman, the train on the gown grew longer, until the penultimate gown appeared: Bethann Hardison's canary-yellow Paris homage with the endless train.

Burrows had managed to get all of his favorite mannequins for the show; the group was predominantly African American but not entirely. The music cued up: Al Green's now classic "Love and Happiness." Burrows eschewed disco music in favor of soul, with its irresistible rhythms, deeply felt groove, and sensuality.

Whenever Burrows had a fashion show, he loved to egg the models on, telling them to have fun and to cut loose. He did not alter that philosophy for the formality of Versailles. In fact, he encouraged them to *really* have fun.

Oozing attitude and confidence, Alva Chinn strutted out in a four-tiered toga of rippling jersey. She'd come from conservative Boston to New York in search of freedom and adventure. That path had brought her to France, and there she was on the stage at Versailles, in front of an audience of swells.

Strutting into the spotlight with her head thrown back, she had arrived at a place she had never imagined.

Amina Warsuma didn't feel nervous. She had worked in Europe before and she loved it. It felt like home. She always felt under scrutiny in the United States; she felt pressure to reach a version of perfection that she could never quite achieve. In France, she felt like she could be herself. She let the music guide her.

Norma Jean Darden, the Sarah Lawrence graduate, was swaddled in a long, color-blocked coat. She was pleased with herself and it showed. Karen Bjornson had been trying to figure out how best to show off her bubble-gum-pink dress with its multiple slinky tiers, each finished in a lettuce hem. She'd been watching Pat Cleveland's whirling charisma. The vitality was contagious. Bjornson, who was typically more reserved on the runway, was invigorated. The shy girl from the Midwest began to stride to the beat of the music.

The Americans were on a tear. They were in harmony with Al Green and dancing across the stage. They were controlling the clothes, bending them to their will. There was no way the clothes could be stiff or static, not as these limber young bodies put them to work.

In hindsight, the kind of extravagant movement that occurred on the Versailles stage was a caffeinated version of what was happening on the New York runways of young designers like Clovis Ruffin. It was akin to the sort of posing and posturing that was the hallmark of the *Ebony* Fashion Fair road show and continues unabashed at amateur fashion shows in the basements of black churches, at sororities on college campuses, and elsewhere. It represents a delight in the clothes, in the woman, and in the sheer pleasure of touting one's own glory.

In 1973, Burrows represented a moment when fashion was connecting to women in ways that were both emotional and practical. In one of Burrows's dresses, a woman's body was free. And she was on her own, for better or worse.

Each model had her moment on the runway, her chance to make herself known. At the end of her walk, she returned to the back of the stage and waited. One of the last models out was Bethann Hardison. She stalked out wearing that long, yellow woven dress—Burrows's homage to Paris couture that he had worked on for so long. "Here comes Bethann walking like a gangster!" Tracy says. "We all backed away!"

Hardison came out onstage, her androgynous figure rocking from side to side in a proud swagger. She arrived downstage and fixed the audience with a death stare. And then she swiveled, the train swirling out behind her, and walked away.

As the segment unfolded, Pat Cleveland was revving up backstage. She would be the last model to make an entrance in Burrows's segment. Her dress, with its angled, color-blocked bodice, had a long, full train, and she began spinning before she even stepped out from the wings. When she emerged into the light, she was spinning like a top. She kept going, faster and faster, with the fabric of her dress fanning out around her tiny frame. As she got closer to the edge of the stage, the entire audience held its breath. She was twirling so fast it seemed as though she might spin right off the stage. She came to the very edge.

And stopped. A perfect landing.

Then, as Burrows and Tracy had planned, all the models who had been posing at the back of the stage moved toward the front one last time en masse. They were an army of Technicolor creatures dripping in bold colors, swaddled in feathers, and styled like exotic birds. When they were as close to the audience as they could get without walking clear off the stage, they froze. And they posed.

"It was the beginning of voguing. They went crazy giving attitude," Tracy says.[31]

The audience shouted its approval, and programs flew into the air like confetti.

"He made such an impact. It was, 'Wow!' There was none of that old regime," Nemy says. "He was the breakout star [because of] everything about it: the models, the clothes. They were clothes that I liked a lot and wanted to wear."[32]

If the American designers were an Olympic relay team, Burrows had just given them a tremendous lead before passing the baton to Blass.

For his *Great Gatsby*–meets–Deauville collection, Blass relied on Cole Porter and re-created the glittering sophistication of the café society upon which he had built his business. His dresses fell to midcalf and had a retro glamour. They were not skin-baring and sexy. They were glamorous and aloof. His models wore little sculptural hats with elegant netting that shielded their eyes. Even his daytime suiting had a sheen of untouchable glamour, thanks to tailored wool jackets topping slim skirts dripping in sequins.

Blass also had Billie Blair.

Tom Fallon's only job—at least the only one that mattered—was getting Blair onstage. As he searched through the freeway of traffic that was calmly whirring backstage, he was frantic. "Where the fuck is Billie Blair?" Fallon called out to no one and everyone. Then he suddenly saw a flash of sequins and found her standing exactly in place. Everything was moving so quickly, she didn't even have time to reassure him as she raced to make her cue.

Blair re-created her star turn in Philadelphia with the marcel waves and the eerie resemblance to Josephine Baker. "When I put on a Bill Blass—the fur and the fabric and the fit—you couldn't tell me I wasn't the most elegant, complete woman. You couldn't tell me anything else."[33]

With the start of Halston's segment, the Americans moved full throttle into evening wear. The star designer had cast his portion of the show with his favorite models and his famous friends. The choreography that Kay Thompson, along with Joe Eula, had devised was simple but dramatic. The models positioned themselves onstage in pitch darkness. And as the spotlight landed on each woman, she was suddenly animated. She would show the clothes and then freeze. And her part of the stage would return to darkness and the spotlight would illuminate someone else.

Halston's music was the moody theme from the 1969 Luchino Visconti film *The Damned*—a film that continues to inspire designers, thanks to its sadomasochistic aesthetic overtones. The clothes were after-hours sexy. Some were elegant, others were nearly scandalous. Shirley Ferro wore a sleeveless gown that swooped seductively in its rear to reveal the curve of her lower back. Heidi Lieberfarb clutched the sides of a satiny, cocoon-shaped cape with a hemline that swept the floor. Nancy North was drenched in a sequined evening gown with a neckline that plummeted to her waist. Karen Bjornson's voluptuous dress was cut on the bias and benefitted from her theatrical pirouettes. Chris Royer sparkled in a pale green sequined gown. Elsa Peretti and Royer posed together in long gowns with smoke swirling upward, cigarettes tucked into long thin holders.

Alva Chinn's one-shoulder toga revealed her naked breast, with only a feather boa providing a hint of cover. Marisa Berenson's sequined gown was literally see-through. China Machado's gown—a term used loosely here—had no bodice, only a large feather fan set in silver that she held at her chest.

The choreography in Halston's portion of the show took full advantage of the wide, deep stage, creating a cinematic tableau to rival the best of Hollywood. He was relying on his boldface names to impress his audience. But Halston had made one miscalculation. While Berenson, whose maternal grandmother was the Paris-based designer Elsa Schiaparelli, was a recognizable part of the jet-setting crowd, the others on Halston's runway mostly were not. Their celebrity was lost on the predominantly French audience.

"They were next to the black girls who knew how to walk," says a still-gloating Oscar de la Renta. "And they were flat."[34]

Still, Halston had done enough to keep the audience entertained, which was no easy feat since it was now almost midnight.

In the finale of the American show, de la Renta had Blair playing the part of a seductive magician. Like the other Americans, de la Renta's rehearsal time had been modest at best and the attention he received from Thompson was distracted. He had been his own choreographer.

The result was hypnotic. His soundtrack was "Love's Theme," an instrumental soul-meets-disco song by Barry White's Love Unlimited Orchestra released in 1973. The music began with the rat-a-tat-tat tapping on cymbals and swelled into an easy dance rhythm with lush strings and insistent drums. And out walked Blair in a filmy green gown, a kind of glamorous caftan, to play fashion's mesmerizing magician.

She dramatically pulled a pink scarf out of her palm and five models emerged wearing pink chiffon gowns. She produced a lilac scarf and five models swanned across the stage cloaked in lilac.

Nicole Fischelis, finally able to take a breather from dressing models, peeked out from the wings and got a look at what was unfolding on stage. "The model was moving with so much grace," Fischelis recalls. "She was different from the French way. There was a ray of light above her and she was just moving her arms above her."[35]

The clothes were positively spare compared to de la Renta's current work, which is far more ornate. At Versailles, his gowns were ethereal. For his finale, the models filed out in a rainbow-colored, serpentine line— Chinn, Cleveland, Warsuma, North, and the rest. "At the end of my show, people are standing and clapping," de la Renta says. "In Paris, they'd never seen girls walking to music. No one had seen people move in that way. . . . There was some magic to it."[36]

Liza Minnelli returned to the stage to wrap everything up. She performed the title song from *Cabaret* in Halston's black cocktail dress, which was dripping with bugle beads. Then all the models joined her onstage, gorgeous in black dresses from all the designers, to sing "Au Revoir, Paris," which Thompson had written for the occasion. "Au revoir, Paris! Au revoir, mes amis!" sings de la Renta, as he remembers how he savored the final moments of the show.[37]

As the curtain came down, the audience of French elite jumped to their feet. Thunderous applause and wild bravos reverberated off the walls of the massive theater. The Americans were astounded.

"The indelible impression was the stunned reaction of the French. The French came out with the old glory backgrounds and those kinds of clothes. After that, the Americans came out with incredible youth and it was like night and day," remembers Nemy. "I didn't watch the show as much as the audience reaction. I'd seen the dress rehearsal. This was a mostly French audience. I couldn't believe what was happening.

"The French social people admitted it," Nemy says. *"Incroyable."*[38]

The audience was both vocal and physical, shouting their bravos from the great boxes of the Théâtre Gabriel and beating their hands in applause. "The American team won because of Kay Thompson," says Pierre Bergé. "It was like a show on Broadway, more or less. The Americans won, not because of the clothes, but because of the choreography."[39]

De la Renta also gives credit to the self-assurance and theatricality of the black models, and how their movement inspired the other women on the American stage. "What made our show was the black American models," de la Renta says. "There is zero question about that."[40]

Jean Fayard, of the French paper *Le Figaro*, wrote: "I would not be telling the truth if I did not say the Americans show their clothes one hundred times better than we. All their models are stars of the stage, each one more beautiful, more lithe, more pantherlike than the other. They march like soldiers and they turn like dancers. In brief, *la mode americaine* brought forth ovations from the cream of Paris who gathered at Versailles."[41]

Eleanor Lambert could not have been prouder. All those years of cajoling and campaigning, waiting and plotting, until finally this one magical, triumphant night. She was seventy years old, a long way from the midwestern kid who'd come to New York with $100. She'd transformed Seventh Avenue. And now, on this stage, American designers had conquered Paris.

"It was as if on this cold night, all the windows of Versailles had been blown open," Lambert cried.[42]

Nancy North (left) and Pat Cleveland arrive at Orly airport for their Versailles adventure. Copyright © 1973 BILL CUNNINGHAM

The Americans had only makeshift workrooms at Versailles. Copyright © 1973 BILL CUNNINGHAM

Karen Bjornson spins on stage in a glittering Halston evening gown. Copyright © 1973 BILL CUNNINGHAM

Alva Chinn, the young model with the conservative Boston upbringing, wears a revealing Halston gown. Copyright © 1973 BILL CUNNINGHAM

Stephen Burrows's presentation at Versailles was filled with his signature color, "lettuce" hemlines, and body conscious jersey. Copyright © 1973 BILL CUNNINGHAM

Ramona Saunders's feathered head-piece casts dramatic shadows across the Americans' spare set during the Stephen Burrows presentation. Copyright © 1973 BILL CUNNINGHAM

Models in colorful chiffon gowns parade in a serpentine line during the Oscar de la Renta presentation at Versailles. Copyright © 1973 BILL CUNNINGHAM

Top: Liza Minnelli, the American models, and the crew take their final bows at Versailles. Copylright © 1973 BILL CUNNINGHAM

Right: Billie Blair and Liza Minnelli hug as the Americans celebrate their dazzling performance. Copyright © 1973 BILL CUNNINGHAM

With her emotions surging, Lambert could only begin to process what had occurred. But she knew what she had seen. The programs flying into the air. The cheers. All for the very essence of American fashion: "So crisp and fresh and to the point. So alive!" Lambert marveled.[43]

After the show ended, guests rushed backstage with congratulations and kudos. Vicomtesse Jacqueline de Ribes was ready to break protocol and shop on the spot—and she did. Others simply wanted to revel in the startling display of expertise. Josephine Baker, who had changed into a see-through Yves Saint Laurent extravaganza with only black feathers camouflaging her breasts and the necessary parts, came looking for Billie Blair, her sweet doppelganger who had been the star of the American segment. "Where is she?" Baker asked Fallon.

"I knew who *she* was," Fallon says. "I went and got Billie. Josephine Baker reached out and touched her face. She said, 'I came to Paris in 1922. And you came to Paris tonight.'"[44]

The French designers were generous with their admiration, in part because it was the performance that had wowed them, not the clothes. The clothes were relatively simple; they were not feats of technical wizardry—not even the yellow dress that had so confounded Burrows. Instead, the magic was the way in which the presentation connected the clothes to contemporary life. The joie de vivre of American fashion had been made plain by the models. The clothes had been shown with personality, movement, and individuality. Givenchy and Saint Laurent were enamored with the way in which Blass and de la Renta had allowed the models—Blair in particular—to bring expressiveness to their work, something that was not part of the French fashion vocabulary. This fashion transformation on the runway was akin to shifting from formal oil on canvas to photography; there was spontaneity, realism, and beautiful imperfection.

Saint Laurent was especially delighted with Stephen Burrows because of the way he bridged the divide between the kinetic energy of contemporary street culture and the atelier. His clothes were alive because of the models. And his models seemed relevant and effervescent because of his clothes. The young man from Newark wasn't in love with French fashion, but a compliment was a compliment.

"To have Saint Laurent tell you, 'You make beautiful clothes,' it was enough for me. It was like the crowning moment of the trip," Burrows says. "Saint Laurent was the king of fashion at the time."

The experience, Burrows says, "made me more worldly. It made me more aware of who those other designers were. I didn't know before. I wasn't even concerned about it. It gave me confidence in my talent."[45]

After the show, the evening continued with a midnight buffet hosted by the Rothschilds, who covered the bill and even loaned a few of their own staff to help serve it. The multicourse dinner was held in the King's Apartments, accessed through the Hall of Mirrors, which was lined with footmen.

The Americans were once again wowed by the grandeur. Burrows, who had just celebrated his thirtieth birthday, eschewed his beloved fringe and mirrored polka-dot pants, trading them in for a traditional tuxedo. It was the first time he'd worn a tux since he'd accompanied a neighborhood girl to her high school prom at the New Jersey shore. His new business partners had made it for him.

Donna Karan couldn't stop staring at the haute cuisine and the formal settings. "The portions were this big," Karan recalls, making a teeny-tiny circle with her fingers. "There were twelve forks and thirteen spoons! It was very formal."[46]

All the key people who worked on the American show were invited to the dinner, not just the designers—even if some of the invitations had arrived at the last minute. Rodney Pearson, the sound engineer, didn't get his invitation until the afternoon of the show. He'd frantically run around Paris looking to rent a tuxedo, relying on his rudimentary, schoolboy French. But the last-minute dash had been worth it. "I don't usually get invited to the king's quarters!"[47]

When the Americans entered the dinner, they were greeted with a standing ovation, cheers, and applause. "I remember floating down in a Stephen Burrows gown with a long train that never ended. It was a rainbow, a butterfly dress. It was just fantastic," recalls Norma Jean Darden. "The French looked at us like we were creatures from outer space."[48]

The guests were seated at eighty-three tables, each covered in royal blue linens printed with gold fleurs-de-lis in an echo of the theater. The tables were scattered across five rooms within the apartments, which were illuminated only by warm, flickering light from white tapers in gold candelabras. There were endless rows of stemware. Each place setting included a large golden gift box of Revlon fragrances. The guests dined on a cold buffet of assorted pâtés, smoked fish, truffle-infused ham, chilled beef and duck, and desserts that reminded Darden of spun gold. It was all accompanied by a 1965 Château Lafite Rothschild and a 1969 Bollinger champagne. No one complained about the wine.

The guests sat shoulder to shoulder, draped in jewels and wrapped in feathers, a glamorous flock clucking in tight-jawed, purse-lipped Parisian French. Burrows, who didn't speak French, found his table, which thankfully was filled with American models. But Baron Guy de Rothschild, in choppy English, invited Burrows to his table, which was situated in a separate room and filled with the glamorous swans of the era. Burrows was curious to meet them; but there was no room at the baron's table for Roz Rubenstein, who was Burrows's close friend and date for the dinner.

"I was a little upset over having to leave Rozy like that. I just thought it was very rude. Suppose I was married, I couldn't bring my wife? I thought it was strange," Burrows says. Still, he went anyway, propelled by excitement and adrenaline. "I met Gloria Guinness and Jacqueline de Ribes and Mrs. Rothschild."[49]

There was no toast that evening, no formal pronouncement of a winner in the runway battle. There was just the insistent chatter of more than eight hundred guests and models against the background noise of unobtrusive music.

"The Americans were in seventh heaven, drunk with joy. They'd had a remarkable exhibition of clothes and creativity," recalls Enid Nemy. "The French were happy too, not miserable. The Americans knew what they had done."[50]

Journalist Pat Shelton, who died in 2013, was writing for the wire service United Press International. She finally left Versailles around 3 a.m., making her way back to Paris and the Hôtel Meurice so she could file a rough draft of her story by 5 a.m. Like so many of her colleagues, Shelton was there to report primarily on the social and cultural aspects of the event. But even in her just-the-facts description of the evening, she acknowledged the American success.

American and European millionaires with checkbooks, furs and jewels sipped champagne until dawn Thursday at the Paris party of the year in an effort to rescue the Versailles Palace from termites and a leaky roof.

The chateau was scarcely heated and women in strapless gowns shivered. One laughed. 'This gets us used to the oil shortage.' There was cold food, no telephones, few toilets.

For this one glorious evening the rich and the royal could forget about the oil crisis and the war, inflation and the sick dollar, and enjoy life as did the 17th century kings of France.

The ladies at the bash were a show in themselves. The sable, minks and ermines checked at the cloakroom could have carpeted the chateau ballroom wall to wall.

The French staged a two-hour show, a style parade by Givenchy and other Paris creators and entertainment by top stars from singer Charles Trenet to Russian ballet star Rudolph Nureyev.

After a champagne intermission, Zizi Jeanmaire drew lottery numbers from a basket and somebody won a Cardin gown, another guest a Dior fur. Nobody in this crowd squealed.

Then on came the first American fashion show ever staged in France—35 fast minutes of breezy music and dancing with Liza Minnelli singing "Cabaret" and mannequins showing the creations of U.S. designers Bill Blass, Halston, and others.

The audience called, "bravo."[51]

Nemy, a society and feature writer, was not expected or asked to focus on the clothes. But she couldn't ignore them in the story she filed: "It was generally acknowledged that the night belonged to 'les Americains.' The French show was held first, but from the moment Liza Minnelli strode on stage, belting out 'Bonjour Paris,' accompanied by models in a symphony of vanilla to brown tone, the blue and gold theater resounded with bravos and sustained applause."[52]

And finally, the great Eugenia Sheppard declared, "It was the robbery of all time."[53]

On that one snowy night at Versailles, the Americans shone brightly onstage, some as brilliantly as they ever would. Black models were a triumph, a thunderclap of glory. The tale unfolded in France, but the story is wholly American: a culmination of social shifts, racial conflict, politics, ambition, idealism, and magic.

Twelve

Success Stories and Cautionary Tales

A fter celebrating Thursday night at La Coupole, most of the victorious Americans returned to New York and plummeted back down to earth. Only a few of the models lingered in Paris. Anne Klein, thrilled by the success of the show and appreciative of the models' hard work, offered to cover the cost of a few additional days in the French capital. (It was a largesse that left Halston complaining that Klein was trying to win the models' loyalty.) "I stayed one or two other days," Barbara Jackson remembers. "I took in the city, rode the Métro, and ate the food. I did all the things I hadn't been able to do while we were working."[1]

In the afterglow of Versailles, there had been rumblings about taking the show to Las Vegas or mounting another extravaganza the following year, as a kind of rematch of a competition that was never meant to be a competition. But everyone knew it was just talk.

Eleanor Lambert dutifully sent out press releases to her usual media contacts. And she repeated the American portion of the show in New York, in far more sedate terms—no Minnelli, no voguing, no big finale—for editors who had not made the trip to Paris. But mostly, the stories had been written. There would be no more.

The hullabaloo, such as it was, was relatively contained. In 1973, there was no social media to take the tale of Versailles viral. Charles Tracy, whom Stephen Burrows and Halston had invited to photograph the show, had mostly been unable to do so. Marie-Hélène de Rothschild, in a bid to heighten the exclusivity, had been ruthless in controlling both the press and the photography. And Liza Minnelli's contract prohibited her performance from being filmed.

Wire photographers were there, however, and society ones, too. And the father of street style photography, Bill Cunningham, went to Versailles, where he stalked the backstage, dress rehearsals, and parties. He printed stacks of images and gave them to some of the models as keepsakes. Walter Cronkite even mentioned the show in a few sentences on the nightly news. And the home audience saw snippets of Josephine Baker performing in her glittering catsuit.

Mostly, though, the details of the event stayed within the insular world of fashion, where Americans savored their triumph. The designers saw themselves as scrappy underdogs who'd trounced the long-standing champions. They'd done themselves, their industry, and their country proud.

But with the success of the Americans at Versailles, fashion was nudged off its presumed path. The French designers continued their work in haute couture, but they also threw themselves into building their ready-to-wear businesses. There was no other way forward.

After Versailles, the French designers returned to their ateliers chastened but not broken—some substantively affected by the experience of showing alongside the American designers, others only subtly, if at all.

Versailles showed French designers how much excitement models could bring to clothes if they were permitted. Movement was an American signature, and it influenced the broader fashion landscape. Hubert de Givenchy was so inspired by what he'd seen on stage at the Théâtre Gabriel that he changed the look and feel of his own shows—changes that came with challenges.

"I went to California and I offered to some [black] models to come to Paris," he says. "I [tried to] make a *cabine* with only black models, but some clients refused to wear the [ensembles] presented by these models. But I still continued."[2]

He added popular music, turning the stilted, silent formality of couture into lively entertainment that, if not exactly au courant, was at least from this century. "It was important to allow [models] to move at their own rhythm," Givenchy says. "So I chose the music of Cole Porter. It was a different and a modern presentation."[3]

Over time, Paris has staunchly protected couture's traditional crafts through unions, private industry, and the educational system. Couture remains a much-admired aspect of French fashion, but it no longer fuels it.

Paris now welcomes and encourages wild creativity from all sources. It markets its fashion as intelligent provocation, brilliant absurdity, daring theatrics, and whimsy. Instead of speaking to an Old World social elite, it whispers sweet nothings to the New World's moneyed class. French designers haven't sent any pumpkin floats down the runway in decades, but there have been steam trains, faux blizzards, naked women, live wolves, and prancing horses.

The industry has grown and changed, becoming more corporate. It's now more a handbag and shoe business rather than one that generates its profits from expensive, pretty frocks. But even its corporate titans like to define themselves as having a special appreciation and patience for the artistic soul, in addition to a talent for moving the merchandise. Even Bernard Arnault, the head of LVMH Moët Hennessy Louis Vuitton, the world's leading luxury conglomerate, says, "The designer must be completely free." He explains, "The creative process is, in a way, not very organized. An artist must be able to organize his day and sometimes you have a meeting organized and he does not show up because he has some other ideas. It is the same as in other areas, like music. They have another way of thinking."

It sounds nice, but he qualifies his open-mindedness, saying, "In fashion, in creativity, what really matters also is commercial success. We are not there to have dresses in a museum. We are there to make dresses used by as many customers as we can."[4]

Paris also has become far more international than it was in 1973. Some of the country's most venerable brands are in the hands of Italian, British, and even American designers now. When the founding designers sell their companies, retire, or pass away, it is rare that the French house will continue to be helmed by a French designer. Oscar de la Renta has designed haute couture for Balmain. Michael Kors led Céline. The historic house of Balenciaga hired the young American Alexander Wang as its creative director in 2012. And, most notably, Marc Jacobs transformed the storied Louis Vuitton into a dynamic, modern, influential, billion-dollar behemoth.

When Givenchy retired from the label that bears his name in 1995, it went through a period of disruption and reinvention that has become a rite of passage for once-revered French houses. The brand was acquired by LVMH and then cycled through British designers John Galliano and Alexander McQueen, and Welshman Julien Macdonald in the course of a decade. In 2005, the Italian designer Riccardo Tisci took up the reins. After a difficult start and several ready-to-wear collections that awkwardly wrestled with the restrained formality of the house, Tisci finally gave Givenchy a darkly romantic point of view that eventually won the affection of an array of Hollywood starlets—the "great beauties" of the modern era.

For the spring 2014 collection, Tisci found inspiration in Africa and Japan—a chaotic collision of cultures. His collection was dominated by draped jersey dresses in earthy hues, graphic prints, and a haughty ease. And in the models who wore sparkling face masks, created with painstakingly hand-applied crystals, one could recall the house's deep couture roots, although put to flashier purposes.

Christian Dior is now another brand controlled by Arnault. He acquired the fashion house in 1984, eleven years after Versailles, when he purchased the bankrupt Boussac textile company of which Dior was a subsidiary. At the time, Bohan was still at the creative helm, but he was producing dull, unremarkable collections. His restraint had devolved into blandness.

To Arnault, Bohan's dullness did not matter. He explains, "Dior is the most magic name in fashion in the world."[5] And he is not being the least bit hyperbolic.

Bohan stayed on until 1989, guiding the brand through fashion's most obnoxiously narcissistic decade with discretion and dignity, if not much energy. He was followed by the Italian designer Gianfranco Ferré, who was known for bold gestures—a dramatic collar, an oversized sleeve, an exaggerated cuff. After seven years, Ferré was out and, in 1996, Galliano was in. The British designer infused the house with his savvy shock factor, his historical romanticism, and his personal flamboyance. Galliano's runway bows, complete with his own costuming—from a pirate to a body builder—were worthy of Broadway. But he was cast out in 2011 after he slurred anti-Semitic insults to patrons in a Paris bar, for which he was later tried in French court and fined.

A few months after that debacle, Arnault expressed shock and sadness over Galliano's behavior. "I'm not trying to diminish the quality of the creativity of John," Arnault says. "But to behave like this is a shame. What can I say? It's really something that took us by surprise. It's a shame."[6]

The modernist Belgian designer Raf Simons replaced Galliano at Dior. He has sought to redefine haute couture for a new generation of women. Respectful of the house's signature silhouettes, its wasp-waisted New Look, its "Bar" jacket, he has streamlined it all, making the shapes easier to wear in a modern era.

For Yves Saint Laurent, Versailles only emphasized what the designer always knew: the energy of fashion lay in young people and popular culture. Saint Laurent was a fan of black models before Versailles, and his affection for them was only heightened afterward. "These women had a sense of movement and attitude," says Saint Laurent's former partner,

Pierre Bergé. "He hated the word 'elegance.' He hated the word 'chic.' He believed in style and attitude."[7]

By the time Saint Laurent died in 2008, he'd retired from haute couture and sold his company to Kering, or what was then called Gucci Group. Tom Ford stepped in as creative director, dividing his time between Saint Laurent and Gucci. After Ford's departure, Italian designer Stefano Pilati took over at Saint Laurent. (Frenchman Hedi Slimane was tapped to take over in March 2012.)

Although it has been a decade since Bergé was actively involved with the brand, he continues to globe-trot, maintaining the Saint Laurent legacy through the Pierre Bergé–Yves Saint Laurent Foundation. He was vocal in his disdain for Ford's work and was not keen on Pilati's either.

But Bergé has been admiring of Slimane's point of view. The fall 2013 collection, Slimane's debut at Yves Saint Laurent, was an homage to California grunge. The spring 2014 offerings, unveiled in an upper chamber of the Grand Palais, included sequin-studded dresses, lip-print one-shoulder party dresses, and riffs on the tuxedo done up in leather. It was anti-elegant, anti-chic, and anti–good taste. But it overflowed with devil-may-care attitude.

Pierre Cardin, Versailles's unapologetic futurist, continued expanding his ready-to-wear business. He became emblematic of fashion's obsession with licensing, a process by which firms pay a fee to the designer for the right to use his name on a host of products.

In 1978, the *Washington Post* covered the unveiling of a Cardin airplane. "It is the penultimate designer label status item, a $2.3 million executive jet, and Pierre Cardin was at Page Terminal Saturday to see his design and to dot the 'I' on his signature near the door," wrote Nina Hyde. "So the Cardin label is now on just about everything: fragrances and furniture, cars and bikes, chocolates and carpets, bathrooms and kitchens, clothes, of course, plus food, wine, and theater. Can there be anything else? Cardin can't think of what it might be, but of course there will be something else."[8]

Cardin, a diminutive man with white hair, continues to control his fashion business, although it now has little bearing on trends, the retail climate, or the manner in which contemporary women dress. But he is supremely wealthy and his holdings include Maxim's, which continues to host parties, as well as tour groups that come to see its art nouveau interior and Cardin's stash of antiques, which is housed upstairs.

Cardin spent several years engaged in an aesthetic fight with the citizens of Venice, Italy, where he had proposed the Palais Lumière: a contemporary skyscraper that was more than eight hundred feet tall. Locals responded with unmitigated disgust. It was an ostentatious trophy building of apartments, offices, and a fashion school. Critics declared it a blight. The critics won. Cardin abandoned the project in 2013.

While Cardin resolutely looks forward, he carefully preserves his history at the Musée Pierre Cardin in Saint-Ouen, a drab, working-class town north of Paris. The museum, situated on the broad Boulevard Victor Hugo, is housed in a former auto garage, just across from the French equivalent of a Home Depot. Covered in blue ceramic tiles, the building is a bright spot on a street dominated by gray concrete.

With its soaring glass ceiling, the museum is a proud monument to Cardin's lifetime of work. One can see the evolution of Cardin's aesthetic, from the bourgeois chic of his time at Christian Dior, where he worked as a tailor creating the New Look, to his jumpsuits, Nehru-collared jackets, big shoulders, miniskirts, sculptural hats, and disco medallions. His furniture, thick with lacquer, is also on display—many of its artisans came from Saint-Ouen. The totality of his accomplishments points toward a future of jetpacks and flying cars—a future that has yet to be.

Emanuel Ungaro also moved aggressively toward fashion's future, with ready-to-wear and menswear. The 1980s, when fashion was full of frilly ostentation, were especially in line with Ungaro's romanticism. His longtime client Lynn Wyatt said, "Emanuel puts a woman on a pedestal, and that's why I feel so feminine and romantic in any Ungaro gown."[9]

His work appeared on the cover of *Newsweek* in April 1988 under the headline THE HEAT IS ON: FASHION GOES FEMININE—AND UNGARO LEADS THE WAY. The Somali-born model Iman wears a short, white, strapless party dress festooned with black polka dots and with a bouquet of red roses tucked into the décolletage.

Of all the French design houses, Emanuel Ungaro had the most troubled transition, after the founder sold the company to Salvatore Ferragamo Spa in 1996. At the time, the business was a success—a rarefied design house sitting atop a lucrative base of licensing, thanks in no small part to businessman Henry Berghauer's early intervention. Following the sale, however, the house plunged into disarray as it was resold and designer after designer was hired, only to be fired or simply flee.

It finally hit its nadir on a Sunday afternoon in October 2009. The troubled actress Lindsay Lohan had been appointed artistic advisor to the brand by its desperate CEO, Mounir Moufarrige. She and chief designer Estrella Archs presented what could be argued was fashion's most ill-conceived collection ever to be unveiled under the auspices of the great Fédération Française de la Couture, du Prêt-à-Porter des Couturiers et des Créateurs de Mode. Relying on a retina-searing palette of shocking pink and safety orange, it included heart-shaped pasties.

The play for publicity, by any means necessary, registered like a death knell for the brand. The fashion press, so dispirited by the spectacle, could find no joy in the schadenfreude.

Several years later, in 2012, under the ownership of the Italian conglomerate Aeffe and with Fausto Puglisi as its creative director, Ungaro was still a mess—one that mortifies its namesake. In the fall of 2013, Puglisi presented a collection at the Chambre de Commerce et d'Industrie de Région Paris Île-de-France—a sober and dignified location for a brand that had become a near laughingstock within the industry. The show unfolded in a sequence of rooms with lofty ceilings, crystal chandeliers, and walls draped in tapestries. Massive French doors opened onto a manicured garden. Dominated by the pairings of teal, sea-foam green, and yellow with black, the collection made an argument for short, ruffled dresses, button-studded shorts, patch pockets, polka dots, and stripes. It was a long way from the sure-handed mix of prints for which the founder was so well known. There was none of his sophisticated, feminine sizzle. And there was nothing to indicate that at one time, Emanuel Ungaro had been rooted in the exacting standards of haute couture. It looked heartbreakingly cheap. But at least there were no pasties.

The success at Versailles brought the American designers newfound respect from the innermost circle of an insulated world. They had managed to overcome their own disorganization, petty grievances, and insecurities. And with a bit of luck that had the French overly confident and overdone, they had shown a small sliver of influential society that there was something unique and original about American style.

Although they didn't know it at the time, the audience at Versailles had witnessed a turning point in the broader culture's relationship to the fashion industry. In the hands of the French design establishment, fashion had always been an elevated form of creative expression for the social elite. For them, fashion emphasized rules, propriety, and order. The French designers doubled down on that philosophy with a spectacle befitting a royal court—not by accident, but by intent. And it was accompanied by all the stiffness, formality, discomfort, and remove of monarchical hierarchies.

The French performances were grand, but they were not contemporary. They celebrated history and tradition. They had nothing to do with the joyous spontaneity of *now* as was epitomized by the new conventions in dance, music, sexuality, and diversity. The French rhapsodized over the past. The Americans thrilled to the future.

The American designers' success was predicated not so much on style as on worldview. The modest American ready-to-wear that appeared alongside the exquisitely made French haute couture was not an aesthetic triumph. Could one of Stephen Burrows's barely-there little jersey dresses be such a thing? No. But it represented something fresh and compelling.

It symbolized a generational shift, a new way of living, a new kind of commerce, and a new understanding of self-definition and control.

Versailles didn't signal that America's off-the-rack garments were *better* than the French, which were crafted by the *petits mains* who'd learned their techniques over generations. Instead, the American success was proof that ready-to-wear was *good enough*. American fashion, and the women who wore it, did not have to aspire to perfection in order to be dynamic and alluring. Clothes could be practical, accessible, and simple. They could be *fun*. A woman could be free. She could be an individual.

Eleanor Lambert, the great "empress of fashion," as she was called, returned to New York and continued to work diligently on behalf of American designers. By 1993, Fashion Week had been reorganized by the CFDA as "7th on Sixth" and shows were centrally located in New York's Bryant Park. No longer were editors perched on little golden chairs in the elegance of the Plaza Hotel. Instead, they sat on bleachers under a big top.

Lambert continued to represent a host of clients, including Bill Blass. She nurtured young publicists, such as James LaForce, who went on to launch their own companies and promote another generation of designers. And Lambert continued to invite editors to her regular Fashion Week brunch.

Lambert died in 2003, at the age of one hundred, at her home on the Upper East Side of Manhattan. She was memorialized at the Metropolitan Museum of Art. Today, the CFDA bestows a Founder's Award in honor of Eleanor Lambert—a prize given to an individual who has made a unique and lasting impact on the industry. Winners have included photographers Irving Penn and Patrick Demarchelier, as well as retailers Joan Kaner, Rose Marie Bravo, Dawn Mello, and Kal Ruttenstein.

After their triumphs at Versailles, Oscar de la Renta and Bill Blass returned to New York freed from the insecurities built up over all those years of working in anonymity—copying Paris and being told that real fashion was born there and there alone. Anne Klein was relieved that she'd had the opportunity to present her work on a world stage and that it had been received with enthusiasm. Despite all the animosity, the arguing, and the frustration, she'd had a once-in-a-lifetime experience. But once she returned to New York, she had to face the difficult subject of her failing health. Halston had lived up to his own hype. He had not disappointed Norton Simon, his company's new owners. His future looked boundless.

And Stephen Burrows's world had expanded by an entire universe. Yves Saint Laurent and Hubert de Givenchy were no longer just names in a fashion school textbook; he'd met them, had been praised by them, and had even bested them. He came home more confident and sophisticated.

Their so-called Versailles victory didn't translate directly into new business opportunities for these five; but they were already on an upward trajectory. That's how they managed invitations to Versailles in the first place. The success was existential for the participants, bringing them to the realization that their different approach to style was not only viable, it had the possibility of thriving in an evolving world.

At Versailles, the French demonstrated how to connect fashion to the breadth of their own centuries-old culture, with its social stratification, accepted doctrine, and rigidity. But the Americans proved that personal showmanship and attitude trumped tradition and formality. To some degree, American style vanquished French substance. The Americans understood the true future of fashion: it was commercial, mass entertainment.

With the exception of de la Renta's, the businesses of the other Americans who shone so brightly at Versailles eventually faded. Today, they no longer are among the dynamic brands of the fashion industry. For Bill Blass and Anne Klein, the death of the founders was a blow from which the brands never fully recovered. Subsequent designers—long lists of them—couldn't redefine the companies' aesthetics in a changing world. Halston ultimately made terrible business decisions that began a domino effect leading to the collapse of his whole enterprise. And Stephen Burrows was never able to move beyond the peculiar circumstances of the era that invented him.

But for a time, they had been stars.

De la Renta's business flourished after Versailles. With input from Eliza Reed Bolen, his stepdaughter from his second marriage, after the death of Françoise, and the financial savvy of his son-in-law, Alex Bolen, his company grew and expanded, with its current estimated global sales in the vicinity of $600 million.[10] In 2012, he moved out of his original offices at 550 Seventh Avenue to expansive and airy new headquarters on West Forty-second Street, across from Bryant Park.

De la Renta remained as socially engaged as ever, whether through frequent dinners with well-connected friends and clients, charity balls, vacations in his beloved Dominican Republic, or via @oscarprgirl on Twitter, an account managed by his savvy communications director.

After a bout with cancer, he still stood tall, with broad shoulders and a sun-kissed complexion. He was terribly self-possessed, a splendid storyteller, a delicious gossip who would happily admit to his own bad behavior. He was attuned to the whims of modern style, able to satisfy his older, loyal customers as well as keep younger ones enthusiastic about the brand. He dressed, for example, Laura Bush as well as her daughter Jenna Bush Hager. Lally Weymouth, daughter of Katharine Graham, media mogul Oprah Winfrey, veteran journalist Barbara Walters, and stateswoman Hillary Clinton all wear his clothes. But so do young entertainers Rihanna and Nicki Minaj. Indeed, one of his dresses—a fuchsia cocktail dress with a billowing skirt—became a symbol of high-flying love and romance on an episode of *Sex and the City* when it was worn by star Sarah Jessica Parker during her character's affair with "the Russian."

There may be no other working designer who dressed such a diverse range of women, all while maintaining his signature high-society aesthetic. De la Renta's fundamental philosophy was always simple: women, no matter their age, want to look pretty. And he dutifully obliged with clothes that spark no controversy. Even if he, himself, occasionally did.

While de la Renta know how to cultivate a broad clientele in a more relaxed, democratic twenty-first century, he came of age when fashion had rules and society had order. And at a certain level in the social hierarchy—at the level of First Lady, for example—those rules matter. In a 2009 conversation with *Women's Wear Daily*, he expressed his disapproval of First Lady Michelle Obama's decision to wear a cardigan to a meeting with Queen Elizabeth II. "You don't," he declared definitively, "go to Buckingham Palace in a sweater."[11]

He was equally vocal and critical when she selected a dress by the British design house Alexander McQueen to host a state dinner for China. But unlike in the 1960s, when the American fashion unions bullied Jacqueline Kennedy into ending her love affair with French designers, de la Renta's comments were fodder for morning television, but little more. Perhaps de la Renta was right aesthetically, historically, and temperamentally, but it didn't matter. Michelle Obama wears what she wears, supporting American designers but refusing to be beholden to them or their arbitrary code of conduct.

De la Renta settled comfortably into the role of the sometimes grumpy, always charismatic éminence gris.

Bill Blass became a friend to First Ladies and a confidant to the first generation of independent dames. When he made a trip to Washington in 1981 for a charity fashion show benefitting the Phillips Collection, no less personages than President and First Lady Ronald and Nancy Reagan attended a cocktail reception in his honor before the $250-a-ticket gala. (They didn't stay for the show, which ultimately raised $49,000.) Blass was solid, safe, fully vetted glamour.

Toward the end of his life, he sold his company for $50 million and retired to his home in Connecticut. After his death from throat cancer in 2002, Bill Blass Ltd. went through years of wrenching spasms as it tried to recapture the jaunty essence of its founder while also pushing the company forward for a new generation of women whose idea of café society is monopolizing a table at Starbucks while logged on to the free Wi-Fi.

The company, which once had sales of $500 million through its own products and more than forty different licenses, went through a half-dozen designers in search of the right alchemy. The midwesterner Steven Slowik, whom Blass had personally approved, barely lasted a year. Lars Nilsson, who had trained in Europe, was fired the day after he showed his fall 2003 collection.

Michael Vollbracht, who was both a friend and colleague to Blass, lasted the longest. He created quietly elegant but decidedly mature looks meant to woo back former customers. He even brought back models from the 1970s, such as Pat Cleveland and Karen Bjornson, to walk the runway. At first, they charmed his audience. Cleveland minced her way down the runway as she used to do in the 1970s, twirling and back-stepping and teasing the guests, who whooped at her antics.

Vollbracht won over many of the customers who had defected. But he couldn't fight the prevailing winds of fashion that demanded charismatic designers, progressive aesthetics, celebrity endorsements, and hype. When Vollbracht repeated his retro model stunt the next season, the audience had lost patience. Most guests sat through the show rolling their eyes, willing Cleveland to just walk down the runway and get it over with.

In 2007, Vollbracht quit and returned to his previous life as an artist. The young New York–based designer Peter Som stepped on board the now sinking ship. Critics often compared Som's signature collection to the work of a young Blass. It displayed an Upper East Side reserve, a playful sense of color, and a strong commitment to tailoring. But by the time Som arrived, the company was in dire circumstances. It was too late. By 2008, the Bill Blass collection was dead.[12] Today, it's little more than licensed products such as watches and luggage.

The days after Anne Klein returned to New York from Versailles were chaotic. In short order, she received the diagnosis that her cancer had returned. She knew she was dying and she began preparing her company for the future.

Businessman Tomio Taki had just bought a significant stake in the brand.[13] Financially, it was on solid ground. Klein planned for her assistant Donna Karan to take the creative reigns, but Karan was unsure. She was recently married, pregnant, and she'd just seen her boss take a beating by colleagues at Versailles. She also didn't yet know how sick Klein was; no one wanted to upset her, she was more than six months pregnant.

As Karan waffled, Klein worked to buttress the creative team. She interviewed Louis Dell'Olio, a friend of Karan's since high school who had also attended Parsons with her. Dell'Olio and Karan had had conversations in the past about his working at Anne Klein—long before Klein's diagnosis made every decision urgent.

"Anne Klein and Co. was the jewel in the crown of American fashion," Dell'Olio recalls. "It was hot, hot, hot. They could do no wrong. It was really the place to be."

Klein had built a company in which the designer was queen. No decision was formal until she'd signed off on it—including her own replacement. In December, Dell'Olio arrived for his interview. Klein's appearance gave no indication that she was ill. "She was one of the strongest women I've ever known," Dell'Olio says. "I don't know many men or women who could do that and not just break down—interview someone to take over a company and you know you're going to die.

"I can't tell you [in] what high esteem I hold this woman."[14]

By the time Karan was ready to give birth, Klein was at Mount Sinai Hospital in grave condition. "I went into labor in the office," Karan says. "Anne's in one hospital; I'm in another.

"The office called and wanted to know: When are you coming back to work? I called the doctor and asked him, 'When can I go back to work?' He says a week, and they sent me home.

"They bring the entire company to the house. I think they're coming to see my baby! How nice!" Karan remembers. "One day, everyone is there. And Betty Hanson [one of the Anne Klein executives] picks up the phone. Every face goes blank. She said, 'Anne just died.'"

It was March 19, 1974, less than four months after Versailles.

"I said, 'I can't believe no one told me just how sick she really was!' They didn't want to tell me; they wanted me to finish the collection. The next day, the collection was supposed to open; instead, there was a funeral. Then I went to work the next day.

"If anybody had said this was going to happen to me, I'd have said, 'You're stark raving mad.'

"I've always thought about Versailles," Karan continues. "It was the turning point in my life. Versailles was the last time I was with Anne."[15]

At only twenty-five years old, Karan, working with Dell'Olio, kept the Anne Klein brand churning until 1984, when Taki and his business partner Frank Mori offered Karan financial backing to launch her own brand. It began with "seven easy pieces"—a pragmatic and feminine mix-and-match take on modern, professional sportswear and an unabashed reflection of Klein's personal philosophy about design.

"Everything I know about fashion," Karan says, "I learned from Anne: sportswear, the body, seven easy pieces."[16]

After Karan's departure, the Anne Klein collection continued on under Dell'Olio until 1993, but then started to slip into decline as other designers began to cycle through. First was Richard Tyler, who was a masterful tailor based in Los Angeles, but his sensibility was more Hollywood flash than businesslike. Then Patrick Robinson, who'd been a lead designer at Giorgio Armani in Milan, stepped in. But he was never able to give the collection enough personality to distinguish it from the now widespread competition.

Before its demise, the company helped usher in the era of bridge collections—modestly priced lines that took their style cues from the flagship brand. But in 1996, Taki and Mori closed the high-end collection, the part of the business that had represented the dynamic, sophisticated new professional woman on the Versailles stage. It had been losing money for years, but it had recently become the target of scathing press reviews. As it was no longer even a positive vehicle for publicity, the owners saw no reason to keep propping it up.

The company enjoyed a brief resuscitation under new owners, Jones Apparel Group, which hired iconoclastic designer Isabel Toledo to create a top-level collection. But in 2007, the company finally succumbed. It was folded into Jones Apparel, where, for six years, they produced $100 dresses and $200 suits before being sold to Sycamore Partners, a private equity firm, in 2013.

If Bill Blass and Anne Klein were slowly extinguished, Halston flamed out like a comet. Halston, who was so proud of the cachet associated with his name, became an enduring symbol of the professional disaster that can strike when a designer loses control of his brand. Whereas Halston had once been "an example of everything a designer could want," read a profile of him in the *New York Times*, he became "an example of everything a designer hopes to avoid."[17]

Halston came back to New York from Versailles full of bluster about how great he had been, how he'd lived up to his superstar billing. He was eagerly pressing onward, building a bigger and bigger brand, all the while luxuriating in the accoutrements of wealth and fame.

After Norton Simon purchased his company, Halston moved from East Sixty-eighth Street into princely offices in the new Olympic Tower on Fifth Avenue. There were limousines, bouquets of orchids, and a view of St. Patrick's Cathedral. There had always been designers who lived well, but Halston began to represent something different. His notoriety broke through the confining walls of the fashion industry and flooded into the popular culture. He was glossy, calculating, and a regular on the party scene, which by 1977 included the legendary club Studio 54.

Studio 54 became Halston's regular haunt. He shifted his work hours to accommodate his new social life. He'd stay out until four or five in the morning and, instead of arriving in his atelier by 8 a.m., he'd saunter in around noon.[18] Halston's reality was, in fact, the dream that his clothes evoked—sexy, glamorous, and unbridled.

Despite being part of a conglomerate, Halston wanted to have a hand in every product, whether it was a tunic, luggage, or perfume. As his company grew, his desire to micromanage became impossible; he was only clogging up the decision-making process. But Halston's business troubles went deeper than an obsessive attention to detail. The products became more diffuse, and in 1983 he agreed to launch a lower-priced collection for JCPenney.

Halston was not bullied into the JCPenney line by corporate money-men. He was enthusiastic about the project. He loved the idea of dressing America. Besides, it would add to his already fat bank account. But this was before high-end designers regularly dabbled in the mass market—before one-off collections for Target and H&M. Halston's longtime sup-porter Bergdorf Goodman, the snooty specialty store that had given him his start, dropped his signature collection once he signed on with JCPen-ney, sending a clear statement that the brand had lost its luster.

By then, as one corporate parent was swallowed by another, the Halston label was getting a new owner every six months. With each transition, Halston became a smaller, less-beloved fish in an ever-expanding pond. By 1984, it had become a division of Beatrice Foods, and the designer was shown the door. "The game plans had all changed and I was invited by them to leave the office, to leave Olympic Tower," he said. "So I left."[19]

He was never able to regain ownership of his trademark and never again designed professionally under his own name.

Halston left New York and moved to San Francisco, where he died of AIDS in 1990. He asked his family to auction the Rolls-Royce he'd pur-chased the year before and donate the proceeds to AIDS research.[20]

Since his death, the label has been in a near constant state of revival, with designers Randolph Duke, Kevan Hall, Bradley Bayou, Marco Za-nini, and Marios Schwab all attempting, unsuccessfully, to resuscitate it. It has also had myriad consultants, from celebrity stylist Rachel Zoe to actress Sarah Jessica Parker. No one has been able to return the once-celebrated fashion house to its glorious apogee. But starry-eyed investors continue to try.

Halston's truest legacy is in the designer Tom Ford. Ford, who was not only inspired by Halston's aesthetics but also crafted himself in a similar guise: as a matinee-idol designer, exuding the same unapologetic confidence and panache. Halston's personal costume was dominated by black turtlenecks and sunglasses; Ford prefers a black suit and a white dress shirt unbuttoned to the middle of a perfectly landscaped chest.

So much of Ford's work during his tenure as creative director of Gucci, from 1994 to 2004, recalled the slithering sexuality of Halston—most notably a collection of simple, white jersey gowns from fall 1996. When models Carolyn Murphy and Kate Moss walked Ford's Milan runway that season, every curve of the derriere, line of the leg, and delicate nipple was apparent, even though the garments themselves were relatively modest in cut. The models' skin glowed as if they'd just emerged from the hot scrum of a dance floor. A single spotlight followed them, and "Under the Influence of Love" played in the background. It was a track from the same 1973 Love Unlimited album that had played for the Americans at Versailles.

"If you're going to be a fashion designer and you're going to be relevant, you have to be part of the time. You also have to have a sense of history and pick up the spirit of those who came before you and then make it your own," Ford said during a 2012 talk at the 92nd Street Y in New York. "You can take a direct line from me to Halston, but you can take Halston back to Madeleine Vionnet."[21]

When Ford added Yves Saint Laurent to his workload in 1999, he did due diligence in researching the house's history. But his work continued to display a louche attitude that recalled the best of Halston.

While Ford was at Saint Laurent, the French dismissed him as a mere stylist—that old-fashioned word the French used to distinguish commercial dressmakers from couturiers. In truth, Ford *was* a commercial designer. He was American, after all. His expertise was not cutting and draping. It was in the equally complex and nuanced realm of seduction, of storytelling. In 2004, Ford left both Gucci and Saint Laurent. He directed the film *A Single Man*, for which actor Colin Firth was nominated for an Academy Award in 2010.

When Ford launched an eponymous women's collection in 2010, he debuted it in a style that Halston would have loved. He gathered his famous friends, from actress Julianne Moore to singer Beyoncé, to walk a mean-dering runway in his New York boutique in front of an audience of some one hundred journalists. Afterward, champagne corks popped and the crowd rushed to congratulate the designer. Amazingly, per Ford's demand, not a single image of the collection leaked to the public before he released photos several months later. The sex appeal, celebrity, and control of that event were pure Halston.

While other American brands faded in the years after their founders passed away, Stephen Burrows's company fizzled on his own watch.

Burrows internalized the Versailles experience, tucking it away in his memory. Unlike his friend Halston, he didn't use it to burnish his reputa-tion. Bragging wasn't in his nature. He shared a few stories about Versailles with friends, telling them about the majesty of the Théâtre Gabriel and the fancy candlelit dinner that followed the show. But Burrows's friends had no idea who the society ladies were; they were unimpressed by the European nobility. They did, however, relate to the sense of victory. "They understood the us-versus-them aspect of the event. *We kicked their asses.* That's what they responded to," Burrows says.[22]

The young designer didn't even bother mentioning the trip to his parents—not even his mother, who'd been so proud of him when he took up residence at Henri Bendel. "She wouldn't know the significance of such a thing," Burrows explains. "She wouldn't know what Versailles meant at all. I'd have to explain that to her." He didn't bother.

Burrows returned from Versailles with a new career waiting on Sev-enth Avenue, where he had opened his own business with ubiquitous in-vestors Ben Shaw and Guido de Natale. The next step was a fragrance, which he was preparing to create with the help of Max Factor. It was to be an answer to Charlie, the fragrance Revlon introduced in early 1973. In 1975, Burrows signed a contract for $50,000 plus royalties.[23] He was the first African American designer with a signature scent. Halston had helped him broker the deal.

After months of sampling possible scents, Max Factor settled on a juice with floral notes, undercurrents of lemon, and a hint of musk. "I liked it, but I liked something else even more because it smelled like a circus," Burrows remembers. "But they don't go with your favorite. They go with what tests well."[24]

He didn't care for the packaging either—a spherical bottle with a donut-shaped stopper. A stylized "S" was carved into the glass. He wanted something more offbeat, something asymmetrical, like what Max Factor had done for Halston. But the company had just gone through the wringer working with Halston on his fragrance. The demanding designer had spent close to a year digging in his heels, determined that his friend the jewelry designer Elsa Peretti would create his bottle. He refused to budge on his affection for her bean-shaped, asymmetrical flask with its off-center opening that defied the efficiency of standard production. "They'd had so much trouble with Halston's bottle, they didn't want to do it again," Burrows sighs.[25]

The result was a scent that was not Burrows's favorite, packaged in a bottle the designer didn't particularly like. Nonetheless, the fragrance, dubbed Stephen B., debuted in department stores and was a million-dollar hit. Advertisements featured a trio of models—including Jaclyn Smith, before her *Charlie's Angels* success—and a smaller image of the designer himself wearing a white suit and red shirt. The copy read: "Meet Stephen B.: the laughing, loving, dancing, fresh and freeing new fragrance from fashion designer Stephen Burrows."

Stephen B. was marketed as a prestige fragrance, and as Burrows traveled around the country promoting it, he was especially proud of its positioning. He may have bragged about wanting to dress the world, but every designer loves a little snob appeal. After a year, however, Max Factor started selling the fragrance to grocery stores and discounters, in search of a more diverse audience. It lost its panache, and Burrows became angry and frustrated. In the throes of endless contract battles over distribution with Max

Factor, he accepted a settlement of about $90,000. He didn't want to fight it out in court. He was done with his own fragrance. And by 1982, Stephen B. was dead.[26]

But Burrows had struggles even before the fragrance debacle. His clothing line had stopped selling. The manufacturing was off. The distributors didn't understand that his jersey dresses would stretch out of shape on hangers. They needed to be folded on shelves, a more time-consuming process and one that made it more difficult for consumers to see exactly what was being pitched to them. Burrows wouldn't make his frustrations heard because he didn't want an argument. He hated confrontations and avoided them at all costs. But he wasn't happy. He began to believe that his decision to move to Seventh Avenue was the cause of all his problems.

In 1976, he went back to Henri Bendel: all was forgiven. Once again he was a paid employee, but this time he was making twice the salary that had caused him to walk out. He was also a partner in the studio. His return was satisfying, though not as electrifying as when he'd first arrived there fresh from O Boutique.

When The Limited Inc. bought Bendel's in 1985, Burrows left again, and once more looked for success on Seventh Avenue. "I couldn't find partners I wanted to work with," he says. Finally, he closed his business. He designed costumes for the off-Broadway gospel musical *Mama, I Want to Sing!* which his old Fire Island cohort Vy Higginsen had cowritten and produced. And he relied on private clients: "Nice Jewish ladies from Fire Island who kept buying my things," he says. "I did a great cash business."[27]

Burrows spent much of the 1990s living quietly, designing a bed-and-breakfast in Harlem and caring for sick family members. The industry lost track of him.

Beginning in 2002, Burrows started making comeback attempts with regularity, each more disheartening than the one that preceded it. The boomerang kid bounced back to Henri Bendel, brought in by a new general manager, Ed Burstell, who welcomed him with a rollicking party during New York's Fashion Week. Burstell called Burrows out of the blue, inspired because what the designer had always done "dovetailed with what was going on in fashion," he says. "There's no denying the incredible talent that spans many, many years. Some of the things from the archive are just as timely today as then."[28]

The plan was for Burrows to once again be a designer in residence, selling the collection through Bendel's and wholesaling it to other retailers. But other retailers didn't bite. The shop closed within a year.

In the midst of his struggles, Burrows was introduced to John Robert Miller. He was an unapologetic Anglophile, a former Halston assistant, and a private-label designer for Bendel's. And, as it turned out, he was a true believer in Burrows's talent.

Miller, a sprawling, barrel-chested man with close-cropped blond hair, wanted to write Burrows's biography. Soon Miller became a near constant presence in Burrows's professional life and his work on the book, which was never finished, expanded into his acting as managing director of the company.

What Miller lacked in financial and marketing expertise, he made up for in devotion. While Burrows's friends privately expressed concern that Miller wasn't the man for the job of turning around a threadbare business, there was no one else to do it. Miller helped to organize fashion shows on shoestring budgets supplied by friends and sponsors. They were disorganized and chaotic, often with novice models who weren't up to the standards of the clothes. One season, Diane von Furstenberg, a friend, opened her New York City Meatpacking District studio to Burrows. The show drew longtime fans, but not much came of it.

In 2006, Burrows was presented with an extraordinary opportunity: a chance to return to Paris for the first time since Versailles. He was invited to present a spring 2007 collection at the Carrousel du Louvre, the subterranean warren of auditoriums attached to the famous museum. It wasn't a landmark event, but still, it was exciting.

Reliable pal Bethann Hardison helped Burrows and Miller organize the Paris show. Burrows wanted to recapture the magic of Versailles.

He encouraged his models to be creative and expressive with their movements. He wanted them to be advocates for his clothes.

When the show opened, the models, a diverse mix of young women, wore a pretty selection of jersey dresses in shades of raspberry, melon, grape, and lemon, all finished with his signature lettuce hem. They began clapping in unison as they marched down the runway. They flirted and twirled and smiled. But as Vollbracht had found when he borrowed from the past at Bill Blass, the effect was sweet nostalgia. It was old-fashioned. Models no longer carry on like that. They'd stopped smiling sometime around 1993, when Kate Moss and other grumpy, awkward waifs began to dominate the industry. There was no going back. Fashion leaves behind those who don't step lively, no matter how glorious their pasts.

The old guard of fashion editors, now retired, came to witness Burrows's return. They remembered how wonderfully innovative he had been. But the new crop of working editors from magazines such as *Vogue, Harper's Bazaar,* and *Elle,* those who had the power to push him back into the spotlight, did not attend. The rows of seats in the small auditorium reserved for the younger members of the American press remained empty. It didn't matter. The show looked terribly out of date—like a bit of fashion history from the 1970s. Instead of saving him, the models did Burrows a disservice.

In 2012, Burrows presented a collection at the Audi automotive showroom on Park Avenue, not far from Grand Central station. If ever there was a soulless place for a fashion show, this was it. The showroom was a bland, open space with late-model cars parked against the walls. A large window faced Park Avenue and armies of suit-and-tie drones passed by, oblivious to the fashion show going on inside.

But the backstage had a reassuring hustle and bustle as John Miller wrangled a few television camera crews and photographers who jockeyed to interview the designer and document the prep work. Two makeup artists and a pedicurist simultaneously groomed a young model from Senegal. With her ebony skin, shoulder-length hair, and gamine figure, she was a quintessential Burrows girl. And the designer, dressed in gray jeans and a black T-shirt, with his trusty fanny pack at his waist, moved to and fro giving directions and offering a preview of the collection from two rolling racks filled with clothes.

In the weeks leading up to the show, Burrows had signed a deal to produce a small dungaree collection with Raven Denim. The jeans were finished with red stitching, a reference to the red zigzag stitching he liked to use on his jersey dresses.

With a few words of encouragement to the models—*"Enjoy yourself!"*—the show began and the young women pranced out. They vamped in front of the showroom's expansive windows—once again, in the old way. And in the same way the models at his Paris show had seemed out of touch, so did those in New York. They were only doing what Burrows asked, but these girls were a long way from the generation of women of the 1970s who knew how to move with ease and confidence on a runway. These young models, only a few years from pubescence, could barely walk.

It seemed Burrows couldn't shake his affection for a decade of parties, nightlife, sexual abandon, and business deals built on a friendly nod and a shared acid trip. He was stuck in the past. No one could convince him to move on. He liked what he liked. More important, however, he had stopped going out. He was no longer embedded in popular culture the way he had been in his youth, the way even de la Renta still was. He knew what was going on in the fashion industry, and he watched other, younger designers, with little professional experience, find financial backing. He waited for someone to come to his rescue. And his friends enabled his acquiescent tendencies. "He's lovable. He's childlike," says Audrey Smaltz. The former *Ebony* fashion editor now runs her own backstage production business, the Ground Crew. "Whatever he asked me to do, I would do it and not even think about it."[29]

In 2012, Hardison stepped in again. She introduced Burrows to the Nigerian-born, London-based designer Duro Olowu, who was a longtime fan. Olowu's star was on the rise. He had smartly fostered relationships with a host of powerful fashion editors and retailers. They were enamored with Olowu's seventies tailoring, his easy caftans, and his urbane African sensibility, all of which had more than a hint of Burrows's signature color and ease.

Hardison and Olowu arranged for the influential Chicago retailer Ikram Goldman—the woman who served as fashion consigliere to Michelle Obama—to view a small, specially created Burrows collection. Goldman was an avid supporter of Olowu and had a reputation for getting behind up-and-coming designers and pushing them toward the light.

The group convened in Hardison's small downtown apartment: Burrows, Olowu, Goldman, and her associates. Two models quietly showed eight looks. Goldman bought five styles—a total of about fifteen pieces. She wanted them in black matte jersey, suggesting the small capsule collection be called "Stephen Burrows Black."

"It was nice to work with her," Burrows reflects. "I liked her idea of a black label. . . . It was simplified, and I like black. It was me, but modern and sleek."[30]

Burrows had finally caught a break. He began to sniff around for financing. A designer used to be able to launch a business with $50,000 and the support of a few friends. Today, that money, Burrows says, would be gone in an hour. In his search for funding, he came up empty and the capsule collection fizzled after that one season.

Burrows is loath to suggest that race either limited or propelled his success. He was never the sort of designer to stand on a soapbox and make an argument for diversity. He believed that through his talent he could make the strongest argument for the merits of black designers.

And for a long time, he did just that. In the generation after Versailles, when racial détente seemed tenuous and fragile, but possible, people were primed to celebrate black models and designers. They did so with enthusiasm and sincerity. And Burrows's achievements opened doors for other black designers whose aesthetics were as diverse as the designers themselves.

Willi Smith, who died in 1987, and Patrick Kelly, who passed away in 1990, both walked through doors Burrows helped open. Smith's Williwear was a true sportswear collection, already a success when the designer received a burst of attention for creating the groomsmen's attire for Caroline Kennedy's wedding to Edwin Schlossberg. Kelly, an overall-wearing Mississippian who built his career on the runways of Paris, was a rebel who reclaimed racist imagery for his own purposes and helped to defuse it of its power to hurt.

Other black designers followed: Jeffrey Banks, Gordon Henderson, Tracy Reese, Olowu. They built signature brands with varying degrees of success. Others, like Edward Wilkerson, who honed his skills working with Donna Karan, have walked tall behind the scenes.

But no other black designer has matched Burrows's series of milestones. He remains the only black designer to have had a signature fragrance, entertainers and sports stars excepted. Since 1981, when the Council of Fashion Designers of America became the preeminent Seventh Avenue organization, the only black person to be honored with the women's wear or menswear designer of the year trophy has been entertainer Sean Combs, aka Puff Daddy, P. Diddy, Diddy, et al., for his Sean John menswear line in 2004. Burrows received a special citation from the board of directors in 2006. Then in 2014, Public School, codesigned by Maxwell Osborne, who is black, won the CFDA's menswear designer of the year award.

Still, more black designers were honored during the days of the Coty Awards than by the modern CFDAs.

Burrows rarely speaks of unfairness, burdens, or hurdles. When he does, the remarks come abruptly, almost as if they have escaped despite his best efforts to contain them. Once, during a particularly exasperating professional moment, he wondered aloud why wealthy black investors focused on white designers instead of struggling black ones. He was speaking specifically about Combs, who after starting his own fashion brand, sank money into the company of Zac Posen, an up-and-coming white designer who was the beneficiary of outsize media attention.

Burrows seems baffled by his inability to regain his footing within the fashion industry. But he never admits defeat. He remains convinced of possibilities just over the horizon.

In October 2012, John Robert Miller died from heart failure. He was only fifty-seven. It was a deeply emotional blow to Burrows. Soon after, Burrows closed his studio.

Several months later, Burrows was honored in an event at the Museum of the City of New York. *When Fashion Danced* opened on March 21, 2013. The first-floor gallery of the museum was packed with well-wishers: members of the fashion community, old friends, folks who had admired Burrows's work from afar, people who had more than a few of his jersey dresses in the back of their closets. Younger designers came to pay homage to a man whose work had inspired their own sense of aesthetics, their own understanding of what it meant to welcome the influence of the street, of music, of life, into the atelier.

Burrows's old cohorts from Henri Bendel were there, too, proud of how contemporary so many of the garments looked even though they were more than forty years old. The jersey, the color-blocking, the playfulness, the sexiness, it all spoke to modern times. Burrows's garments called to mind the work of Marc Jacobs, Anna Sui, Lisa Perry, Costello Tagliapietra, and a host of other designers and labels. Burrows's career may not have endured, but his work had.

His model friends were there, as well. Pat Cleveland danced around for the cameras, her body so thin it looked as if a nudge could break it in half. Now a yoga instructor, Alva Chinn was there to offer her pal a hug. Karen Bjornson-Macdonald, who'd gotten married and raised a family in Connecticut, beamed with pride over Burrows's talent and over having been there when it was in full bloom. Iman donned a color-blocked Burrows gown that he'd made for her years earlier. It looked magnificent on her curves. Bethann Hardison, collaborator and protector, was by his side throughout the dinner. So was the photographer Charles Tracy, whose images from the 1960s and '70s filled the pages of the exhibition catalog. And Burrows's buddy Daniela Morera, who he'd met one night many years ago in a limousine headed to yet another party, wrote a celebratory essay for it.

The evening of the opening, the retailer Target, which sponsored the exhibition, hosted a small dinner to toast Burrows. It wasn't the King's Apartments at Versailles, but still, it was a breathtaking setting. A single long table, running the length of a narrow white gallery on the upper level of the museum, was decorated with a rainbow of flowers, their green stems coiled into clear glass vases. Everyone dined on Maine lobster, black bass, and honey-lacquered duck. Ginger tarts and chocolate ganache followed. And of course, there was plenty of wine.

Throughout dinner, a soundtrack of Burrows's favorite songs played, but mostly the room was warm with the chirping of old friends and young fans. Hardison thanked everyone for coming and expressed her deep affection for Burrows. There was much laughter as Iman and Tracy kibitzed from their seats. And then all eyes shifted to the man of the hour. But Burrows did not make a speech. He said nothing at all.

If the American designers returned to New York more confident and secure in their work, the models came home positively triumphant. The one thing everyone agreed on after Versailles was that the models' showmanship had altered expectations of what a fashion presentation should and could be. And it was the black models at Versailles who were most responsible for the transformation of those expectations.

For them, the road to Versailles had been cleared by a social storm in the United States—an upheaval in which fashion played an active role. The black models had been building their careers, leaping all sorts of hurdles and wrestling with cultural stereotypes. Many of them had been given their breaks by men like Clovis Ruffin and Burrows who liked to unleash movement and energy on the runway. They had been inspired by dancers, musicians, and performers, by the *Ebony* Fashion Fair, and by the rhythm of the times. They were denizens of the New York discos full of gay men, black men, and women searching for liberation. They danced down the runways because that was a style that felt natural to them; it was encouraged; it was allowed because their very presence broke so many rules that the rules simply ceased to apply. And their exuberant presence influenced their white counterparts.

At Versailles, Charlene Dash, Alva Chinn, Norma Jean Darden, and the others were not aiming to make a political statement. They were not trying to stand out as exotic or representing some kind of "otherness." They wanted to be accepted on their own terms; but they also wanted to be part of the fashion community. The Kerner Report had been clear and true. What the models—what the "Negro"—wanted was simple: "fuller participation in the social order and the material benefits enjoyed by the majority of American citizens."[31]

The black models did not see Versailles as a triumph for their race because there were more than black models onstage. For them, it was a victory for Americans. And that meant more than anything else. That's all they ever wanted it to be. Even for someone like Bethann Hardison, the born rebel, Versailles was not about being black. It was about being good.

Their presence anywhere, however, then as now, raises the subject of race—how far society has progressed toward equality, how segregated society remains, and how fearful people are about continued disenfranchisement. Those in the audience did not simply see American models; they saw models of color. The designers did, too. So did the media. The women were described as "light-skinned blacks," "the black model," and so on. It didn't matter how the models saw themselves. For anyone who knew anything about what happened at Versailles, it wasn't merely an American success story. There was a separate African American one, too. These models were still categorically, uniquely, exotically black. They had yet to be just great girls.

The show elevated the profile of black models into the stratosphere. The Versailles models didn't reinvent themselves for their trip across the ocean. In France, they were the models that they had always been. But contrasted with their European counterparts, who moved with such precise and precious calm, the Americans seemed vivid and alive. The difference wasn't just obvious; it begged for judgment. And the media obliged.

Explained writer Phyllis Feldkamp in a story for the *Christian Science Monitor* in 1974:

New York models are dancier. They move faster than their Paris counterparts and have a greater knack for dramatizing what they are wearing. Many of the New York girls whose profession it is to show clothes have real star quality—as Parisians discovered when the New York models brought down the house at the Franco-American fashion gala last November in the palace of Versailles.

Some of the girls—like Billie Blair, the reed-slim, dark-skinned beauty who moves like quicksilver—are superstars who hold their audience with disciplined performances on the runway. Hers were the kind of theatrics that brought New York's big looks to life and put the clothes across more effectively than was the case in Paris.

New York's black models have been transforming the traditional stilted walk and frozen-face manner of presenting clothes by strutting or gliding sinuously like dancers to dramatize the fashions they are displaying.[32]

The designers were not longing for the models' static beauty, their richly colored skin, or their bone structure. Their beauty in repose did not drive their popularity. It was the swivel of their hips and the swing of their shoulders that propelled them toward success.

Versailles opened all sorts of doors. In the 1970s, the trickle of black models into the business that had begun as a matter of social engineering became a steady stream. Black women enjoyed solid careers. They became stars in the industry and racked up landmark moments with a dynamic presence that was in demand for nearly a generation.

In 1974, Beverly Johnson became the first black model to appear on the cover of American *Vogue*. That year, she made an estimated $100,000. Two years after her notable cover, Iman stepped into the spotlight and soon pushed black models into the "super" realm. Her enduring career as a model, and now as a businesswoman, began with an elaborate discovery myth that described her as an exotic, almost wild creature plucked from the African veldt by the photographer Peter Beard. In a boring truth, Iman was actually a diplomat's daughter.

The black models of Versailles also stayed busy, even if they did not become brand names. When Jennifer Brice returned to New York, Studio 54 became one of her regular haunts. And she participated in one of the most eccentrically elaborate weddings of the twentieth century: the union of singer Sly Stone and model Kathy Silva in 1974. The couple said their vows onstage at Madison Square Garden before twenty-three thousand fans. Brice was one of a dozen models dressed in black and carrying golden palm fronds who walked in the ceremony. Her dress was by Halston; she'd been chosen for the show by Stephen Burrows. She was not paid. "You get popular first," she said at the time, "then rich."[33] Brice left New York in 1987. She had not gotten rich. By 1994 she'd settled in Atlanta, a married woman with four children, one of whom she lost to cancer.

Alva Chinn moved up to being a $2,500-a-day model in New York and Europe.[34] Charlene Dash and Norma Jean Darden continued to work the runway for nearly a decade. Dash retired in New York and settled into life as a bureaucrat in the city government. Darden, who was left with a significant scar after misdiagnosed peritonitis, left fashion and built a restaurant and catering business, Spoonbread, Inc., based on family recipes. She successfully operates from a home base in Harlem.

Pat Cleveland continued to build her career in New York, but really came into her own in Europe. She was a star there and continues to occasionally walk a runway even as her daughter Anna van Ravenstein carries on the tradition. Amina Warsuma moved to Los Angeles and tried her hand at acting and filmmaking. Barbara Jackson eventually moved to Los Angeles, as well, where her first husband was in the music business. She modeled until the birth of her second child. She's now remarried and a content grandmother who volunteers with Dress for Success. Ramona Saunders passed away in the mid-eighties. The circumstances of her death remain stubbornly cloudy, but Burrows remembers that she had returned to Brazil.

The great Billie Blair stayed in New York for two decades. In her younger years, no one was counseling her on the wisdom of stashing money away for retirement. All she knew was that she was getting a check and it was hers to spend at a time when it was good to be young, in New York, and flush with cash. She lived the fast life at nightclubs for many years before finally burning out.

In 1987, she returned home to Flint, which had become a depressed, half-empty city—dull and nearly defeated. She enrolled at Saginaw Valley State University intent on becoming a parish nurse, a registered nurse who incorporates religion and spirituality into her practice. But she only lasted about a year; it was spreading the word of God that interested her, not organic chemistry. The model was called to minister.

"It was around October 7, 1987, when I knew that God had a calling on my life," Blair says. "I was in Detroit at Straight Gate [International] Church," which is nondenominational.

"I saw a silhouette of Jesus in a vision. I was crying. I had my hands lifted and my eyes were closed and I talked to Him. I wanted the truth," Blair says. "I saw the shape of His head and shoulders. There were no blue eyes; there was no flat nose. I saw a silhouette and beams of light from around His head.

"And there He was. He just covered me," Blair says. "It was quick. Quick as quick! Amen."[35] It was not a conversion as gripping as that of Saul on the road to Damascus. But for Blair, it was a moment of clarity, reassurance, and rebirth.

Blair no longer has the angular, wispy silhouette of her youth. Time has allowed her figure to become more solid. But she remains a tall, slender woman with a sleek blond bob, who relies on a pair of stylishly rectangular glasses for reading. She has retained the effervescence that designers found so compelling during her heyday. She speaks in emotional fragments, sharing fully realized and cherished memories and deeply felt mini-sermons about the power of God and the richness of His blessings.

As if moved by the memory of her sacred conversion vision, as if possessed by the Holy Spirit—or believing herself to be—Blair murmurs in an unintelligible tongue. She tilts her lineless face to the heavens, extends her arms in supplication, and speaks aloud in the prophetic tradition. Without a hint of self-consciousness, Blair engages in a public communion with her God.

Raised in the Baptist church, Blair had always been spiritual. She'd regularly recite a quiet prayer before every fashion show. Evangelism, however, came as a revelation. It gave her a new purpose and a soft landing after a high-flying career. Blair was ordained as a minister in 1995 by the nondenominational Faith Tech Ministries Bible School.[36] She followed friends to Defiance, Ohio, where she manages on a fixed income of Social Security benefits.

"The first time I had to pay taxes, my mother and father had worked and they got money back. I thought I was going to get money back, but they said I had to pay. I was sick for three days!" Blair says. "I appreciate the models who came along later and did something and took this business to another level, like Tyra [Banks]. There are some others. Maybe not as well known. Another model has a vintage store. A lot of little businesswomen came out of this. My business? I'm about my Father's business. Ministry."[37]

Defiance is an incongruous place for a former model, particularly an African American one without any familial connections, to spend her retirement years. With a population of about seventeen thousand, plus forty thousand more who live in the county, Defiance is a deeply conservative, working-class community with an economy ruled by General Motors and a cultural life dominated by Catholicism and Republicans. It is 88 percent white, with an African American population of less than 4 percent.

Blair often feels isolated there and at odds with neighbors who have led far more constricted lives than hers. And she sees racism in the slights and unkind words from some of them. She stays because it is too expensive to move and because the town is home to Defiance College, a small liberal arts school with about one thousand students. The school is affiliated with the United Church of Christ, a denomination that believes in prophetic worship. It's where Blair is studying theology. "Eventually I'll have a PhD," she says. "I'll be a theologian."[38]

O n into the 1980s and early '90s, black models walked the runway with gusto and flair. People knew their names, and in some cases they were more famous than the designers whose clothes they wore. Almost all of these black women had a distinctive runway style. The caricature of the high-stepping model, whose hips whiplashed violently from side to side as one foot crossed the other in a death-defying act of balance, was born during this time.

This was the era that brought a teenage Naomi Campbell to the fore. She was a striking Londoner with close-cropped hair and dance training. She walked the runway like she was personally hunting her evening meal. With her distinctive strut, Campbell solidified her place in history as part of a triumvirate of models with Linda Evangelista and Christy Turlington, women who dominated the runways, ratcheted up the pay scale, and became celebrities beyond the catwalk.

Around that same time, Tyra Banks bounced, sashayed, and flirted down the runway. Her stage presence was so compelling that the fashion industry welcomed her pinup-girl cleavage, which would traditionally have disqualified her from a career that demands that a woman have the figure of a twelve-year-old boy. Banks became the first African American *Sports Illustrated* swimsuit-cover model in 1996.

And Detroit's Veronica Webb swanned down the international runways, maintaining an expression of silent amusement, as if she was just a little too sophisticated for the catwalk silliness. By 1992, Revlon had signed Webb to a cosmetics deal, making her the first African American model to represent a makeup brand.

In the 1980s and '90s, designers didn't just encourage models to emote, they treated their runway presentations like dance parties. In the early 1990s, some of the hottest invitations were those for the shows of designers like Todd Oldham and Anna Sui who used popular music to create a joyful energy. Beside their runways, the crowd shrieked with delight, encouraging the models to really whoop it up, to really strut. People expected to see the clothes, but they came to see the girls—many of whom were black—and the antics, too. They came for contemporary entertainment.

It's no surprise that during this period a black drag queen named Ru-Paul rose to fame. She served as a hyperbolic version of the black runway diva. RuPaul is part caricature, part adoring fan, part savvy entrepreneur. Her style of exaggerated strutting remains a beloved trope of neighborhood drag queens, *Mahogany* fanatics, schoolgirls, and amateur models "working it" on makeshift catwalks in fellowship halls, university auditoriums, and hotel ballrooms.

Black models succeeded and thrived in ways only fantasized about back in the 1970s. They became cultural stars and crossed boundaries. Bethann Hardison, who retired from modeling and opened her own talent agency in 1984, was a player in many of these success stories—nurturing, supporting, and in some cases helping to broker contracts. Thanks to her natural temperament and upbringing, Hardison became a leading activist for diversity within the fashion industry. And in 1989, she cofounded the Black Girls Coalition to celebrate the successes of black women in fashion and to organize their collective good fortune for philanthropic purposes.

But her greatest industry accomplishment might well have been the breakthrough success of a black *male* model she managed: Tyson Beckford.

In 1993, designer Ralph Lauren signed Beckford as the face of his Polo men's division. In doing so, Lauren shrewdly exploited the frisson of race as aesthetic, identity, and stereotype. With his almond-shaped eyes, high cheekbones, and dark skin, Beckford was a distinctly black man who was unabashedly muscular and macho. His presence was freighted with prejudices yearning to define him as dangerous, thuggish, and uncivilized. Lauren, at the height of his fame as a designer of preppy fashion, dressed Beckford in everything from anoraks to tailored suits—the most idealized versions of the Establishment's uniforms for work and play. In doing so, he created powerful images that upended cultural ideals regarding privilege and power.

But despite his daring, Lauren only exploited simmering racial tensions. He didn't defuse them. As Lauren went on to win countless awards and become a prince of Wall Street with a stratospheric initial public offering, the broader culture had yet to be fully convinced of a wider definition of the aesthetics of American success and beauty. Lauren's company would be accused of racial discrimination in its treatment of employees more than once in successive years. Incidents would flare and the company would tamp them down like a stubborn fire.

By the mid-nineties, the industry's affection for black models began to wane. Contemporary designers, in both New York and Paris, mostly stopped hiring models based on their ability to show the clothes—to sell them through gesture and personality. Designers wanted a new runway aesthetic. They wanted total control over their vision, including how it was presented on the catwalk. They now aimed to create a cohesive runway tableau. They wanted women whose stage presence would not compete with the clothes or the designers themselves.

Oh sure, designers would still indulge in elaborate sets. And the clothes would sometimes take on the look of art projects. But the models? They were walking hangers. Only rarely were there exceptions. John Galliano, in his early years, asked his models to emote on his runway. But they were playing a character of Galliano's choosing. They were not revealing their own personalities.

The industry no longer had call for models who were defined as boldly individual, which meant the industry no longer had much need for black models who had always been connected to personal showmanship.

Black models were pushed aside to make room for the gawky, grunge sensibility of Kate Moss, Stella Tennant, Kristen McMenamy, and the like. Not only were models purposely more homogenous in appearance, any hint of personality or individuality was stage-directed out of them.

The generation of models who had starred at Versailles could only look at what had become of their industry and shake their head in disappointment and bewilderment. They hadn't gotten rich from Versailles, but in their scrapbook of memories, they thought they'd made a difference. But what had so entranced the industry was something other than their high cheekbones, brown skin, and slim hips. The French were not captivated by the *beauty* of the American models, but by their physicality. As Pierre Bergé noted, the success was in the choreography—Thompson's professional version and the designers' amateur instructions—and the American models' execution of it.

Did the models of Versailles help the fashion industry see that black was beautiful? Truly, fundamentally beautiful? Or did it only see trendy, politically correct mannequins executing a beautiful performance that reflected the particular rhythms of an era? In the ensuing years, in matters of race, laws, language, and business, practices changed. But hearts? The answer is not so definitive.

The default standard of beauty had always been white and it remains so. It doesn't matter that the increasingly commercial and global fashion trade has, as its fastest growing markets, regions such as Asia, India, and South America.

Hardison closed her agency in 1996, which meant the loss of one of the few firms that made a pointed effort to recruit models of color. By the start of the twenty-first century, designer preferences had turned to the blondes of Scandinavia. Then they drifted to Brazil—but only the most fair-skinned women of that diverse South American country. The era of the Brazilian bombshell, led by Gisele Bündchen, mostly left out black models. After they grew bored with Brazil, model scouts swarmed the streets of Russia, the Czech Republic, and the myriad countries that were once part of the Soviet Union. In the first decade of the new millennium, were it not for the Ethiopian-born Liya Kebede, black models would have practically disappeared from the runway.

The number of working black models in high-profile runway presentations or appearing on the covers of magazines became so dire that stories began appearing in the mainstream media about the "whitewashing" of the runway and what it meant for cultural perceptions of beauty, femininity, and worth. The homogeneity continued for a decade. Finding success on the runway was already a bit like winning the lottery, genetic and otherwise. But if fair-skinned women were having a run of good luck, their darker-skinned colleagues were stuck in a losing streak.

By 2007, activists went public with their dissatisfaction in town hall meetings. Hardison, joined by Iman and Naomi Campbell, led the effort. Around this time, Anna Wintour, editor-in-chief of American *Vogue*, admitted that while the industry was flush with Asian models and a few black models had made headway—such as Jourdan Dunn, Chanel Iman, and Joan Smalls, who is from Puerto Rico—"sadly we don't see as many African American models as we could."[39]

An Italian publication would make the strongest visual argument on behalf of black models. In 2008, Franca Sozzani, the editor of *Vogue Italia*, produced "The Black Issue." It featured only black models in its fashion editorials. After it sold out its initial print run of 120,000 copies, it was reprinted for the German, British, and American markets, where readers had turned it into a collector's item. Two years later, Sozzani reflected that the issue was born out of activism, business acumen, and personal boredom with runways.

"All the girls looked the same," Sozzani said in 2010. "The only one who stood out is Liya Kebede. Everything she wore, I liked. I started to question myself."

"We go looking for tall, thin, and blue eyes. But we have to scout in Africa, everywhere," Sozzani said. "I decided to do an issue only with black girls. People say, 'It's a ghetto.' But we do thousands of issues with Russian girls and it's not a ghetto."[40]

The attention to diversity was not sustained. By 2013, Hardison had begun hand-counting the numbers of black models on the runways in New York and Europe. And in shows where she found only one black model, or none, she spoke up. "I'm not calling anyone a racist," Hardison explains, "but the result is racist. It's a racist act.

"I do think there has been progress," she adds. "But I don't see the progress as well as the stability."[41]

Versailles was a mile marker along a very long, twisting highway that has had more than a few hairpin turns.

"Maybe I won't see it in my life," said Naomi Sims in 1968. "But there will come a day when it will be quite common to see a Negro face on the cover of *Harper's Bazaar* or *Vogue*."[42] Sims died in 2009. And the sight of a black model on the cover of any mainstream fashion magazine remains uncommon.

There is no political push for the fashion industry to keep its ranks diverse. Fashion isn't deemed important enough today to demand that attention—not like when the authors of the Kerner Report were at work. But there is at least one steady point of pressure: Hardison. She continues to cajole, embarrass, and insist. And in 2014, the Council of Fashion Designers of America honored Hardison for her work on diversity at its annual awards gala.

During the decade of the Versailles show, prominent women in political, social, and intellectual circles still publicly discussed their wardrobes and reporters soberly chronicled their purchases—not merely out of gossipy interest, but because what these women wore meant something. Their choices influenced the masses, their attention to style raised the profile of designers, and the sales were good for the economy. Fashion was equated with dignity and duty.

The Versailles show was meant to speak to these women. And it did. It changed their perception of American fashion, and, eventually, of fashion in general. Fashion, as seen through the eyes of designers like Klein, Halston, Burrows, and those who followed immediately in their footsteps, ceased to focus on hemline rules, social propriety, and enshrining beauty in a perfect couture suit. The rules of dress began to disintegrate, and society became more informal. Women looked to fashion as a source of freedom, workplace costuming, and aesthetic delight. And for a time, fashion complied, with the introduction of Diane von Furstenberg's wrap dress, Liz Claiborne's modest separates, Donna Karan's seven easy pieces, and even Italian designer Giorgio Armani's seductive, menswear-style tailoring.

But by the 1980s and into the new millennium, fashion's cultural influence and symbolism exploded and evolved until it became what it is today: an enormous and unwieldy global business ostentatiously fueled by entertainment, status, and the artfully esoteric. And as fashion changed, its intimate relationship with its main customers—women—frayed.

Women became distrustful of fashion, doubtful that it had anything important to say either to them personally or about their place in the world. What did crinoline underskirts, grunge, dropped crotch trousers, and logo-infested jackets have to do with climbing a corporate ladder or running a political campaign? Freed of fashion's tyranny, women have been at turns vengeful and dismissive of the industry. They regularly decry the disconnection between "real women" and those depicted in the pages of fashion magazines. Instead of understanding a model to be a fanciful, dynamic stand-in for the average woman, they see her as an underfed, underage alien.

Very few people now care what socialites are wearing—that is, unless they have been propelled onto their own reality show through purloined sex tapes, mudslinging divorces, or some other sordid spat. The only women happily detailing the designer of every garment on their back, right down to their Spanx, are starlets, who are dressed and given their talking points by professional stylists and gifted their gowns by designers whose marketing departments have determined that the starlet reflects the "brand."

The new breed of influential women, women of authority, freed from fashion's oppressive demands and with myriad options for moving up in life—options that do not involve marrying well—see fashion as belittling, too dangerously glitzy and superficial to even engage. They avoid discussing fashion. There is little upside. Power and fashion do not go together.

In 2009, a reporter asked then–Speaker of the House Nancy Pelosi, the first woman to hold the position, who designed the evening gown she was wearing as she arrived at the White House for a state dinner. The question was posed as Pelosi walked across the marble foyer of the Booksellers area, the White House equivalent of a red carpet, a place where such questions are standard. She responded with an expression of stony, glaring silence.

Pelosi later explained that her expression had not been intended to shame the questioner for chauvinistic effrontery, but was rather the result of frustration at her own inability to recall the designer's name.

Taking Pelosi at her word, why *should* she remember some designer's name? The power structure has grown increasingly suspicious of women who are more than a little fashionable. When the stylish Desirée Rogers arrived in Washington from Chicago in 2009 to take on the role of social secretary in the Obama administration, the media celebrated her for giving the nation's capital a dash more glamour. The former corporate executive had a fashion-forward wardrobe that was age appropriate, sophisticated, but with a bit of whimsy.

But Rogers's White House career imploded when two reality television show stars crashed the Obamas' first state dinner. Rogers wasn't responsible for security, but her office was in charge of the dinner. She was on the hot seat and the furor over her glossy public persona only added to the heat. Rogers had been tucked into the front row at New York's Fashion Week. She wore Nina Ricci. She had worn an avant-garde Comme des Garçons dress for that infamous state dinner, and it was far more notable than the gown worn by the First Lady.

In a flurry of controversy, congressional hearings, and brutal calls for her head, Rogers resigned. Her replacement was Julianna Smoot, an experienced political operative and fund-raiser whose public style could be summed up as reassuringly beige.[43]

There is now a stubborn, artificial divide. Serious women wear *clothes*. Fashion is a shallow, flaccid amusement. Our culture is losing faith in fashion's ability to empower, to change the world. Fashion is left to exist in an ever-expanding, mesmerizing bubble. Until the bubble finally bursts.

Fashion was once a kind of cultural currency with profound value. It commanded respect. Models could uplift a race. The economics of fashion resonated from Seventh Avenue to Pennsylvania Avenue. Creativity in the atelier evoked national pride. Aesthetics spoke eloquently of freedom: sexual, gender, political.

The success of Versailles gave the American designers a jolt of confidence, but it had an even broader impact. As American sportswear and informality gained legitimacy, it helped fuel a transformation that made fashion less dogmatic, more democratic and invigorating. Fashion became a flashy, exuberant, open party that *seemed* to welcome everyone. That openness was an enormous shift from the past, in which fashion was a private club for society's elite.

Following Versailles, fashion was no longer an artful tool for organizing, taming, and understanding society. It became brash entertainment— suspect to many, but irresistible. Fashion ceased being discreet and precise. There was no longer a singular lingua franca of fashion. It was broken down into countless dialects, leaving room for misunderstandings and gaffes.

Fashion became a form of tribal communication. It allows myriad groups to speak to each other, at each other, and over each other through wardrobe decisions that are at once simple and provocative. Everything from designer handbags and shoes to sneakers are now a measure of status and power. Hoodies, baggy jeans, and oversized T-shirts complicate race relations. Short skirts, tight blouses, leggings, and thongs have become lightning rods in gender conflicts.

Fashion feeds a constant cultural conversation with intermittent spikes of media saturation and personal punditry. The Academy Awards, for example, are as much a fashion show as they are a celebration of cinema, with viewers debating the fashion choices with as much vigor as the winner of Best Actress or Best Picture. The presidential inauguration marks a day when every American becomes a fashion critic and the inaugural gown becomes emblematic of national pride. Periodically a politician wears something out of the ordinary, inappropriate, or provocative. And voters admire, criticize, and gawk. The Internet is littered with blogs, online magazines, and fan sites devoted to fashion. Everyone is a fashion authority.

Fashion speaks more loudly than it ever did. It isn't quite a tower of Babel, but it is a daily cacophony of crosstalk. It is more important than ever to listen. Fashion has ceased to be the religion of women, revered and followed on pure faith. After Versailles, fashion broke free of the ateliers, its cherished cathedrals, and entered the public square.

Fashion no longer serves as a way of unifying the culture. Instead, it delineates the differences and forces the difficult question: How much do those differences matter?

Team Vicious performs at the Rick Owens spring 2014 show in Paris.

In Our Own Way

We knew we had a huge success. But as the years have gone by, the event itself has become, in the minds of the people, bigger and bigger. At the point when we went to Versailles to do the show, we never thought for a single second it would become a date or moment in time people would talk about twenty or thirty years later.[1] —OSCAR DE LA RENTA

O ver time, the Grand Divertissement à Versailles was nearly forgotten. But at a luncheon on January 24, 2011, it was remembered with great fanfare.

Few locations, except perhaps the Théâtre Gabriel, can rival the Temple of Dendur at New York's Metropolitan Museum of Art as an exotic and glorious setting for a luncheon. Dating from 15 B.C. and given to the United States by the Egyptian government, the sandstone temple sits amid the angled glass walls of the museum's Sackler Wing, which backs onto Central Park. Its architecture is noble, important, and enduring.

The January luncheon had been organized by the Met's Costume Institute and Multicultural Audience Development Initiative to celebrate the models who had been the stars of that 1973 Franco-American fashion show.

Over the years, the gala at Versailles has been occasionally resurrected as an academic footnote in fashion history. In 1993, for example, it served as the foundation for a Met exhibition on American style. Richard Martin, the late curator of the Costume Institute, and Harold Koda, his assistant at the time, mounted *Versailles 1973: American Fashion on the World Stage.* The exhibition defined the Versailles show as a moment of blossoming for American design akin to the 1913 Armory Show, which thrust avant-garde European art into the sightlines of American collectors.

In describing the intent of their exhibit, Martin and Koda noted: "There is something Emersonian in this inquiry, wanting to see what is definably American in this country's experience."[2]

The exhibition showcased the varying influences that continue to make American style distinct from its European counterpart: informality, pragmatism, Hollywood-wattage glamour, and multiculturalism. The show explored the work of a wide range of American designers, not merely those who were at Versailles. It sparked reminiscences from the fashion industry about Eleanor Lambert and her keen promotional skills and elicited a few stories in the press about how the French had been put in their place.

By the time of the 2011 luncheon in the Temple of Dendur, only six of the ten designers who participated in the Versailles gala were still alive. Klein, Blass, Halston, and Saint Laurent had all died. De la Renta would pass away in 2014 at his home in Kent, Connecticut. Givenchy, Ungaro, and Bohan had successfully retired from the fashion industry. Cardin, an enormously wealthy man, continues to work, although he spends most of his time on quixotic ventures unrelated to frocks. Oscar de la Renta and Stephen Burrows played masters of ceremony that afternoon at the Met.

The museum had planned to highlight all ten black American models who were at Versailles, but the staff had not been able to locate them all—and Saunders had passed away. But those who could be found arrived from all corners of the country: California, Georgia, New Jersey, Ohio, and a few blocks north in Harlem.

De la Renta, Donna Karan, and Pat Cleveland presided over one table. At the time of the luncheon, the fashion industry was very publicly grappling with a lack of diversity on its runways. The industry was being dogged by activists, bloggers, and even some exasperated insiders for its startlingly homogenous ways. It did not seem to matter that the country as a whole was becoming more diverse.

As those at the table discussed the dearth of black models on the contemporary catwalk, de la Renta became exasperated by the whole conversation, not because he wasn't concerned about diversity, but because the solution seemed so simple and obvious: just hire great models regardless of their race. He hated it when talent agents called to tell him they had "a great black girl" they wanted him to meet. Why couldn't they just say they had a "great girl"? And yes, the fashion industry still refers to models as "girls" even when they have long passed the age of majority.

Later, de la Renta, Burrows, and Karan gathered around a lectern to reminisce about the show and take questions from the audience. De la Renta held court, Karan chimed in, and Burrows stood quietly. Journalist Teri Agins, who is black, raised her hand. Burrows knew what she was going to ask before she even opened her mouth. She had given him advance notice. What was it like being the only black designer at Versailles?

Burrows hemmed and hawed. His discomfort was obvious and painful. De la Renta quickly spoke up: Burrows was at Versailles because he was a brilliant designer! Not because he was a black designer! It was a nice sentiment, but it wasn't entirely true. Race was an important aspect of what made Versailles so special. It had helped determine the participants as surely as social connections and political favors had.

Versailles was a high point on society's journey toward making peace with its own diversity. As a moment of racial enlightenment, it was one that grew out of fear, economics, practicality, and radical chic. Social justice was a momentary by-product, not an end goal reached by moral or righteous deliberation.

In 1973, race was a dilemma that needed to be confronted. And some folks thought fashion was part of the solution. Inclusiveness in matters of beauty, dress, and style was part of the nationally prescribed antidote to the anger and despair that had ripped apart American cities in the 1960s. "Blackness" was topical, and in the 1970s, it inspired new aesthetics. Exoticism sent a frisson of excitement through the liberal elite.

Burrows was a young man with a fashion point of view that was unburdened by aggression, despair, or political disruption. His clothes were joyful and exuberant. He worked with a community of friends that was multiethnic. Burrows made people feel good about all that ailed the culture. His race was important.

As the luncheon came to a close, guests chitchatted their way to coat check, mulling over the ultimate meaning of Versailles. People desperately sought a narrative with a coda of triumph, transformation, and uplift. In Burrows, they hoped to see a designer who had forever broken the color barrier by simple virtue of his talent. But in matters of race, things are always more complicated than that. Barriers fall when the right person arrives at the opportune time and under the perfect circumstances. And the first person to clear a hurdle does not always win.

Guests also wanted to revel in a feel-good story about how an open-minded industry embraced black women. They wanted to assign to the black models who had dazzled at Versailles the title of trailblazer, suggesting that they had cleared a path for others. But had they? If they had opened the door for other black models, why is it that all these years later one of the most contentious debates in the fashion industry is on the subject of diversity—specifically, the lack of it?

Race played a powerful role in the American triumph at Versailles, but it did not transform the lives of the black models who made such a memorable statement. The victory gave the participating American designers bragging rights, but it did not guarantee their business success or professional endurance. Still, the story of how Americans outdid the French made Seventh Avenue's young students, designers, and entrepreneurs more confident in themselves, in their culture, and in their industry. Every subsequent generation of designers has been secure in the knowledge that they did not have to emulate the methods and sensibilities of Paris in order to succeed or be taken seriously. Versailles helped free American designers to think like the entertaining capitalists that they were.

In 1973, the Americans bristled at being called "commercial." To this day, New York designers' feathers get ruffled when a collection is deemed "wearable," because that is equated with its being banal. But such fretting can now be done with the comforting knowledge that theirs is a $200 billion industry. Couture has become a charming niche art that is worth admiring but wields little influence. Contemporary dressing is American-style dressing: full of ease, sportiness, and fun.

Ralph Lauren, born in 1939, was part of the first generation of American corporate titans within the fashion industry. Lauren and his cohort of designers turned fashion into a barometer of our financial hopes, physical insecurities, gender ideals, and racial politics. They never bothered with couture and never harbored any self-doubt about their lack of couture training. Their success was foreshadowed at Versailles, where unabashedly commercial, personality-driven ready-to-wear captivated an international audience. Polo Ralph Lauren is now a nearly $5 billion corporation.

Calvin Klein, who'd shared a Coty Award with Burrows in 1973, made a fortune from underwear and that most mundane of American garments, blue jeans. Klein sexualized jeans with the help of a precocious fifteen-year-old brunette named Brooke Shields. He idealized the emaciated woman-child and the hypermuscular man with underwear advertisements starring Kate Moss and Mark Wahlberg. And he mainstreamed homoeroticism, both black and white, with his multistory billboards of Adonises in briefs.

More recently, in 2011, Michael Kors leveraged the fantasy of America's own golden-haired leisure class into a hugely successful initial public offering. The once struggling Michael Kors Holdings Ltd. is now a $1.3 billion company.[3]

America's fashion entrepreneurs continue to go to Paris. Sometimes they have been sent for, asked to lead a grand French house in search of youthful vigor and commercial savvy. Sometimes they go on their own. The place that once held American designers down, suffocating their imagination, is now the city where they go to let loose. They go looking for a stage big enough to support their expansive curiosity and daring.

"To have a commercial collection in Paris doesn't make sense," says Didier Grumbach, honorary president of French fashion's governing body. "It has to be advanced, a little perverse, a little shocking. If it's not a little surprising and shocking it doesn't work in France.

"In Paris, if everybody likes a collection, that means it's bad."[4]

American designers go to Paris in search of understanding and fuller participation in the global fashion business. They want to be part of an international dreamscape. They may be awestruck by the sheer size and reach of the Paris stage, but the French no longer intimidate them. They don't bother paying homage to haute couture the way Burrows did with his canary-yellow dress. They come to brush up against history, but they are focused on the future. And while it's nice to be invited to show in Paris, they do not feel compelled to await a summons.

To show in Paris on the industry's official calendar, a designer must be invited. Only a handful of Americans have been asked to show their collections in Paris over the years. There were the five intrepid Versailles designers, of course. Patrick Kelly, the African American designer from Vicksburg, Mississippi, who turned golliwogs and mammy culture into high style and political commentary in the 1980s, showed there. Ralph Rucci, who was deeply influenced by French technique, debuted his version of couture in Paris in July 2002.

Others, with an overabundance of American confidence and ebullience, have simply arrived in the City of Light, rented space, and sent out invitations. They are lured by the traditions, by the thrill of playing before an enormous global audience, and by the desire to test themselves creatively. The French fashion system might be closed, but Grumbach admits that "Paris is an open city."[5]

The iconoclastic entertainer Kanye West debuted his women's wear in

Paris in 2011, off the official calendar, at the Lycee Henri IV, one of the city's many architecturally grand cubbies. It was an aesthetically confusing, ill-fitting collection, a spring line dominated by fur—including a Brobdingnagian white fur backpack.

Backstage after West's show and with his soundtrack still blaring, he appeared shell-shocked when asked about his inspiration for the collection. His eyes went wide and his head began to swivel left and right in a frantic search for his publicist. "I'm so nervous," he said, looking at the three reporters standing in front of him. "I'm so scared. I'm so distracted. Turn down the music," he implored to the room in general.[6] Paris still has the capacity to make even a Grammy-winning music star break into a cold sweat when it comes to fashion.

In 2003, thirty years after Versailles, the California-born designer Rick Owens, who has a penchant for gothic darkness and flowing garments that work in opposition to conventional notions of beauty and luxury, began showing his collections in Paris. "I think France is about romance and it's about poetry," Owens said that first season. "I think if you do too much of that in the States, you get marginalized into an art school category. I think people look at things a little differently here."[7]

Owens brings his full, unique American self to the City of Light. Over the years, that has occasionally been dazzling. For his spring 2014 presentation, Owens decided to try something altogether different. He eschewed professional models. Instead, he flew in a group of college-age women who were members of four different "step" teams. With its roots tangled in the history of the African diaspora in America, stepping was popularized by black fraternities and sororities. It is synchronized movement using the body as the sole instrument. Stomping and clapping out a rhythm with military precision, the performers move in unison. They are bold, aggressive, confident, and a bit haughty. It is a display of group solidarity, cultural cockiness, and street credibility. The intent is not a display of prim, socially approved beauty. Instead, step teams honor movement, the power of the body, the control and ownership of one's body.

Owens's work has always defied the traditional lines of "pretty" or "sexy" clothes. Instead, his garments are often rather modest, revealing little skin and only a hint of the female form. His color palette is murky. His shapes are sometimes no more inspiring than a sack. But in his refusal of the classic markers of beauty, he finds a unique elegance, sophistication, and a strong, forthright poetry.

Owens unveiled his collection in one of the performance spaces at the Palais Omnisports de Paris-Bercy. There were no uniformed footmen standing by with cocktails. No one was wearing a formal gown or a tiara. And the setting had all the opulence of a warehouse. In the darkness, the first pair of models appeared on high platforms set atop spare, industrial scaffolding. They began a rhythmic stomping. They slapped their chests and their arms bounced toward the sky in harmony. As they descended two sets of stairs—one on either side of the metal tower—more models followed in exuberant, foot-stomping precision. The girls held expressions of fury, toughness, confidence, disdain, fearlessness, and pride. Some forty girls, predominantly—but not all—black, captivated a jaded, globe-trotting audience who hollered and cheered. And in the ultimate sign of approval in the twenty-first century, people in the crowd held their camera phones aloft to capture it all for history. It was a tremendous display that transformed Owens's reliably loose-fitting, comfortable separates into the costumes of warrior goddesses.

Backstage after the show, many of the performers were in tears; they couldn't believe that only a few months before they had been coeds at Howard University or the University of Maryland and suddenly, thanks to YouTube videos and long-shot go-sees, they were swept into the fashion world, flown to Paris, and onstage in front of the industry's kings and queens. Everyone was a sweaty mess in the crowded backstage space, which was swarming with steppers, dressers, editors, and photographers. In the center of the chaos, his shoulder-length, jet-black hair clinging to his long, pale, sweaty face, Owens beamed. The girls had been magnificent.

There were some critics who complained that the girls' intimidating expressions were an extension of the "angry black woman" cliché and that their performance was a gimmick. But those expressions weren't focused on churning, interior anger. They ranged from roaring fearlessness to exaggerated hauteur that mimicked the old posture of couture models. And, well, of course it was a gimmick—in the same way that Billie Blair played a magician for Oscar de la Renta and Bethann Hardison walked with a gangster's lean for Stephen Burrows. Modern fashion shows are fueled by gimmicks. They are, after all, entertainment.

Just as Blair, Pat Cleveland, and Alva Chinn made full-length cashmere T-shirts and slinky jersey dresses exciting, sexy, and irresistible, a new group of models made Owens's rompers, T-shirts, and shorts breathtaking. The clothes were in keeping with Owens's long-standing, familiar sensibility. The fresh thrill was the models' doing. They made the clothes dynamic. They instilled them with personality and audacity. They delivered.

Forty years earlier, national urgency to improve race relations had helped propel ten black models onto the Versailles stage. In their professional lives, they were accustomed to having to work harder, be better, than their white colleagues. And as a result, they made it their business to sell the clothes, to liven them up, to distinguish them. They worked the runway as a matter of necessity because their beauty alone was not going to do the job.

Back then, a black woman's beauty was not of equal stature to that of a white woman. Her looks were trendy; they were chic. But a white woman's beauty was the standard; it was the norm. Black models had to bring something else. They brought their physicality and their individuality. Both of those things overrode any judgment on the color of their skin, the shape of their noses, or the texture of their hair.

The particular legacy of the black models of Versailles was on display at Owens's show. The young women onstage didn't fit into the narrow confines of the fashion industry's definition of beauty either. They were not classically good-looking in the way that has been portrayed in the pages of *Vogue* over the generations. And they were not the all-American girls as our culture understands that description.

Owens had been attracted by their gritty, defiant independence—by their decision to be more than society outlined. "It was such a *fuck you* to conventional beauty," he recalls. "They were saying, 'We're beautiful in our own way.'"[8]

In our own way. That is the legacy of Versailles.

Versailles did not change the dominant standard of beauty. But it proved that veering away from the accepted and the expected can produce winning results. So every time the fashion runway makes a place for a plus-size woman, an eccentric tomboy, an awkward aristocrat, or four dozen sorority girls, it is a nod to Versailles. That was a moment when the individual trumped the group, when five Americans triumphed not because of the cut of the clothes or any extraordinary embellishments, but because of the spirit in which they were worn. American individualism showed its best face. And we inched forward.

Every now and then, that happens again.

And we rejoice.

Acknowledgments

This book began with David Kuhn, who had an idea and invited me to coffee one spring day in 2011. It exists because he led me by the hand, talked me down from the rafters, and never let me get lost in my own thoughts. I cannot begin to thank him and everyone at Kuhn Projects.

There can be no calmer, kinder, wiser, and more reassuring editor than Colin Dickerman. He has endless patience for fretfulness, self-doubts, and neediness. His enthusiasm and understanding of what this book could be buoyed me and guided me. The clear-eyed Whitney Frick, who has no tolerance for murky language, unsatisfying tangents, or distracting indulgences, is my hero. Copy editor Greg Villepique is a god of accuracy and precision and kindly corrected my mortifying misspellings without comment. I'm so proud to be part of Flatiron Books and its wonderful team.

I am forever indebted to a small army of people who made this, my first book, possible. Thank you to every single person who is quoted here, as well as those whose wisdom is reflected but whose names are not mentioned.

In particular, this book would have been impossible without the help and enthusiasm of those surviving designers and models who made history at Versailles.

The gracious Oscar de la Renta brought Versailles vividly to life with humor and honesty. Thank you to Erika Bearman and Alex Bolen for helping me tell this story.

Stephen Burrows opened his life to me and I was honored to be allowed in. His joie de vivre is inspiring. Like him, I sorely miss John Robert Miller, a stalwart optimist whose enthusiasm helped propel this book forward.

Donna Karan gave voice to Anne Klein and transported me backstage at the Théâtre Gabriel on that fateful night. You are a masterful storyteller.

The models of Versailles dazzled me, not just with their beauty and grace, but also with the stories of their dreams and hurdles. Thank you all.

The wisdom of the special collections researchers, Karen Cannell and April Callahan, at the Fashion Institute of Technology's Gladys Marcus Library was invaluable. They provided access to Eleanor Lambert's papers as well as those of the former *Washington Post* fashion editor Nina Hyde.

To the readers of rough drafts, editors extraordinaire, keepers of wisdom, and fashion consiglieri, thank you: Steve Reiss, Deborah Heard, Kevin Merida, Hank Stuever, Jennifer Beeson, Richard Aldacushion, Ann Gerhart, James Grady, Robert Janjigian, Marylou Luther, Clifford Pugh, Booth Moore, Maria Valentino, Nancy Moran, Paul Wilmot, Patti Cohen, Liberty Jones, Hamish Bowles, André Leon Talley, Sandy Schreier, Connie Uzzo, Joel Kaye, Ralph Rucci, Rosina Rucci, Louis Dell'Olio, Diane von Furstenberg, Steven Kolb and the Council of Fashion Designers of America, Jimmy Pihet and the Fédération Française de la Couture, du Pret-à-Porter des Couturiers et des Créateurs de Mode, John Tiffany, Anne Vegnaduzzo, Sandra McElwaine, Jean Rosenberg, Marion Greenberg, Audrey Smaltz, Megan Salt, Nancy Chilton, Madison Cox, Judy Taubman, Lisa Immordino Vreeland, Bronwyn Cosgrave, Maryann Wheaton, Bethann Hardison, Melissa Balmer, and Timothy Macdonald.

Patty Sicular appeared as if by magic with a Rolodex of names nearly lost to history. You were unbelievably generous.

Deeda Blair has encouraged me to write a book for years; she filled this one with her wisdom, her memories, and her generosity.

The scholars, curators, and historians who shared their expertise made me look smarter and encouraged me to think more deeply. Thank you, Harold Koda, Timothy Long, Patricia Mears, Valerie Steele, and Phyllis Magidson.

The splendid journalists who bore witness to Versailles, how I appreciated your eagle eye for detail! Thank you Enid Nemy and the late Patricia Shelton. Nancy North and Billie Blair, you don't have journalism degrees, but your keen memories and wonderful stories were a salvation.

Thank you, Ginny Power, for your research and your fluent French.

The great Bill Cunningham, your kindness leaves me speechless.

Where would I have been without the support and hospitality of Edward Hogikyan, Marcos Rodriguez, Blanca Rodriguez, Susan Rolontz, Richard Drezen, Basil Kyriakou, Gary Lee, and Teri Agins? Thank you.

To Teresa Wiltz, Debra Humphreys, and Nancy Pearlstein, you helped me see it all through. And to my parents, I have nothing but love and gratitude.

Notes

One: French Rules

1. Didier Grumbach, Paris interview in his office, 2012.
2. Ibid.
3. Ibid.
4. Hubert de Givenchy, Paris e-mail interview, 2013.
5. Grumbach, 2012.
6. Givenchy, 2013.
7. "Babe Paley," Vogue.com, www.vogue.com/voguepedia/Babe_Paley.
8. Marylou Luther, New York interview in her home, 2012.
9. Lynn Wyatt, Houston telephone interview, 2013.
10. Timothy Long, London telephone interview, 2013.
11. Jonathan Reynolds, "Gowns or Butter?" *New York Times*, April 20, 2003.
12. Givenchy, 2013.
13. Christopher Petkanas, "The Hostess with the Mostest," *New York Times*, November 9, 2008.
14. Enid Nemy, "Marie-Helene de Rothschild, 65, Worldly Hostess Extraordinaire," *New York Times*, March 7, 1996.
15. Deeda Blair, New York interview in her home, 2013.
16. Dreda Mele, Paris interview in her home, 2012.

Two: Copycats and Salami

1. Marc Levin, director, *Schmatta: Rags to Riches to Rags*, 2009.
2. Into the 1960s, the garment unions continued to wield great clout. During John F. Kennedy's presidential campaign, Jacqueline Kennedy was pressured to break her expensive French fashion habit in order to satisfy the union bosses. The new first lady turned to fashion editor Diana Vreeland for counsel and Oleg Cassini for clothes, not because he excelled at design, but because he excelled at "being inspired" by French couture. He could re-create the French fashions for which Mrs. Kennedy longed, and she could still "buy American."
3. Madelyn Shaw, "Hattie Carnegie," *Contemporary Fashion* (Detroit: St. James Press, 1995), p. 85.
4. Margaret Case Harriman, "Very Terrific, Very Divine," *The New Yorker*, Oct. 19, 1940.
5. John Tiffany, *Eleanor Lambert: Still Here* (New York: Pointed Leaf Press, 2011), p. 20.
6. Louis Dell'Olio, New York telephone interview, 2013.
7. Ibid.
8. Luther, 2012.
9. Tiffany, *Eleanor Lambert*, p. 19.
10. Joan Kaner, Florida telephone interview, 2013.
11. Pierre Bergé, New York interview at the Pierre Hotel, 2013.
12. Alexandra Palmer, *Couture & Commerce* (Vancouver: UBC Press, 2001), p. 77.
13. Bergé, 2013.
14. Ibid.
15. Timothy Long, London telephone interview, 2013.
16. Ibid.
17. Nina S. Hyde, "Paris 'Originals' at Ohrbach's: Fashions by 'Monsieur X' a Hit with Kennedy Women," *Washington Post*, September 26, 1972.
18. Nina S. Hyde, "Paris 'Originals' at Ohrbach's."
19. Long, 2013.
20. Oscar de la Renta, New York interview in his Seventh Avenue studio, 2011.
21. Stan Herman, New York telephone interview, 2012. Herman began his career in 1961 at a business typical of the time, Mr. Mort, a successful ladies' apparel brand, founded by Mortimer Goldman. It was known for its pleasant midmarket frocks until Herman, a small-framed, dapper man, was hired as a backroom designer. He had been attempting to make a go of a career in show business, but he wasn't making much headway. With an eye for translating the rhythms of contemporary life into jersey dresses, Herman clawed his way up

the workroom ladder until the label finally read MR. MORT BY STAN HERMAN. It was the beginning of a lucrative but quiet career. "I bit the edges off fashion," Herman says.

Three: Four Gentlemen and a Powerhouse

1. Tiffany, *Eleanor Lambert*, p. 53.
2. Tiffany, *Eleanor Lambert*, p. 30.
3. Herman, 2012.
4. Luther, 2012.
5. "The President: February 1968. MP893," YouTube video, LBJ Library.
6. Eugenia Sheppard, "Style Show to Make History," *Deseret News*, Feb. 28, 1968.
7. "The President: February 1968."
8. Barbara Cloud, "The First and Last White House Fashion Show," *Pittsburgh Post-Gazette*, March 26, 2006.
9. De la Renta, 2011.
10. Ibid.
11. Ibid.
12. Angela Taylor, "Coty's Winnie Given to Oscar," *New York Times*, June 30, 1967.
13. No author, "Francoise de la Renta," *Women's Wear Daily*, June 20, 1983.
14. No author, "Heart of Blass," *Women's Wear Daily*, June 24, 1982.
15. Ibid.
16. Bill Blass interviewed by Charles Gandee, "1950s," *Vogue*, April 26, 1999.
17. "Heart of Blass."
18. Bill Blass interviewed by Charles Gandee, April 26, 1999.
19. Enid Nemy, "A Decade Ago, Bill Blass Wouldn't Admit He Was a Designer," *New York Times*, April 1, 1970.
20. Elaine Gross & Fred Rottman, *Halston: An American Original* (New York: Harper-Collins, 1999), pp. 7–8.
21. No author, "The Halston Looks," *New York Times Magazine*, February 11, 1973.
22. Lisa Belkin, *New York Times Magazine*, March 15, 1987.
23. Bill Blass, *Bare Blass* (New York: HarperCollins, 2002), p. 20.
24. Luther, 2012.
25. Ibid.
26. Dell'Olio, 2013.
27. Frances Patiky Stein, Paris telephone interview, 2012.
28. National Institutes of Health, "Cancer," October 2010, http://report.nih.gov/nihfactsheets/viewfactsheet.aspx?csid=73.

29. Tomio Taki, New York interview at Parsons The New School for Design, 2013.
30. Stephen Burrows, New York interview in his studio, 2011.
31. Ibid.
32. Vy Higginsen, transcript of interview with John Robert Miller, 1999.
33. Burrows, 2011.
34. Ibid.
35. Diane von Furstenberg, New York interview in her showroom, 2013.
36. De la Renta, 2011.
37. Ellin Saltzman, Florida telephone interview, 2013.

Four: Cities in Flames

1. Report of the National Advisory Commission on Civil Disorders, p. 1.
2. Report of the National Advisory Commission on Civil Disorders, p. 7.
3. Report of the National Advisory Commission on Civil Disorders, p. 133.
4. Report on the National Advisory Commission on Civil Disorders, p. 386.
5. In the contemporary fashion industry, the low number of black designers is a regular cause for despair among those who track and attempt to encourage diversity. Educators note that the paucity begins with the fact that black students are underrepresented in design school. African Americans make up 13–14 percent of college students in general, but in 2010 they comprised only 4.7 percent of fashion design students, according to Joel Towers, dean of Parsons The New School for Design. Striving black designers lament the difficulty in attracting financial backing from banks, venture capitalists, or angel investors. And most are unable to rely on family wealth or community connections, as white and Asian designers often do. And the few established black designers have watched with dismay as Seventh Avenue is more enthusiastic in its embrace of black musicians and athletes who use fashion for branding purposes than it is of those folks who have devoted their professional lives to the métier.
6. Margaret Crimmins, "Designed with Soul," *Washington Post*, May 21, 1969.
7. Judy Klemesrud, "Bergdorf's Gives Boost to Fashion by Blacks," *New York Times*, May 21, 1969.
8. John Lichfield, "Egalite! Liberte! Sexualite!: Paris, May 1968," *The Independent*, Feb. 23, 2008.
9. Pamela Golbin, Paris interview at the Musée des Arts Décoratif, 2012.
10. Robin Givhan, "Fashion Great Saint Laurent Hangs Up Hat," *Washington Post*, June 9, 1998.
11. Lizzy Duffy, "Parisian Women Now (Officially) Allowed to Wear Pants," NPR .com, February 4, 2013.

12. Joseph Carroll, "Police Move on Student Barricades," *The Guardian*, May 25, 1968.

13. Joseph Carroll, "Paris Students in Savage Battles," *The Guardian*, May 7, 1968.

14. Givenchy, 2013.

15. Lichfield, "Egalite! Liberte! Sexualite!"

Five: Apostasy

1. Grumbach, 2012.

2. Ibid.

3. Marylou Luther, New York telephone interview, 1998.

4. Bergé, 2013.

5. Marc Bohan, e-mail interview, 2013.

6. Teri Agins, *The End of Fashion* (New York: William Morrow and Company, 1999), p. 32.

7. Nina S. Hyde, "Pierre Cardin," *Washington Post*, September 11, 1978.

8. Musée Pierre Cardin, permanent exhibition, Saint-Ouen, France, 2013.

9. Renée Taponier, Saint-Ouen interview at the Musée Pierre Cardin, 2013.

10. Grumbach, 2012.

11. Taponier, 2013.

12. Givenchy, 2013.

13. Ibid.

14. Golbin, 2012.

15. Ibid.

16. Stein, 2012.

17. Marian Christy, "Is Paris Fashion Dying?" *Boston Globe*, September 4, 1973.

18. Federal Reserve Bank of St. Louis, "France/U.S. Foreign Exchange Rate (Discontinued Series)," French Franc to One U.S. Dollar, March 8, 2006, http://research.stlouisfed.org/fred2/data/EXFRUS.txt.

19. Jimmy Pihet, communication manager of the Fédération Française de la Couture, Paris, e-mail interview, 2013.

20. Patricia Shelton, "Paris Threat Worries U.S. Dressmakers," *Christian Science Monitor*, April 24, 1971.

21. Valentine Lawford, "Versailles, Its Persuasive Curator," *Vogue*, August 1, 1967.

22. Ibid.

23. Ibid.

24. Paul Lewis, "Gerald Van der Kemp, 89, Versailles' Restorer," *New York Times*, January 15, 2002.

25. Mary Blume, "The Man Who Gave Versailles Back to the French," *Los Angeles Times*, October 26, 1975.

26. Valentine Lawford, "A Fresh Wind Through Versailles," *Vogue*, August 1, 1967.

27. Blair, 2013.

28. Ibid.

29. Nina S. Hyde, "At Home . . . In Versailles," *Washington Post*, January 5, 1978.

30. Lawford, "Versailles, Its Persuasive Curator."

31. Hyde, "At Home . . . In Versailles."

32. Blair, 2013.

33. Blume, "The Man Who Gave Versailles Back to the French."

34. Enid Nemy, "C. Z. Guest, Society Royalty, Dies at 83," *New York Times*, November 9, 2003.

35. Blair, 2013.

36. Hugo Vickers, "Obituary: Marie-Hélène de Rothschild," *The Independent*, March 12, 1996.

37. Mele, 2012.

38. Mele, 2012.

39. Pat McColl, "Designer Finds New Home at Hartnell," *Los Angeles Times*, February 1, 1991.

40. Blair, 2013.

41. Marian Christy, "Marc Bohan of Dior Still Favors the Starkly Classic," *Reading Eagle*, October 15, 1971.

42. Christy, "Marc Bohan of Dior Still Favors the Starkly Classic."

43. Bohan, 2013.

44. Ibid.

45. Christy, "Marc Bohan of Dior Still Favors the Starkly Classic."

46. Henry Berghauer, Paris interview at his home, 2012.

47. Henry Berghauer, Paris interview at Café Flore, 2012.

48. Berghauer, his home, 2012.

49. Agins, *The End of Fashion*, p. 62.

50. Grace Mirabella, *In and Out of Vogue* (New York: Doubleday, 1995), p. 147.

51. Nina S. Hyde, "Ungaro: The Influence of Low Flash," *Washington Post*, April 22, 1973.

52. Ibid.

53. Grace Mirabella, New York telephone interview, 2013.

54. "Yves Sparks Elegant Reign of Terror," *Women's Wear Daily*, August 5, 1966.

55. Bergé, 2013.

Notes

Six: Disco Balls and Divas

1. Mitra Toossi, "A Century of Change: The U.S. Labor Force, 1950–2050," *Monthly Labor Review*, May 2002.
2. As I interviewed those who lived at full throttle during the 1970s, many of them shared a similarly blurred memory of the decade. Whether it was designer Diane von Furstenberg, model Bethann Hardison, or Stephen Burrows, they had the ability to recall their emotional pleasures, but the specifics—even the broad strokes—were typically lost.
3. Lisa Robinson, "Boogie Nights," *Vanity Fair*, February 2010.
4. Eric Wilson, "Naomi Sims, 61, Pioneering Cover Girl, Is Dead," *New York Times*, August 3, 2009.
5. Eugenia Sheppard, "Americans in Paris," *Los Angeles Times*, November 29, 1973.
6. De la Renta, 2011.
7. Gross & Rottman, *Halston: An American Original*, p. 19.
8. Stein, 2012.
9. Eleanor Lambert, "Anne Klein press release, November 1973," Nina Hyde Collection, Special Collections and FIT Archives, Gladys Marcus Library, Goodman Resource Center, Fashion Institute of Technology–SUNY.
10. De la Renta, 2011.
11. Burrows, 2011.

Seven: Stephen Burrows's World

1. Burrows, 2011.
2. Ibid.
3. Jean Butler, "Burrows Is Back with a Little Help from His Friends," *New York Times*, June 5, 1977.
4. Burrows, 2011.
5. Stephen Burrows, New York interview in the office of his licensing associate, 2013.
6. Higginsen, 1999.
7. Charles Tracy, New York interview in his home, 2013.
8. Ibid.
9. Ibid.
10. "Vogue's Own Boutique of Suggestions, Finds and Observations," *Vogue*, April 15, 1969.

11. Burrows, 2011.
12. Ginia Bellafante, "A Fallen Star of the 70s Is Back in the Business," *New York Times*, January 1, 2002.
13. Nina S. Hyde, "With Plans 'to Dress the World,'" *Washington Post*, November 12, 1973.
14. Eric Wilson, "Geraldine Stutz Dies at 80; Headed Bendel for 29 Years," *New York Times*, April 9, 2005.
15. Shirley Clurman, "Gerry Stutz Is Hardly Just Window Dressing at Bendel's— She Owns the Store," *People*, October 13, 1980.
16. Kaner, 2013.
17. Marion Greenberg, New York telephone interview, 2013.
18. Kaner, 2013.
19. Burrows, 2011.
20. Herman, 2012.
21. Butler, "Stephen Burrows Is Back with a Little Help from His Friends."
22. Audrey Smaltz, New York telephone interview, 2013.
23. Roz Rubenstein-Johnson, interview transcript from John Robert Miller, 1999.
24. No author, "12 U.S. Designers Get Fashion Awards," *Wilmington Star-News*, October 18, 1973.
25. Smaltz, 2013.
26. Ibid.
27. Ibid.
28. Ibid.
29. Hyde, "With Plans 'to Dress the World.'"
30. Burrows, 2011.
31. Hyde, "With Plans 'to Dress the World.'"
32. Burrows, 2011.

Eight: Insecurity and Egos

1. De la Renta, 2011.
2. Burrows, 2011.
3. De la Renta, 2011.
4. Eleanor Lambert, "Monsanto memo," Eleanor Lambert Collection, Special Collections and FIT Archives, Gladys Marcus Library, Goodman Resource Center, Fashion Institute of Technology–SUNY.
5. Charlene Dash, New York telephone interview, 2013.
6. Billie Blair, Toledo interview at the Toledo Museum of Art, 2011.
7. Sheppard, "Americans in Paris."

8. Karen Bjornson-Macdonald, Connecticut telephone interview, 2013.
9. De la Renta, 2011.
10. Ibid.
11. Ibid.
12. Sheppard, "Americans in Paris."
13. Jonathan C. Randal, "Let Them Eat Cake and Drink Chateau Lafite," *Washington Post*, November 30, 1973.
14. Enid Nemy, New York telephone interview, 2013.
15. "Versailles File," Eleanor Lambert Collection, Special Collections and FIT Archives, Gladys Marcus Library, Goodman Resource Center, Fashion Institute of Technology–SUNY.

Nine: Muses, Marijuana, and Mayhem

1. Tom Fallon, New York telephone interview, 2012.
2. Barbara Summers, New York telephone interview, 2013.
3. Ibid.
4. Judith Martin, "New High Fashion Trend Is to the Black Model," *Washington Post*, October 27, 1968.
5. Blair, 2011.
6. Ibid.
7. Billie Blair, Defiance telephone interview, 2013.
8. Blair, 2011.
9. Ibid.
10. Ibid.
11. Fallon, 2012.
12. Ibid.
13. Enid Nemy, "Jerry Zipkin, Who Lunched and Listened, Is Dead at 80," *New York Times*, June 9, 1995.
14. Fallon, 2012.
15. Ibid.
16. Ibid.
17. Ibid.
18. Not much has changed in the contemporary American industry. Models become favorites because of designers' lemminglike habits, fear of missing out, and general insecurities. Everyone always wants the hot girl who is often only hot because everyone wants her.
19. Blair, 2011.
20. De la Renta, 2011.

21. Bethann Hardison, New York interview in her apartment, 2011.

22. Ibid.

23. Ibid.

24. Ibid.

25. Bjornson-Macdonald, 2013.

26. Pat Cleveland, New Jersey telephone interview, 2013.

27. Blair, 2011.

28. Amina Warsuma, Los Angeles telephone interview, 2012.

29. Ibid.

30. Ibid.

31. Anne-Marie Schiro, "Scott Barrie Is Dead; Designer, 52, Made Jersey Matte Dresses," *New York Times*, June 11, 1993.

32. Warsuma, 2012.

33. Ibid.

34. Ibid.

35. Charlene Dash, New York telephone interview, 2013.

36. Ibid.

37. Eric Wilson, "Dorothea T. Church, 83, Pioneering Model, Dies," *New York Times*, July 23, 2006.

38. Norma Jean Darden, New York telephone interview, 2013.

39. Ibid.

40. Ibid.

41. Marian Christy, "Alva Chinn's Journey," *Boston Globe*, June 12, 1983.

42. Alva Chinn, New York telephone interview, 2013.

43. Ibid.

44. Carol DiPasalegne served as commentator for *Ebony* Fashion Fair from 1965 to 1967. She also worked as a United Airlines flight attendant and a nightclub singer, performing under the name Carol Denmark. According to a 1988 story in the *Chicago Tribune*, upon DiPasalegne's death on April 27, 1982, her husband at the time, Herbert Cammon, was accused of murdering her to collect a $250,000 life insurance policy. The couple had had a two-month courtship and had been married only sixteen days when she was found strangled and stabbed in the face twenty times. The life insurance policy had been taken out three days before her death. A 1984 trial ended in a hung jury. In 1988, Cammon was acquitted after a bench trial before a Cook County Criminal Court judge. As a motive, prosecutors argued that Cammon was gay and had been living with a male roommate for five years prior to his marriage to DiPasalegne and moved back immediately after her death.

45. Barbara Jackson, phone interview, 2014.

46. Ibid.

47. Anne-Marie Schiro, "Eugenia Sheppard, Fashion Columnist, Dies," *New York Times*, November 12, 1984.

48. Jennifer Brice, Atlanta telephone interview, 2013.

49. Nina S. Hyde, "A Fashionable Kind of Benefit," *Washington Post*, November 15, 1973.

50. Jennifer Brice, Washington interview at the Jefferson Hotel, 2013.

51. Ibid.

52. Ibid.

53. Ibid.

54. Ibid.

55. Dash, 2013.

56. Warsuma, 2012.

57. Emily Nussbaum, "Liza Must Go On," *New York* magazine, November 30, 2008.

58. Sam Irvin, *Kay Thompson: From* Funny Face *to* Eloise (New York: Simon & Schuster, 2010), e-book.

59. Irvin, *Kay Thompson*, e-book.

60. Nussbaum, "Liza Must Go On."

61. Irvin, *Kay Thompson*, e-book.

62. Darden, 2013.

63. Gross and Rottman, *Halston: An American Original*, p. 21.

64. Brice, Atlanta telephone interview, 2013.

65. Irvin, *Kay Thompson*, e-book.

66. Marie-Antoinette Esterhazy, column, *Women's Wear Daily*, November 26, 1973.

67. Dash, 2013.

68. Blair, 2011.

69. Warsuma, 2012.

70. Marie-Antoinette Esterhazy, November 26, 1973.

71. Jonathan C. Randal, "Glad Rags Rite," *Washington Post*, November 28, 1973.

72. Randal, "Glad Rags Rite."

73. Dash, 2013.

74. Marie-Antoinette Esterhazy, November 26, 1973.

75. Enid Nemy, "Paris Is in a Tizzy, but Then It's Not Just Another Fashion Show," *New York Times*, November 28, 1973.

76. Nemy, "Paris Is in a Tizzy, but Then It's Not Just Another Fashion Show."

Ten: Waiting

1. Donna Karan, Washington interview at Reagan National Airport, 2011.

2. Warsuma, 2012.

3. In 2013, Sheryl Sandberg, the chief operating officer of Facebook, published *Lean In: Women, Work, and the Will to Lead*. Its signature premise is that regardless of the hurdles women encounter in the workplace, excuses don't help the situation. Instead, they should believe in themselves and "lean in" to the action.
4. Louis Dell'Olio, New York telephone interview, 2013.
5. Karan, 2011.
6. Hardison, 2011.
7. Karan, 2011.
8. Jennifer Brice, Jefferson Hotel, 2013.
9. Sam Irvin, *Kay Thompson*, e-book.
10. Pat McColl, "Palace Coup," *New York Times*, August 19, 2001.
11. Burrows, 2011.
12. Ibid.
13. Hardison, 2011.
14. Pat McColl, "Palace Coup."
15. Nemy, "Paris Is in a Tizzy, but Then It's Not Just Another Fashion Show."
16. Nemy, 2013.
17. Bellafante, "A Fallen Star of the 70s Is Back in the Business."
18. McColl, "Palace Coup."
19. Randal, "Glad Rags Rite."
20. McColl, "Palace Coup."
21. Randal, "Glad Rags Rite."
22. Alan Riding, "Jean-Louis Barrault, 83, Director and Actor in the French Theater," *New York Times*, January 23, 1994.
23. John Calder, "Obituary: Jean-Louis Barrault," *The Independent*, January 24, 1994.
24. Tracy, 2013.
25. Warsuma, 2012.
26. De la Renta, 2011.
27. Warsuma, 2012.
28. No author, "Louis XIV, We Are Here," *Newsweek*, December 10, 1973.
29. "Rybar & Daigre—Decorative Magicians," Christie's press release, March 24, 2003.
30. Christopher Petkanas, "Fabulous Dead People: Alexis, Baron de Redé," *New York Times*, April 8, 2011.
31. Alexis de Rede, *Alexis: The Memoirs of the Baron de Redé* (Dovecote Press: 2005), excerpt at http://scalaregia.blogspot.com/2009/01/oriental-ball-in-1969-has-been.html
32. Petkanas, "Fabulous Dead People: Alexis, Baron de Redé."
33. De Rede, *Alexis: The Memoirs of the Baron de Redé*.
34. Enid Nemy, "Paris Is in a Tizzy, but Then It's Not Just Another Fashion Show."

35. Rodney Pearson, California telephone interview, 2013.

36. Ibid.

37. Karan, 2011.

38. Sam Irvin, *Kay Thompson*, e-book.

39. Fallon, 2011.

40. Nemy, 2013.

41. Bjornson-Macdonald, 2013.

42. Tracy, 2013.

43. De la Renta, 2011.

44. Fallon, 2011.

45. Ibid.

46. Nemy, 2013.

47. "Great Day," by Edward Eliscu, Billy Rose, and Vincent Youmans, 1929.

48. Mary Tannen, "Inside Whiff; Mink Dew," *New York Times*, February 25, 2001.

49. Lynn Hirschberg, "Lyn's Lost World," *W*, January 2012.

50. Eugenia Sheppard, "Parties Precede Paris Shows," *Los Angeles Times*, November 29, 1973.

51. Carolyne Zinko, "Double Trouble: High Anxiety in High Society?" *San Francisco Chronicle*, April 15, 2007.

52. Pat Shelton, Shreveport, Louisiana telephone interview, 2011.

Eleven: One Night at Versailles

1. Mark Twain, *The Innocents Abroad*, e-book.

2. No author, "Louis XIV, We Are Here," *Newsweek*, December 10, 1973.

3. Fallon, 2011.

4. Karan, 2011.

5. Simone Levitt, New York telephone interview, 2014.

6. Wyatt, 2013.

7. Monique, "Fashion Kings Merge in a Surge of Elegance," *Chicago Tribune*, December 1, 1973.

8. Eugenia Sheppard, "Yanks Pull Off Fashion Heist in Paris," *Los Angeles Times*, December 2, 1973.

9. No author, "The Versailles Caper," *Women's Wear Daily*, November 29, 1973.

10. Karan, 2011.

11. Grumbach, 2012.

12. Shelton, 2011.

13. Jonathan C. Randal, "Let Them Eat Cake and Drink Chateau Lafite."

14. Sheppard, "Yanks Pull Off Fashion Heist in Paris."

15. Randal, "Let Them Eat Cake and Drink Chateau Lafite."
16. Alessandra Codinha, "Ringside Seat: The 'Battle of Versailles' in WWD's Eye," *Women's Wear Daily,* July 9, 2012.
17. Bergé, 2013.
18. Gunilla Lindblad, New York telephone interview, 2014.
19. Monique, "Fashion Kings Merge in a Surge of Elegance."
20. Givenchy, 2013.
21. Enid Nemy, "Fashion at Versailles: French Were Good, Americans Were Great," *New York Times,* November 30, 1973.
22. Sheppard, "Yanks Pull Off Fashion Heist in Paris."
23. Fallon, 2011.
24. Bergé, 2013.
25. Grumbach, 2012.
26. Fallon, 2011.
27. Jackson, 2014
28. Nemy, 2013.
29. Nicole Fischelis, Paris interview at Le Printemps café, 2012.
30. Karan, 2011.
31. Tracy, 2013.
32. Nemy, 2013.
33. Blair, 2011.
34. De la Renta, 2011.
35. Fischelis, 2012.
36. Ibid.
37. Ibid.
38. Nemy, 2013.
39. Bergé, 2013.
40. De la Renta, 2011.
41. Phyllis Feldkamp, "Versailles Divertissement," *Christian Science Monitor,* December 17, 1973.
42. Tiffany, *Eleanor Lambert,* p. 267.
43. Linda Gillan Griffin, "Time for U.S. Designers to Shine," *Houston Chronicle,* November 4, 1993.
44. Fallon, 2011.
45. Burrows, 2011.
46. Karan, 2011.
47. Pearson, 2013.
48. Darden, 2013.
49. Burrows, 2011.
50. Nemy, 2013.

51. (Pat Shelton), "Elite Sip Champagne to Save Versailles Palace," *Los Angeles Times* via United Press International, November 30, 1973.

52. Nemy, "Fashion at Versailles: French Were Good, Americans Were Great."

53. Eugenia Sheppard, "Yanks Pull Off Fashion Heist in Paris."

Twelve: Success Stories and Cautionary Tales

1. Jackson, 2014.

2. Givenchy, 2013.

3. Givenchy, 2013.

4. Robin Givhan, "The French Connection: Bernard Arnault Built a Fashion Empire. But Don't Expect Any Air Kisses," *Washington Post*, April 28, 2002.

5. Givhan, "The French Connection."

6. Bernard Arnault, Paris interview in his office, 2011.

7. Bergé, 2013.

8. Hyde, "Pierre Cardin."

9. Teri Agins, *The End of Fashion*, p. 66.

10. Julia Reed, "Oscar de la Renta's Next Big Act," *Wall Street Journal*, Feburary, 23, 2012.

11. Bridget Foley, "Dressing Michelle: Major Designers Wait for First Lady's Call," *Women's Wear Daily*, April 2, 2009.

12. Eric Wilson, "The Long Fall of the House of Blass," *New York Times*, December 25, 2008.

13. Mary Rourke, "Made for the U.S.A.: Designer: Louis Dell'Olio, the Man Behind the Anne Klein Label, Specializes in Translating European Fashions into Classic American Styles," *Los Angeles Times*, February 22, 1993.

14. Dell'Olio, 2013.

15. Karan, 2011.

16. Ibid.

17. Lisa Belkin column, *New York Times Magazine*, March 15, 1987.

18. Ibid.

19. Ibid.

20. Bernadine Morris, "Halston, Symbol of Fashion in America in 70's, Dies at 57," *New York Times*, March 28, 1990.

21. Rosemary Feitelberg, "Tom Ford on Family, Fashion and Film," *Women's Wear Daily*, May 9, 2012.

22. Burrows, 2011.

23. Jean Butler, "Burrows Is Back with a Little Help from His Friends."

24. Burrows, 2013.

25. Ibid.
26. Ibid.
27. Burrows, 2011.
28. Robin Givhan, "Déjà Vu," *Washington Post*, August 1, 2005.
29. Smaltz, 2013.
30. Burrows, 2013.
31. Report on the National Advisory Commission on Civil Disorders, p. 7.
32. Phyllis Feldkamp, "'Motion' Clothes for Fall," *Christian Science Monitor*, May 20, 1974.
33. Marion Clark and Nina S. Hyde, "Black Beauty: A Washington Model Shoots for the Top," *Washington Post*, November 10, 1974.
34. Marian Christy, "Alva Chinn's Journey."
35. Blair, 2011.
36. David Yonke, "Model's Pathway Led to Pulpit as Minister," *Toledo Blade*, September 4, 2010.
37. Blair, 2011.
38. Ibid.
39. Robin Givhan, "Fashion Statement," *Washington Post*, November 28, 2010.
40. Givhan, "Fashion Statement."
41. Bethann Hardison, New York telephone interview, 2013.
42. Martin, "New High Fashion Trend Is to the Black Model."
43. Robin Givhan, "White House Social Secretary Could Take a Page from the Fashion Industry," *Washington Post*, April 25, 2010.

Epilogue: In Our Own Way

1. De la Renta, 2011.
2. Metropolitan Museum of Art Costume Institute, *Versailles 1973: American Fashion on the World Stage* press release, August 10, 1993.
3. Lee Spears and Elizabeth Wollman, "Luxury Beats Tech as Michael Kors Tops IPO Ranking," *Bloomberg Markets* magazine, July 17, 2012.
4. Grumbach, 2012.
5. Ibid.
6. Robin Givhan, "Kanye West's Paris Flop," *The Daily Beast*, October 2, 2011.
7. Robin Givhan, "In Paris, Shredding the Fabric of Class: Fall Collections Revel in Unraveling Haute Couture," *Washington Post*, March 8, 2003.
8. Rick Owens, Paris interview backstage at his spring 2014 show, 2013.

Index

Designers are listed by surname, e.g. Cardin, Pierre. Their companies are listed by the full company names, e.g. Pierre Cardin company. GDV stands for Grand Divertissement à Versailles.

LVMH Moët Hennessy Louis Vuitton, 223, 224

Macdonald, Julien, 224
Machado, China, 150, 212
Madame Grès, 31, 86
  clothing by, 198, 199
Mademoiselle magazine, 158, 159
Mahoney, David, 128, 168–69, 180
Mainbocher company, clothing, 199
Maison Lemarié, 10
Maison Lesage, 10
Malraux, André, 84
"mannequins" (models), 152
manufacturers, American, 30, 31, 34
Marie Antoinette, Queen, 9–10
Marshall Field company, 31
Martin, Judith, 141
Martin, Richard, 267–68
Max Factor company, 126, 170, 240–42
Maxim's, Paris, 227
  Norton Simon company party at
    (November 26), 180–83
Max's Kansas City, 152
McCardell, Claire, 24, 27, 28
McGee, Arthur, 63
McMenamy, Kristen, 258
McQueen, Alexander, 224, 233
media, news about blacks, 60–61
Mele, Dreda, 20–21, 85–86, 88–89
Mellon, Rachel "Bunny" Lambert, 14
Messmer, Pierre, 135
Metropolitan Museum of Art, New
    York
  Temple of Dendur, 267
  See also Costume Institute
Michael Kors Holdings Ltd., 271
Miller, John Robert, 243–44, 248
Minnelli, Liza
  biography, 165, 195
  invited to the GDV, 125

morale building by, at Versailles,
    173, 178, 191, 194, 205–6
  role in GDV, 128, 150, 189, 205–6,
    213, 222
  social world, 47, 174, 182, 190
  at Versailles, 168, 171, 179
Minnelli, Vincente, 195
Mirabella, Grace, 94, 95, 208
Miss Dior boutique, 72
models
  of 1970s compared to today's, 148
  black. *See* black models
  careers of, 139, 148, 287n18
  costume changes by, 124, 207
  dresses first presented on live models
    (by Worth), 11
  fees of, 127, 137
  gawky, grumpy, grunge style, 244,
    258
  at the GDV. *See* models at the GDV
  lack of diversity in, 258–60, 268
  male, 146, 150, 256–57
  music with, 223
  print girls, 138
  racial categories of, 258–60
  runway walkers, 6, 138, 148–49, 191,
    249–50
  singing, acting, and dancing by,
    205–6, 222–23, 249–50
  walking hangar style, 257–58
models at the GDV, 124–27, 149–64
  influence of, 258
  later life, 249–55
  in Paris, 173, 221
monarchy, role in French fashion,
    9–12
Mondrian, Piet, 95
Monsanto, 126
Moore, Julianne, 240
Moreau, Jeanne, 73
Morera, Daniela, 249